SHAKESPEARE'S MERCUTIO

"I like his friend Mercutio that gets killed. He is a man."
OWEN WISTER, *The Virginian*

JOSEPH A. PORTER

Shakespeare's Mercutio

HIS HISTORY AND DRAMA

The University of North Carolina Press / Chapel Hill & London

© 1988 The University of North Carolina Press

Library of Congress Cataloging-in-Publication Data

Porter, Joseph Ashby, 1942–
Shakespeare's Mercutio: his history and drama / Joseph A. Porter.
p. cm.
Bibliography: p.
Includes index.
ISBN 0-8078-1824-0 (alk. paper)
1. Shakespeare, William, 1564–1616—Characters—Mercutio.
2. Shakespeare, William, 1564–1616. Romeo and Juliet. 3. Mercutio
(Fictitious character) 4. Mercury (Roman deity) I. Title.
PR2831.P67 1988
822.3'3—dc 19
88-17236
CIP

The paper in this book meets the
guidelines for permanence and durability
of the Committee on Production Guidelines
for Book Longevity of the
Council on Library Resources.

Printed in the United States of America
92 91 90 89 88   5 4 3 2 1

8901120

This book is for Yves Orvoën.

CONTENTS

ILLUSTRATIONS

ACKNOWLEDGMENTS

THANKS and more thanks are due Peter H. Burian, Ronald R. Butters, Thomas Cartelli, Maurice Charney, Michael Cohen, A. Leigh DeNeef, Joel Fineman, Mary E. Gardner, Shirley Nelson Garner, Jonathan Goldberg, Michael Goldman, George D. Gopen, Barbara Hodgdon, Melissa Kelly, Frank Lentricchia, Jill Levenson, Barbara Mowat, Stephen Orgel, Yves Orvoën, Dale B. J. Randall, Lawrence Richardson, Kent J. Rigsby, James R. Siemon, Jane Tompkins, George Walton Williams, fellow participants in the 1987 Folger Summer Institute and in seminars at annual meetings of the Shakespeare Association of America since 1982, the staffs of the Folger Shakespeare Library, the Duke University Libraries, and the University of North Carolina Press, the faculty and staff of the Department of English of Duke University, the Andrew W. Mellon Foundation for a Mellon Leave Fellowship in 1985, and the many others who have helped bring this work to fruition.

SHAKESPEARE'S MERCUTIO

INTRODUCTION.

MERCUTIO'S BROTHER

I n *The Most Excellent and Lamentable Tragedy of Romeo and Juliet* 1.2 Romeo obliges Capulet's illiterate servant by reading the guest list for Capulet's feast, whereupon Benvolio remarks that, since "the fair Rosaline, whom thou so loves" (1.2.85)[1] is among the invited, Romeo should attend. Since Capulet has just invited Paris in person on the spur of the moment, we don't expect to find his name in the list. We do find the name of Tybalt, who has skirmished with Benvolio in the first scene, but otherwise the play has not yet identified any of the dozen or so named guests with their unnamed but listed daughters, beauteous sisters, and lovely nieces. In particular, the play has not yet provided any handle for the two guests named in line 68, one of whom soon proves memorable, the other of whom is never again mentioned: *"Mercutio and his brother Valentine"* (1.2.68).

Valentine is a kind of ghost character, one of those "introduced in stage directions or briefly mentioned in dialogue who have no speaking parts and do not otherwise manifest their presence" (Smidt, "Absent Characters," p. 398). If Valentine is ever onstage, it is as a guest at the feast in 1.5. But if so, nothing in the text suggests anything to distinguish him from the other guests—nothing like, for instance, a word with his brother. Mercutio himself, it is true, goes into a kind of suspended animation in 3.1 with Benvolio as Tybalt recognizes and prepares to fight not Benvolio again (as we might expect) but rather Romeo. And it is true that none of the other ghost guests has a speech or stage direction. Still, none of the other ghosts is linked to the main action as firmly as is Valentine by the bond of brotherhood, so that we might reasonably expect him to bear some small part in the action. Unless he is unexplainedly absent from the feast, then, Valentine is as retiring as Rosaline at the same occasion.

Romeo and Juliet, by the way, seems marked by an unusually high degree of corporeal or ontological indeterminateness. Benvo-lio, pretty constantly onstage until the middle of the play, inexpli-cably vanishes thereafter. In 3.1 Paris may be "certainly . . . pres-ent at the feast though he is not mentioned in direction or dia-logue" (Newman & Williams, "Paris," p. 16n), or it may be that "not only Rosaline but Count Paris, too, is a defaulter at Capulet's feast" (Smidt, p. 402). In such a world it is perhaps understandable that even as informed a commentator as Brian Gibbons should hal-lucinate an unquestionably absent character as present when he writes that, in the scene with the guest list, "Romeo, Benvolio *and Mercutio* [emphasis added] learn by accident from Capulet's illiter-ate servant of the ball" (p. 41). Only Romeo, Benvolio, and the ser-vant appear in the scene.

Valentine, though, is less present in the play than even Rosaline. Absent from Smidt's treatment of absent characters, he is a ghost of a ghost, and he raises interesting questions of ontology. In the re-sponses and memories of the play's audience he is far less real than, say, Queen Mab. On the other hand he may have as good a claim to actual onstage presence at the Capulet feast as do Rosaline and Paris. And this ghostly Valentine's effective momentary presence in Shakespeare's mind raises other sorts of questions as well: what is he doing in the play at all, where does he come from, what are we to make of him? Who is Valentine really? Frivolous though it might seem to pose such questions, attempting to answer them leads quickly into deep waters.

THE obvious place to begin a search for answers to these questions is Arthur Brooke's 1562 translation from the Italian of Bandello, *The Tragicall Historye of Romeus and Juliet,*[2] Shakespeare's source and one he followed with unusual faithfulness. Were Valentine in Brooke, his presence in Shakespeare might be attributable to a cer-tain inertia of imagination. But in Brooke there is no Valentine.

Indeed Mercutio himself makes a very brief, though tantalizing, appearance in Brooke, at the Capulet feast where Romeus has adroitly seated himself next to Juliet's chair while she dances:

Fayre Juliet tourned to her chayre with pleasant cheere
And glad she was her Romeus approached was so neere.
At thone side of her chayre, her lover Romeo
And on the other side there sat one cald Mercutio,

A courtier that eche where was highly had in pryce,
For he was coorteous of his speeche, and pleasant of devise
Even as a Lyon would emong the lambes be bold,
Such was emong the bashful maydes, Mercutio to behold.
With friendly gripe he ceasd fayre Juliets snowish hand.
A gift he had that nature gave him in his swathing band,
That frosen mountayne yse was never halfe so cold
As were his handes, though nere so neer the fire he
   dyd them holde.
Within his trembling hand her left hath loving Romeus caught
                                                    (ll. 251–64)

.   .   .   .

[to Romeus, Juliet] sayd with smyling cheere
Mervayle no whit my heartes delight, my only knight and fere,
Mercutio's ysy hande had all to frosen myne
And of thy goodness thou agayne hast warmed it with thine.
                                                    (ll. 287–90)

The passage contains hints of Mercutio's characterization and story
in Shakespeare, and thereby, indirectly some of Valentine's raison
d'être. Here Mercutio has the same name, social station, and apparent approximate age as in Shakespeare, and Brooke's characterizing
touches of assurance, sensuality, and precipitateness (ll. 257–59,
263) all flower in Shakespeare. But the differences between Brooke
and Shakespeare are perhaps more striking than the similarities.

Nothing in Brooke establishes that Mercutio even knows Romeo,
much less that they are boon companions. Instead, Mercutio in
Brooke is a bested rival or would-be rival for Juliet's attentions. He
doesn't stand a chance, as the first two quoted lines make clear,
and Juliet's rejection of him provides her with an occasion to open
conversation with the more tremulous (l. 264) Romeus. And then
there are Mercutio's icy hands (ll. 260–62), that disarming detail
few commentators can resist.[3]

Shakespeare resisted incorporating them directly into his play,
perhaps because such fabulous iciness would have been inappropri-
ately comical on the stage. But the detail seems too remarkable to
have simply disappeared as Mercutio came into Shakespeare. The
coldness of Mercutio's hands in Brooke may have figured in the
early demise Shakespeare gives the character—in Brooke he merely
drops from sight. It may also be (and here, as will be seen, Valentine

lingers in the wings) that Shakespeare responded to a certain inconsistency between the friendliness of Mercutio's *gripe* (l. 259) and
the coldness of his hands. That inconsistency in Brooke's Mercutio,
I would argue, gives him an instability that makes him ripe for the
development he undergoes as he comes into Shakespeare, a development in which Valentine plays a key part.

Another detail from Brooke that may well have influenced Shakespeare's transformation of Mercutio and creation of his brother is
the rhyme of

> At thone side of her chayre, her lover Romeo
> And on the other side there sat one cald Mercutio
>
> (ll. 253–54).

While in Painter and in other versions Juliet's lover's name has the
form Shakespeare uses (despite Painter's spelling to Holofernes's
taste, "Rhomeo"), he is "Romeus" in Brooke everywhere except
here. Warned by Shakespeare's play against being too cavalier about
what's in a name, we may give some weight to the fact that Romeus
becomes Romeo for the sake of a rhyme with Mercutio. "Now for
this one pair of lines, and because of me," Mercutio might have
said, "now art thou Romeo; now art thou what thou art." He might
have added, "Now art thou sociable," too. The association, merely
phonetic at this point in Brooke, becomes crucial in Shakespeare,
where it characterizes Mercutio far more than Romeo, and where
Mercutio's attribution of it to Romeo amounts to a sort of wishful
thinking.[4]

Neither in this passage nor elsewhere in Brooke is there any mention of Mercutio's brother Valentine. To find where he comes from,
how he is in solution in Brooke, and why he precipitates out in
Shakespeare, one must look further. Two questions are at issue.
First, why does Mercutio generate a ghost brother in the transition
from Brooke into Shakespeare? Second, why is that brother named
Valentine, or, where does the name come from? Let me address the
second question first.

THE name Valentine, a diminutive of the present participle of the
Latin *valeo*, was of course familiar to Shakespeare in the form of St.
Valentine. Two or three saints seem to have been conflated for the
saint on whose February 14 feast day birds traditionally begin to
court.[5] And Shakespeare uses the name twice before *Romeo and*

Juliet for nonghost characters—for a very minor role in *Titus Andronicus* and for one of the protagonists in *The Two Gentlemen of Verona*. We might expect earlier Elizabethan dramatists to have capitalized on the name's Italianate amorousness (as did the creators of Rudolph Valentino), but in fact Shakespeare seems to be the only English dramatist to have used the name for a character before *Romeo and Juliet*. Therefore his earlier uses of the name have a special relevance.[6]

In *Titus Andronicus* Valentine is a kinsman of Titus with a single nonspeaking appearance. In *The Two Gentlemen of Verona*, however, where Valentine the constant lover is tested by his fickle friend Proteus's temporary rivalry in love, we have Shakespeare's only extensive use of the name. Although the main source for *The Two Gentlemen of Verona* is an English translation (from French) of the Spanish *Diana Enamorada* of Montemayor, the source for several incidents is Brooke's *The Tragicall Historye of Romeus and Juliet*.[7] In those incidents, without exception, the antecedent for the Valentine of *The Two Gentlemen of Verona* turns out to be Brooke's Romeus. Thus Shakespeare's association of the name Valentine with the Brooke version, and in particular with the character of Romeus, dates back at least to the composition of *Two Gentlemen*. Once established, the association lies dormant for a couple of years until Shakespeare uses Brooke again, more extensively and exclusively, for a play about other gentlemen of Verona.[8]

But where then does *Two Gentlemen*'s Valentine come from?— for the name does not appear in the play's sources. Clifford Leech advises that "the name suggests 'lover'" (*Two Gentlemen*, p. 2n) and that the connotations and associations of the saint's name may have figured in Shakespeare's choosing it for the play's constant lover. In addition to "lover," the name could well have suggested "brother" to Shakespeare, specifically "one of two brothers approximately the same age," and this because of two other Valentines perhaps known to Shakespeare.

Valentine and Orson, the English prose romance of the Charlemagne cycle, which was translated by Wynkyn de Worde's apprentice Henry Watson from the French *Valentin et Orson*, appeared in three sixteenth-century editions.[9] Furthermore, in the work's most recent edition, Arthur Dickson (*Valentine*, p. li) observes: "That our romance was well known in sixteenth-century England is indicated by the appearance of Valentine and Orson in the coronation pageant of 1547; Sidney's allusion to Pacolet's horse in the *Apologie for Poetrie*; the use of *Valentine and Orson* in *The Seven Champions of Christendom*; the record of two lost plays; and the account of a boy's reading given by Robert Ashley." Thus Shakespeare might well have had some familiarity with the romance in 1595. Dickson (p. lix) and others also have seen an allusion to the romance in the reference to stories of wolves and bears suckling children in *The Winter's Tale* 2.3.186–88 (a surmise that gains credence from the numerous other resonances between *Romeo* and *Winter's Tale* discussed below passim).

The titular heroes are twins separated at birth when a bear carries Orson off to feed her cubs. She relents and raises Orson as her own (hence his name). Through the course of adventures (involving, for instance, a magician, a dragon, and a green knight) the brothers meet, fight each other, and then join forces; Orson learns to speak and eventually they learn that they are brothers. Valentine is a model of knightly virtues, including constancy in love; Orson falls a bit short of that, and some other virtues, and may be the more interesting thereby.

Memories of the romance may have figured in Shakespeare's choice of the name Valentine for the more constant lover of *The Two Gentlemen of Verona*. Proteus does not especially recall Orson, but in *Romeo and Juliet* one may find a touch of the rough-and-ready Orson in Valentine's brother Mercutio. Indeed an associative resonance might seem the more likely with the latter play inasmuch as the earlier of the two lost plays (both titled *Valentine and Orson*) mentioned above by Dickson is entered in the *Stationers' Register* for 1595, the date customarily given to *Romeo and Juliet*.[10]

The name Valentine may also have suggested to Shakespeare "one of a pair of brothers" because of the brotherhood of Valentinianus, Roman emperor of the West 364–78, and Valens, emperor of the East 364–75. Because of the number of their joint edicts contained in the Theodosian Code and in the many anthologies of legal *sententiae* available by the sixteenth century, their names were customarily coupled.[11] Nor was knowledge of the two emperors confined to the legal profession. For instance, a character in the 1598 *Courtiers Academie* speaks of "another testimoniall of *Valente* and *Valtentino*."[12]

Familiarity with these paired brother emperors would have given the name Valentine a valence suitable for one of the protagonists in *The Two Gentlemen of Verona* and for the character referred to only as Mercutio's brother in *Romeo and Juliet*. Indeed Shakespeare's presumed familiarity with the paired emperors' names probably made Valentine in line 68 of the Capulet guest list call up another ghost three lines later: "*Signor Valentio and his cousin Tybalt*" (1.2.71).

In light of these earlier Valentines—the saint, the bear's foster child's brother, and the emperor—one may begin to see why it is that Mercutio in his passage from Brooke to Shakespeare should generate a brother so named.

S H A K E S P E A R E' S most extensive use of the name Valentine is in *The Two Gentlemen of Verona*, "a play on the *debat*-theme of love versus friendship" (Leech, ed., *Two Gentlemen*, p. lxxv), of the amatory versus the amicable or fraternal. Leech associates the name with "the great mass of friendship-literature that extends through the Middle Ages to the seventeenth century" (*Two Gentlemen*, p. xxxv). His use of Brooke as a source for certain episodes of that play has, I suggest, a similar effect: that use associates Brooke firmly with the tradition of friendship literature. Therefore when the playwright returned to Brooke in 1595 he may well have seen the love-tragedy as if through a filter, with a residual idiosyncratic coloring of the fraternal and amicable.

That coloring is nowhere more notable in *Romeo and Juliet* than in the character of Mercutio, transformed from a bit part as Romeus's rival in love to Romeo's friend, the scoffer at love whose death "is the keystone of the plot's structure" (Hosley, "Children," p. 171). And Valentine, I suggest, figures importantly if briefly in Mercutio's transformation.

Mercutio develops a brother, however ghostly and evanescent, in *Romeo and Juliet* because of the increased brotherliness and decreased amorousness he also develops there. Valentine is thus a symptom or by-product of Mercutio's transformation; he also facilitates that transformation in quite specific ways. At their first mention in Capulet's guest list Valentine serves as an object of what is to be an essential characteristic of Mercutio, his brotherliness: Valentine is there to begin the characterization of Mercutio as fraternal. At the same time, Valentine by his name serves as a sort of lightning rod to draw off and embody whatever residual amorousness Mercutio retains from Brooke. Valentine by his brief appearance, then, initiates the characterization of Mercutio that blossoms in the man's strong brotherly friendship and scorn of love. Valentine's name, because of its amorous and fraternal associations (including its previous uses by Shakespeare) was peculiarly, perhaps even uniquely, suited for its function in *Romeo and Juliet.*

Mercutio's brotherliness manifests itself in his confraternity with Benvolio and Romeo. An easy camaraderie links each with the other two. But as for Benvolio, though he appears in the play before either of the others, and though he is given a few intriguing touches of characterization—such as the troubled mind he says led him out for a predawn walk (1.1)—still a certain blandness in him makes him begin to dissolve into good wishes toward both his friends even before he slips out of the play midway through, not anchored even by his cousinship with Romeo.

The important friendship bond is thus that between Mercutio and Romeo. Mercutio is Romeo's "very friend" (3.1.108). Their friendship leads Mercutio to take Romeo's part against Tybalt, leads Romeo to rush between them and, after Tybalt has thrust under his arm and given Mercutio his deathblow, to fight and kill Tybalt. And the profoundly consequential friendship and fraternal loyalty between these two gentlemen of Verona may shed a bit more light on the ghostly Valentine.

Who is he really? In a sense Valentine is a possibly subliminal double of the play's lover-hero Romeo. By virtue of that ancestry they share—

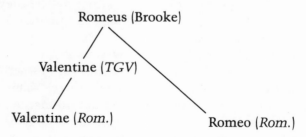

a certain equivalence or deep identity obtains between Valentine and Romeo. I call Valentine a possibly subliminal double because, while Shakespeare would hardly have been unaware of his earlier use of the name in *The Two Gentlemen of Verona*, and while the various associations noted above for the name would have been available to him, nevertheless those associations seem unobtrusive enough to have gone unnoticed in the quick forge and working house of thought. Even the precise bearing of the earlier tale of Verona on the new one may well have been, in the phrase of Armstrong (*Imagination*, p. 55), "below the level of full awareness" on Shakespeare's part.

However conscious it was, the evolution that leads to Mercutio's brother Valentine looks something like the following. The potential triangle from Brooke—Mercutio . . . Juliet . . . Romeo—with each young man holding one of Juliet's hands, and with the men perhaps not even acquaintances, undergoes a sea change as it comes into Shakespeare, where, in its new configuration—Mercutio . . . Romeo . . . Juliet—Romeo has traded places with Juliet and taken the center for himself. Brooke's empty Romeo-Mercutio bond is thus filled, with a friendship strong as brotherhood, and simultaneously the Mercutio-Juliet bond is erased. And thus Mercutio's first mention in *Romeo and Juliet* marks him as brotherly rather than amorous, and at the same time, as it were, creates the role Romeo is to fill, that of Mercutio's amorous brother.

The question of Mercutio himself remains. Why, that is, should Shakespeare have found the sketchy portrayal in Brooke worthy of, or necessitating, its huge development—of which the generation of a ghost Valentine is after all a minor component—in the movement into the play? Who really was the Mercutio Shakespeare found, who did he become, and how, and why? Such are the sorts of questions the remainder of this study attempts to answer. And as with Valentine, so the more with Mercutio: throughout, I assume that the answers I propose must be at once provisional and overdetermined, complex and incomplete. Jones (Review, p. 359) expresses a nearly universal assumption when he writes that "Shakespeare's method of composition, much of which was no doubt outside his conscious control, was complexly accretive." The same may be said of the long communal thought process in which a particular god, Mercury, composes himself to become a major constituent of Shakespeare's Mercutio. Similarly with that character's transformation through four centuries. That is, just as with the thresholds

Valentine passes to appear for half a line in *Romeo and Juliet,* so too
as we turn to Valentine's brother Mercutio: the evolutionary cross-
ings are complex in the extreme, and tracing some parts of them
involves considerable shuttling back and forth in the intertextual
web.[13]

PART ONE.

SHAKESPEARE'S MERCURY

IN the introduction above I have tried to tease out how some of the features of the Mercutio Shakespeare found in Brooke (such as the cold hands) may have prompted his development of the figure. But Brooke's Mercutio's most significant feature for the Shakespeare of 1595 would seem to have been his name. While its ending may have determined the form Romeo takes in the play, most of Mercutio resonates—must have resonated consciously or not in the playwright's mind—with the name Mercury. In the following pages, after a preliminary glance at Mercutio's mercuriality, and at those few moments in Shakespeare's plays when a character mentions the god, I then attempt to arrive at an approximation of Shakespeare's received notion of Mercury, considering the god's appearances in relevant classical and medieval texts (chap. 1) and in Renaissance pictorial representations and texts (chaps. 2 and 3).

Once stated, the resonance between the character so attractive he had to be killed off midway through to keep him from stealing the play (Dryden, "Defence," p. 174) and the Olympian whose "attributes are the most complex and varied of those of any of the major gods" (Zimmerman, *Dictionary*, pp. 124–25) may seem obvious enough. The very phonetic similarity of their names, in the context of a play obsessively concerned with nomenclature and spelling, establishes a kinship further deepened and solidified in their common associations with dreams, death, and the phallus, and their common antagonisms to love. The Mercurial resonance in Mercutio often seems just beneath the surface, as with the petasos-like form Mercutio's visor takes when worn as a cap by John McEnery in the Zeffirelli film, and occasionally rises to the surface, as with Altman's (*Tudor Play of Mind*, p. 123n) passing description of Mercutio as "Mercury-turned-Vice." And yet so much is so far beneath the surface (as the following pages attempt to demonstrate) that

Shakespeare himself may not seem quite aware of the god's role in his character's genesis.

Shakespeare's handful of uses of the name Hermes-Mercury (hereafter Mercury, Shakespeare's form on all occasions but one) provides an initial conspectus of Shakespeare's notions of the god. The seven appearances of the god's name that precede *Romeo and Juliet* have especial relevance to Mercutio. Of these, three occur amid the heavy classicizing of *Titus Andronicus*. In two of these (4.3.55 and 4.4.14) Mercury simply makes one with the generally undifferentiated gods to whom Titus shoots his arrows. Since as the arrows carry messages and the two mentions of them are closely followed by the dispatch and delivery of Titus's letter to Saturninus, it might be argued that Mercury thereby stands in a higher relief than his fellows. Still, these two are the baldest of Shakespeare's references to the god.

Considerably more interesting is the earlier mention of Mercury in *Titus Andronicus*. In 4.1, after the mutilated Lavinia has directed her father's and uncle's attention to the story of Tereus and Philomela in young Lucius's dropped copy of the *Metamorphoses*, Marcus asks, "Apollo, Pallas, Jove, or Mercury, / Inspire me, that I may this treason find" (ll. 66–67). Perhaps because this pantheon is more selective than Titus's toxophilitic one—three of these gods are obvious granters of intellectual powers, and Jove by virtue of his office and power is a de facto fourth—the prayer is granted and Marcus is inspired to show Lavinia how to become a speaking picture of written speech, with the scribal staff extending from her mouth. But which god is responsible for the inspiration? The moment's emphasis on conundrum solving and on reading and writing would seem to select the god most closely identified with the science of interpretation and with writing.[1]

Mercury's case gains further weight from the specific word Marcus chooses to write in his demonstration of the oral-pedal scribal technique. It is his own name, which chimes with Mercury far more closely than with any of the other three gods' names. Furthermore the Elizabethan *er-ar* equivalence, as with "clerk," gives the Mercury-Marcus chime an added resonance, of a sort that functions to activate the *mark* in Mercutio (see chap. 5). Assuming then that Mercury is to be credited for Marcus's hermeneutical inspiration, this early quicksilver and largely subliminal visitation of the god in Shakespeare's text heralds a career of some elusiveness.[2]

Mercury appears in his most conventional guises when he is mentioned in *Richard III*, both times by Richard, and it is quite in keeping with the play and character that the god should so appear, circumscribed and instrumental in Richard's wit. To Edward's "Is Clarence dead? The order was reversed," Richard replies, "But he (poor man) by your first order died, / And that a wingèd Mercury did bear: / Some tardy cripple bare the countermand" (2.1.87–90), the tardy cripple being Richard himself. A similar kind of reduction of Mercury to a counter in Richard's play of wit happens later when Richard exclaims, "Then fiery expedition be my wing, / Jove's Mercury, and herald for a king!" (4.3.54–55), neatly equating himself with Jove, as Evans observes (Harbage, *Works*, p. 585n).

In *King John* Mercury makes a less token appearance when John urges the Bastard, "Be Mercury, set feathers to thy heels, / And fly like thought from them [restive nobles] to me again" (4.2.174–75). This is Shakespeare's first explicit mention of Mercury's talaria, the accoutrement he most often gives the god.[3] Heels have been mentioned shortly before, in conjunction with "harsh-sounding rimes" (ll. 149–50) that foreshadow the harsh words of Mercury at the ending of *Love's Labour's Lost*; in such a context, the mere mention of "foot" (l. 170) may have called up Mercury in l. 174. Preceded by the appearance of "Messenger" (l. 103), and framed with talk of news, dreams, prophecy, and prodigies of nature (ll. 144–53, 182–86), Mercury here has an ominous resonance the brevity of the immediate reference may belie. And the simile "like thought" (l. 175) makes the canon's first explicit statement of Mercury's traditional tie with ratiocination (forecast in *Two Gentlemen*, "herald thoughts," 3.1.144).

Some of the same features are apparent in the last mention of the god before *Romeo and Juliet*. The very uncertainty of attribution surrounding the concluding sentence of the Quarto *Love's Labour's Lost*—"The words of Mercury are harsh after the songs of Apollo" —befits the god of margins and trickery.[4] However gnomic, the line provides a more comprehensive statement of Mercury's significance than do any of the preceding mentions—indeed than does any other in the canon—and many of the pages that follow are devoted to an unfolding of that significance. But several features deserve noting immediately. Instead of a more or less selective pantheon in which Mercury is one among a group, here we have the most forcefully significant arrangement possible, a binary opposition.

Berowne earlier has established the operative conception of Apollo in his aria on love, "as sweet and musical / As bright Apollo's lute, strung with his hair" (4.3.337–38). He is patron of music and poetry, all the rhapsody in which the little academy abandons its studies for love. Mercury by contrast represents forces inimical to song and love. His words' harshness comes not only from their unmetricalness but also from the fact that they state truths the academy-become-court-of-love would ignore. In particular, of course, Mercury in the person of Marcade, the messenger who nearly bears his name, brings the news of death that darkens and chills the comedy's ending.

Berowne's taffeta phrases partly rehearse Romeo's kissing by the book. Indeed as Snyder, ("*Romeo*," p. 391) remarks, *Romeo and Juliet* differs from Shakespeare's other tragedies in its shift out of comedy into tragedy, a movement for which the ending of *Love's Labour's Lost* may stand as a rehearsal. Marcade-Mercury, the pivotal figure for the comedy's shift out of the world of amorous lyricism, may thus stand as a rehearsal for Shakespeare's most important simulacrum of the god: Mercutio who, with his harsh words and his death, leads the way into the tragedy of *Romeo and Juliet*.

SHAKESPEARE'S remaining uses of the god's name, all succeeding *Romeo and Juliet*, may be dealt with in shorter order even though in general they are more elaborated than the preceding ones. Mercury's winged heels are mentioned on two occasions. In *Henry V* the youth of England follow the mirror of all Christian kings "With winged heels, as English Mercuries" (2.Prol.7).[5] These Mercurys of the Chorus are "all on fire" (l. 1) with expedition. By contrast, Troilus's "chidden Mercury" (*Troilus* 2.2.45) figures a warrior led by "reasons" (l. 38) to flee. This fleet Mercury of the battleground seems implicit in Imogen's commentary of the headless body she supposes Posthumus's, "this is his hand, / His foot Mercurial, his Martial thigh, / The brawns of Hercules" (*Cymbeline* 4.2.309–11), and is explicit in Vernon's description of "young Harry . . . like feathered Mercury" (*1 Henry IV* 4.1.104–6).

The other winged Mercurys are heralds. Hamlet's lovely "herald Mercury / New lighted on a heaven-kissing hill" (*Hamlet* 3.4.59–60) probably derives from Virgil's description of Mercury alighting on Mount Atlas, and may be influenced by pictures based on the Virgil (Jenkins, *Hamlet*, p. 322n59; Thomson, *Shakespeare*, p. 118).[6]

Cleopatra thinks of the envoy Mercury when she says from her monument to Antony below, "Had I great Juno's power, / The strong-winged Mercury should fetch thee up / And set thee by Jove's side" (*Antony* 4.15.34–36). And as noted above, Mercury's winged heels may be present by implication in the mention in *Henry V* 3.7.17. Since this is Shakespeare's only use of the name Hermes, and only mention of Hermes' pipe, the two attributes may well have been associated in his mind. Mercury's best-known use of the pipe is in lulling Argus asleep to kill him, so that the Hermes-harms pun may have operated here to select the god's Greek name.

Falstaff's "But what says she to me? Be brief, my good she-Mercury" to Quickly in *The Merry Wives of Windsor*, 2.2.74–75, in its roundabout way emphasizes the god's own gender. Otherwise this is one of Shakespeare's most conventional Mercurys. Falstaff's use of the god's name as a near-synonym for "messenger" shares Richard III's reductionism, if not quite his wit.

The remaining three namings of Mercury show him in a different guise, as the crafty and deceptive "patron god of cheating, thieving and lying . . . known to the Elizabethans chiefly from Ovid (*Fasti* 5.625–38) or from the mythographers dependent on Ovid" (Thomson, *Shakespeare*, p. 128). Feste tells Olivia, "Now Mercury indue thee with leasing [lying], for thou speak'st well of fools" (*Twelfth Night* 1.5.92–93). Thersites speaks of the serpentine craft of Mercury's caduceus and of his power over "wit" (*Troilus* 2.3.11–12).[7] Finally, the god of thieves appears in "My father named me Autolycus, who being, as I am, littered under Mercury, was likewise a snapper-up of unconsidered trifles" (*Winter's Tale* 4.3.24–25). Shakespeare's entire characterization of Autolycus, named for the son of Mercury and grandfather of Ulysses, inherits a good deal from the idea of Mercury as it has evolved through Shakespeare's career. Autolycus thus figures in the reprise and processing of *Romeo and Juliet*, and specifically of Mercutio, that Shakespeare effects in *The Winter's Tale*. As discussed below passim, the resonances include Hermione's name, her "death," her "statue," and its sculptor's name, as well as Autolycus.[8] It seems peculiarly just, then, that this final explicit Shakespearean mention of the god, this last tip of the iceberg, should involve retrospection to the site of Shakespeare's major incarnation of his received Mercury.

CHAPTER ONE.

TO THE RENAISSANCE

Mercury appears as he does in Shakespeare largely because of the long and intricate history, some of which will be touched on here, that brings him from pre-Homeric Greece to Renaissance England. Originally of course he is Hermes, whose prehistoric and even prehuman origins Burkert (*Greek Religion*, p. 156), locates in boundary marking and phallic display: "*herma* is a heap of stones, a monument set up as an elementary form of demarcation. Everyone who passes by adds a stone to the pile and so announces his presence. In this way territories are proclaimed and demarcated. Another form of territorial demarcation, older than man himself, is phallic display, which is then . . . replaced by erected stones or stakes." By the time of his appearances in Homer, Hesiod, and the Homeric "Hymn to Hermes," the *herma* has become Hermes, herald or messenger of the gods, trickster and psychopomp (or, conductor of souls to the place of the dead), patron of thieves, merchants, shepherds, scribes, and travelers, and associated with manual skill, oratory and eloquence, luck and wealth, roads, wind, sleep, and dreams. Hermes in time becomes identified with the Roman Mercurius, god of trade, *merx* (Zimmerman, *Dictionary*, p. 124; Harvey, *Companion*, pp. 204–5, 267).

Sociological factors account for some complexities of the god's nature, according to Brown (*Hermes*, pp. 1–19), who traces the concept of Hermes the thief to earlier concepts of the god as trickster and magician and draws connections between these notions and the myth of Hermes the herald, "expert in runes and other forms of word-magic" (p. 31). Since the assistance of such a figure is particularly needed in intercourse with strangers, Hermes becomes a god of boundaries and roads, and the sacred stone heaps associated with the cult of Hermes are boundary markers.[1] In particular, Hermes becomes associated with the primitive trade taking place at interterritorial boundaries (pp. 39–45).

As for "the other sacred object in the cult of Hermes, the [often priapic] phallus," Brown (*Hermes*, p. 34) notes that symbols of it "were placed on mountaintops, rural waysides, state boundaries, city streets, in the doorways and courtyards of houses, in gymnasia and libraries, in sacred precincts, and on graves. . . . in fact found in much the same locations as the stone-heap, with which it was often combined." Brown argues that the Hermetic phallus is an apotropaic amulet rather than, as has sometimes been claimed, a fertility symbol. It frequently appeared as part of the remarkable statues called herms, in which from the neck or arms down the god's body has become a quadrangular pillar, with only his genitals remaining in place (see below, chap. 2). Like the stone heaps, the herms could mark boundaries, and they also could serve to mark roads, to honor the god, and to celebrate his association with locations or institutions such as the gymnasia. We may remember that North's Plutarch, in "Life of Alcibiades" (North, *Lives*, 2:131–37), speaks of the latter sort of herm, telling of the consternation caused in Athens by their nocturnal mutilation, a sacrilege attributed by some to Alcibiades and his followers. Certain of the herms manifest an ambiguity of age intermittently characteristic of the god throughout his history and reemergent in his avatar Mercutio: as Burkert, p. 158, notes, while the early border-marking herms have bearded heads, the patron of the gymnasia is a youthful, "phallic, homoerotically tinged" Hermes.

The institution of kingship around the fifteenth century B.C., Brown maintains, brings about a subordination of Hermes to Zeus that reflects class differentiation and the subordination of merchants, craftsmen, pioneers, unskilled laborers, and the other members of the Third Estate to the monarchy. The rise of the city-state brings trade from the perimeter to the agora, and Hermes follows.

> This did not, however, result in the obliteration of his original cult centers, on the boundaries, in the wild wastelands, and on mountaintops . . . antique monuments of the cult of Hermes, situated in the wilderness, retained a prominent place in public religion throughout the classical period. This disjunction in the location of the cult is paralleled by a disjunction in the mythological representations of Hermes current in classical times. On the one hand he is the god who was born in the mountains of rugged Arcadia, the companion of the . . . deities of the

wilds, the friend of shepherds. . . . On the other hand he is the friend of merchants . . . the very type of the "city slicker" or "man of the agora." (Brown, *Hermes*, p. 43)

These cultural changes were in full swing in the ninth century, and Brown (pp. 52–65) attributes Hesiod's disapproval of the god allied with the new professional class to his reactionary nostalgia. Finally, Brown (pp. 66–101) holds that the Homeric "Hymn to Hermes" reflects the sixth-century urban and commercial civilization, with Hermes a figure of the rising lower classes in their struggle with the aristocracy represented in the "Hymn" by Apollo.[2]

Mercury comes from these or other origins to Shakespeare in 1595, to Mercutio, in textual (and other) representations through manifold routes. Looking back through the historical palimpsest, we may see that at every step of the god's journey, to varying degrees and in a great variety of manners, familiarity with earlier representations thickens and weights his figure. At the same time the god in any of his representations may leap many generations in a single bound. None of this is news, of course. I mention it here merely by way of noting the multiple and shifting focus I will adopt here to account for so complex a situation.

While translations provide important shortcuts for the god, few such Greek-English routes were available in 1595. Tusser, *Hundreth Good Points of Husbandrie*, based on Hesiod, goes through numerous editions after 1557, but Tusser's sanctimony has screened out mention of pagan deities, and Chapman's translation of Hesiod does not appear until 1618. Nor are Apollodorus, Apollonius Rhodius, or Pausanias yet Englished, although they have begun to infiltrate the language in learned citations. Hall, *Ten Books of Homer's Iliades*, 1581, provides no more of Mercury than his conservatorship of Agamemnon's scepter mentioned in 2, and his rescue of Mars from the brazen jar in 5: "Euribea . . . Mercurius . . . besought / In favour of the God distrest, who stale him in a braide, / And secretly convayde him forth" (sig. M4); and Chapman's Homer does not begin to appear until 1595 and is not complete until 1615. All the same, since the Greek Mercury was available in Aldine and other editions, and in Latin and some continental translations as well as, importantly, in mythographies and other compendiums (see chaps. 2 and 3), and since his Greek literary embodiments directly influ-

enced the Latin ones more available to Shakespeare, the Greek
god's broad outlines contribute to Shakespeare's Mercury.

In the *Iliad*, where Iris performs the function of Zeus's messenger, Hermes appears as one of the independent Olympians, a figure
of helpfulness as well as stealth. In addition to rescuing Ares from
the brazen jar (5.390), he uses "his rod, that hath the grace / To shut
what eyes he lists, with sleep; and open them againe / In strongest
trances" (Chapman, *Whole Works*, sig. Ff4v) to charm the Greek
guards as he leads Priam to Achilles and away with Hector's body.
While in the *Odyssey* Hermes in his role of messenger is more
subordinated to Zeus, he still maintains considerable autonomy.
He leads spirits of the dead in Hades (12.626, 24.1, 10, 99), he be-
friends Autolycus "who, th'Art / Of Theft and swearing ... / ...
first adorn'd / Your witty man withall" (Chapman, *Crowne of
Workes*, sig. Cc5v), and he declares that he would gladly lie beside
Aphrodite even though it meant being ensnared like Ares by He-
phaestus (8.323–42).

In Hermes' two most extended and important appearances in the
poem, as bearer of a particular sort of message, he looks forward to
Virgil's Mercury and beyond to Mercutio. In the first, he comes to
Calypso to advise her to let Odysseus go back to his friends (1.38,
42, 84; 5.28–196). Later at the threshold of Circe's palace Odysseus
is met by Mercury "in / A yong mans likenesse, of the first-flowr'd
chin, / Whose forme hath all the grace, of one so yong" (Chapman,
Crowne of Workes, sig. O4v); Mercury has brought moly and instructions about how Odysseus's men are to be freed from Circe's
enchantments.[3] In essence, the god's behest to the hero is the same:
end your infatuation—escape Calypso, leave Circe, abandon Dido,
cure yourself of "this drivelling love" (*Romeo* 2.4.91).

In Hesiod, *Works and Days* (ll. 42–104), Mercury's role in the
story of Pandora marks "a new stage in the evolution of the mythology of the god" (Brown, *Hermes*, p. 53). Whereas Athena gives
the newly created woman skill and Aphrodite gives her beauty,
Mercury endows her with "the mind of a cur and a stealthy disposi-
tion." He leads her to Epimetheus, who accepts her against his
brother's advice, whereupon she opens the jar and fills the earth
with ills. While there may be some mitigation in Mercury's acting
under Zeus's instructions, this may be his most sinister moment
yet, given the outcome.

Last and perhaps most important of the early Greek textual representations of Mercury is the Homeric "Hymn to Hermes," an account of the eventful first day of the god's life, during which on Mount Cyllene he kills a tortoise at the threshold of the cave of his mother Maia and invents the lyre using the tortoise shell; steals and hides the cattle of his brother Apollo and vows to gain the same status as Apollo; protests his innocence of theft but, commanded by his amused father Zeus, reveals the cattle to Apollo; and then, swearing to steal nothing of Apollo's, takes part in a compact of friendship with his brother. The "Hymn" ends:

> And thus, with Gods and Mortalls Hermes liu'd,
> Who truely helpt but few; but all deceiu'd
> With an undifferencing respect; and made
> Vaine words, and false perswasions his Trade.
> His Deeds, were all associats of the Night;
> In which, his close wrongs, car'd for no mans Right.
> (Chapman, *Crowne of Workes*, sig. L4)

This disappproving conclusion, suiting ill with the poem's generally approving picture of Mercury's trickery, may as Brown suggests be the work of an Apolline reviser attempting to correct the poem's favor of the god of craftsmen, merchants, thieves, and the lottery whose "use . . . in the selection of Athenian public officials was the supreme expression of the democratic principle of the absolute equality of all citizens" (Brown, *Hermes*, p. 101)[4] over the more aristocratic Apollo. The poem in any case contributes key elements —including playfulness, thievery, and prevarication—to the developing character of the god.

FROM these and other Greek origins[5] Mercury moves to the Latin embodiments Shakespeare would more likely have known directly or in translation, particularly the works of Plautus, Horace, Virgil, Ovid, and Apuleius. In Plautus's *Amphitruo*, which Shakespeare probably read in the original Latin, and which he used as a model for *The Comedy of Errors*, Mercury's role is that of the wily and impudent slave. Impersonating the mortal slave Sosia, Mercury assists as Jove, impersonating Amphitruo, enjoys the favors of Amphitruo's wife Alcmena. The portrayal of the gods is notably "gross and irreverent" (Harvey, *Companion*, p. 25), and Mercury in particular is thoroughly subordinated, not only playing a slave but also, as he says, made a slave by his father Jove (Plautus, *Amphitruo*

1.178). At the same time Mercury is the most engaging male in the play. His asides and long prologue make the audience complicit in his mockery, some of which is of Jove's infatuation (1.541). Of additional interest with respect to resonances with *Romeo and Juliet* are Mercury's remarks in the Prologue, ll. 50–63, about the genre of the play to follow. He calls it a tragedy and then, prompted by frowns he says the word has brought to the audience's foreheads, vows to convert it to a comedy without changing a line. Immediately he amends this remarkable proposal in the interests of decorum—since out-and-out comedy won't do with gods on the boards, the play will be a tragicomedy. While this genre instability remains hypothetical in the entirely comic *Amphitruo*, *Romeo and Juliet* has a more realized and poignant analogue. "Other tragedies have reversals, but in *Romeo and Juliet* the reversal is so radical as to constitute a change of genre" (Snyder, "*Romeo*," p. 391). And it is Mercutio, jesting with the lover the Chorus has labeled death-marked (and then in his own death initiating the irrevocable tragic movement), who most brings into his play suggestions of the subversive instability of genre that Plautus's Mercury playfully hypothesizes.

H O R A C E ' S most extended account of Mercury is Ode 1.10, a beautifully modulated recapitulation of the received portrayal. In the first of the Ode's five stanzas Mercury is a culture hero who has provided humankind with speech itself and who is patron of the wrestling ground. In the second stanza Horace calls Mercury messenger of the gods and inventor of the lyre, and strings together the attributes of cleverness, playfulness, and stealth. The next stanzas glance at two of the god's adventures—his theft of Apollo's cattle and his guiding Priam through the Greek camp. In the final stanza Mercury is psychopomp, marshaling ("coerces," l. 18) with his caduceus the throng of souls of the pious to their final homes. The picture is almost entirely favorable but even here, in the power of the caduceus and in a certain wilfulness, Horace admits traces of the more frightening god of Ode 1.24, where the caduceus is a gruesome wand ("virga . . . horrida," l. 16) wielded by an obdurate ("non lenis," l. 17) warden of the spirits of the dead, who would not open the gates of death even though entreated to by Virgil himself.

Mercury has another touch of the chthonic in Ode 3.11, which opens with an address to the god and to the lyre he invented. In tribute to Mercury's skill in music Horace mentions the god's having taught Amphion to play the lyre, which instrument has supernatural powers including power to charm Cerberus and beguile the dead.[6]

Two other appearances in the odes deserve mention. In 2.7 Horace recalls the battle of Phillipi and his own "basely abandoned shield" (l. 10) and flight that, as Commager notes (*Odes*, p. 171), reminds some of Falstaff at Shrewsbury. In that crisis Mercury assisted Horace as he assisted Priam in the Greek camp: "sed me per hostes Mercurius celer / denso paventem sustulit aere" (ll. 13–14), "But me in my terror Mercury bore swiftly through the foe in a dense cloud" (Bennett, *Odes*, p. 123). And in Ode 1.2, addressed to Octavian, Mercury appears in periphrasis—"almae / filius Maiae," "son of benign Maia" (ll. 42–43)—as the last and most elaborately presented in a catalog of gods, the one whose earthly embodiment is Caesar.[7]

In *Aeneid* 4 Mercury, as with Odysseus, and like Mercutio with Romeo, urges the hero to end his romantic entanglement. It is a role that would have impressed itself on Shakespeare by virtue of the grandeur and sonorousness the god takes on in Virgil, and also of course because of the nationalism resonating between the stories of Aeneas and Brute. Shakespeare could have known the Virgilian Mercury in the original, in continental translations, and in English versions of Caxton (1490), Douglas (1553), Surrey (1557), Phaer (1558), and Stanyhurst (1582), as well as via the innumerable imitations and allusions occasioned by Virgil's prestige.

In this famous episode, 4.222–78, after Jupiter gives Mercury the message for Aeneas that he should leave off his dalliance and set sail for Italy, Mercury dons his golden talaria, takes the caduceus (whose powers Virgil lists), and sets out on the awesome flight imitated by Ronsard and Milton, and possibly recalled in *Hamlet* (see above, "Part One: Shakespeare's Mercury"), a flight that gains power from its brief prefiguration when Mercury makes the same voyage in *Aeneid* 1. Skimming the clouds he sees the peak and slopes of Atlas, where he pauses and then plunges down to fly low over the waves like a seabird, between earth and sky, to the shore of Libya. He sees Aeneas and delivers Jupiter's admonition, not verbatim but with some more pointed and exact word choices, so demonstrating his eloquence (see Welch, *Mercury*, p. 30). While still speaking he vanishes into thin air, leaving Aeneas dumbfounded, his hair on end.

Later in the same book, as Aeneas sleeps on board his ship, the god reappears to him in a dream—"omnia Mercurio similis, vocemque coloremque / et crinis flavos et membra decora iuventa" (ll. 558–59); "in all points like to Mercury, in voice and hue, in golden hair and the graceful limbs of youth" (Fairclough, *Satires*, p. 433)— to urge him to set sail immediately to escape Dido's fury. The speech ends with a touch of Hesiodic misogyny: "varium et mutabile semper / femina" (ll. 569–70); "A fickle and changeful thing is woman ever" (Fairclough, *Aeneid*, p. 435). Mercury melts into the darkness, leaving Aeneas once again frightened ("exterritus," l. 571) by his visit.

Mercury appears so, with some differences of emphasis, in the five English versions available to Shakespeare. Caxton's prose *Eneydos*, a fairly close translation of a very free French paraphrase, omits one of the caduceus's powers, the "lumina morte resignat" (l. 244), "unseals eyes in death." This is "an allusion to the Roman custom of opening the eyes of the dead on the funeral pyre" (Fairclough, *Aeneid*, p. 413) that troubles later translators.[8] Otherwise, Caxton's is the most long-winded Englishing, with the description of Atlas greatly expanded (*Eneydos*, sig. E3v–E4) and with Virgil's Mercury's terse "uxorius" (l. 266) expanded as "effemynate, wythout honour, rauysshed in to dileectacion femynyne" (sig. E4).

Douglas's translation in heroic couplets in Scots English and Surrey's in blank verse are linked since, while both worked with Virgil's Latin, Surrey also used Douglas (see Ridley, "*Aeneid*," pp. 13–29). Douglas "freely amplifies to explain, and to give his picture life and vividness by means of explicit, concrete detail which Surrey, striving for compactness, omits" (Ridley, p. 39). The formal demands of the couplet sometimes also lead Douglas into a wordiness Surrey is comparatively free of. A case in point is Virgil's "uxorius." Douglas (*Eneados*, sig. M3v) gives "exercit, in ane wyiffis seruice," Surrey uses "wifebound" (*Aenaeis*, sig. E4). But both provide more or less faithful renderings.

So too does Phaer, although his use of fourteener couplets, fondness for alliteration, and general lack of vigor dilute the god somewhat. Phaer introduces wordplay, as when he makes the purple of Aeneas's cloak Moorish (rather than Tyrian as Virgil and the earlier English translators have it) in order to say that the cloak hangs

"Morisko gise [guise]." But in the couplet in question Phaer (*Enei-dos*, sig. I3v) backs into a solecism worthy of the 1980s: "And shining read in roabe of Moorishe purple, *mantle wise*, / He stood, and from his shulders down it hing Morisko gise" (emphasis added). Phaer (sig. I3v) translates Virgil's "uxorius" with two half-lines: "doting dost thy mind applye / To pleas thy lusty spouse."

Nashe ("Preface," p. 319) praises Phaer but he, like many later critics, has nothing kind to say of Stanyhurst's *Aeneis* in unrhymed quantitative hexameters.[9] The style of his Mercury, like the rest of his translation, is "decidedly queer" (Haar, "*Aeneis*," p. 8), but the god survives his "Thrasonicall huffe snuffe" (Nashe, "Preface," p. 319) and "foule lumbring boystrous wallowing measure" (Nashe, "News," p. 299) intact enough. Virgil's "uxorius" becomes "with youre braue bedfelo sotted" (Stanyhurst, *Aeneis* sig. L2v). The misogyny of Mercury's second visit to "the duke Aeneas" does have some huff snuff—"a wind fane changabil huf puffe / Always is a woomman" (sig. M3)—but, given the general strangeness of Stanyhurst's style, his presentation of Mercury is succinct and memorable, as for instance with the god's exit from his first speech to Aeneas (Stanyhurst, *Aeneis*, sig. L2v):

> When this round message thee Cyllen Mercurye whisperd,
> In myd of his parling from gazing mortal he shrincketh:
> From lookers eyesight too thinnes he vannished ayrye.

However he comes to Shakespeare, the Virgilian Mercury has a number of traits important for the characterization of Mercutio. These include his youthfulness, uncanniness, and misogyny. Of additional importance for Shakespeare, it would seem, are the substance of the messages Virgil's Mercury brings—leave Dido, get about your proper business—and the fact that at the end of each of his speeches he exits memorably before Aeneas can reply. The first of these exits is the more impressive: "tali Cyllenius ore locutus / mortalis visus medio sermone reliquit / et procul in tenuem ex oculis evanuit auram" (ll. 276–78). The translators (including Stanyhurst in the lines just quoted) all do it well, and so too with the briefer second exit: "sic fatus nocti se immiscuit atrae" (l. 570), "So he spake and melted into the black night" (Fairclough, *Aeneid*, p. 435). Finally, Virgil's portrayal of the god's flight to Mt. Atlas and Libya would seem likely to have lodged itself in Shakespeare's mind.

Of all classical representations of Mercury, Ovid's would have been most familiar to Shakespeare. Ovid's Mercury makes a number of disconnected appearances and displays a variety of characteristics within which some constants and patterns appear. Ovid retells certain of the Mercurian stories already treated here, adding his own coloring and emphasis. Treating the story of the theft of Apollo's cattle (*Metamorphoses* 2.679–707), Ovid recounts almost nothing of the actual theft, adding only that it was Apollo's distraction by thoughts of love that permitted the cattle to stray in the first place. Instead Ovid turns to the episode of Battus, bribed by Mercury to keep the theft secret, tricked into tattling by the disguised god, and finally turned to stone as punishment. While Ovid gives Mercury's disguise simply as "versa pariter cum voce figura" (l. 698), "with changed voice and form" (Miller, *Metamorphoses*, p. 109), Golding, *Metamorphoses*, 1–4 (1565, complete 1567), gives Mercury (sig. C2) the disguise of a vigorously realized rustic dialect:

> Ich heartely bezeche,
> And if thou zawest any kie come royling through this
> grounde,
> Or driven away, tell what he was and where they may be
> vownde.
> And I chill gethee vor thy paine an Hecfar and hir match.

The episode emphasizes Mercury's dangerous trickery, his peremptory vindictiveness, and a certain nonchalance, as with the episode's conclusion:

> And with that word strayt to a stone he turnde his
> double heart,
> In which the slaunder yet remains without the
> stones desart.
> The bearer of the charmed Rod the suttle Mercurie
> This done arose with wauing wings and from that place
> did flie.
>
> (sig. C2)

As if having developed a taste for petrifaction, Mercury in the following incident punishes Aglauros the same way, for her attempting to bar his entry at the threshold of Herse's bedchamber. Mercury acts even more summarily than with Battus and then, after Aglauros has undergone the frightening experience, he flies off without another thought of Aglauros or of the Herse whose beauty had earlier led him to primp like an Augustan or Elizabethan dandy.

Ovid mentions three other objects of Mercury's amorous attentions. While he touches in passing on the parentage of Hermaphroditus (*Metamorphoses* 4.288), he recounts Mercury's fathering of Autolycus at greater length in 11.301–15. This story pairs Mercury and Apollo once again, and in a way that incidentally seems to foreshadow Mercutio's transformation from Brooke to Shakespeare. The two gods see the beautiful Chione "bothe at once, and bothe at once where [were] tane in love" (Golding, *Metamorphoses*, sig. T4; "pariter, pariter traxere calorem," 11.305). The rivalry that seems incipient fails to materialize since Apollo defers his suit until night. Mercury, however,

> could not beare delay. He stroked on the face
> The mayden with his charmed rod which hath the powre to
> chace
> And bring in sleepe: the touch whereof did cast her in so dead
> A sleepe, that Hermes by and by his purpose of her sped.
> (Golding, sig. T4)

After nightfall Apollo treats Chione similarly when he takes "the pleasure which the sonne of Maya had forehent" (Golding, sig. T4), and the sons Chione bears in due time reflect their respective fathers' characters. While Apollo's Philammon is musical, Autolycus

> provde a wyly pye,
> And such a fellow as in theft and filching had no peere.
> He was his fathers owne sonne right: he could mennes eyes
> so bleere,
> As for to make the black things whyght, and whyght
> things black appeere.
> (Golding, sig. T4)

Since Autolycus is mentioned only once elsewhere in the *Metamorphoses*, his main function here would seem to be to layer his thievery and deceptiveness onto his father's impatience, casual Ovidian sexist brutality, command of sleep, and his peculiarly conjured and deferred fraternal sexual rivalry.[10]

Mercury's third amour is with the nymph Lara in Ovid's *Fasti* 2.608–16. Jupiter having punished her loquaciousness, he instructs Mercury to convey her to the underworld. On the way there Mer-

cury forces himself on the silently protesting nymph, who then
gives birth to the Lares, twin spirits of crossroads and Mercury's
most ambiguous progeny.[11]

For the most part though, as with Battus above, Mercury's Ovidian adventures have little to do with amorousness. The most extended characterization, analogous to the Horatian Ode, is from
Fasti 5.663–72 (Frazer's translation):

> Thou arbiter of peace and war to gods
> . . . who dost ply thy way on winged foot; thou who
> dost delight in the music of the lyre, and dost delight
> too in the wrestling-school, glistening with oil;
> thou by whose instruction the tongue learns to discourse
> elegantly. . . . All who make a business of selling
> their wares give thee incense and beg that thou
> wouldst grant them gain.

Ovid goes on to describe a merchant reciting prayers to Mercury,
begging leniency for his past deceptions and perjuries so that he
may commit more, and asking that Mercury grant him profits and
pleasure in cheating. Mercury laughs, remembering his own theft of
Apollo's cattle (ll. 681–92).

Ovid does not reveal whether the laughing Mercury grants the
merchant's prayer. That indeterminateness, part and parcel of all
divinity, seems particularly suited to the god of chance. Mercury's
laughter too seems to come from the heart. The occasion for it
characterizes him memorably, and laughter makes for the particular sociability he has in two of Ovid's stories, stories similar enough
to magnify their effects in the god's characterization. Both tales are
examples of the archetype of hospitality extended to a disguised
god.

Lelex in *Metamorphoses* 7.618–724 (Golding, sig. P2) tells the
story of the welcome Baucis and Philemon give to a pair of strangers who are in fact "The mightie Iove and Mercurie his sonne in
shape of men." In this famous story of rustic hospitality rewarded,
Mercury's disguise may recall his more particularized one in the
story of Battus. However, Jupiter too is disguised here, and there is
no other evidence of Mercury's tricksiness nor, indeed, of most of
the traits thus far noted, unless one count the excessiveness of the
retribution meted out to the thousand households guilty of inhospi-
tality: looking back from a hilltop the old couple "saw / How all

the towne was drowned saue their lyttle shed of straw" (sig. P3). But since the gods pronounce sentence in unison—"For wee bee Gods (quoth they) and all this wicked towneship shall / Abye their gylt" (ll. 868–69)—the vindictiveness like the deception is attenuated by being shared. In fact, Mercury's sharing of roles—traveler, punisher, rewarder—with Jupiter seems quite as important as any of the specific parts he plays. It is a collegiality in which the lightest of subordination dissolves into a kind of fraternity.

Much the same situation obtains in *Fasti* 5.493–534. Here the trio of disguised wayfaring gods Mercury, Jupiter, and Neptune reward Hyrieus's hospitality by granting his wish for a child, engendering Orion by urinating together onto the skin of an ox Hyrieus has slaughtered for them. This genital fraternization in a femaleless (or worse, the slaughtered hide possibly representing the female) procreation of another male stands as an extreme toward which Mercury tends persistently throughout his evolution. As will be seen, traces of that disturbing extreme appear in Mercutio.

The above-noted appearances of Mercury in *Metamorphoses*, as well as a few other minor ones,[12] are all colored by the role he plays in the story of Io in the first book of the poem (1.668–721; Golding, 1.831–903). In this tale, alluded to directly by Shakespeare in *The Taming of the Shrew*, *Love's Labour's Lost*, *The Merchant of Venice*, and *Troilus and Cressida*,[13] Jupiter attempts to hide one of his peccadilloes from Juno by changing Io into a heifer. Juno demands the heifer as a gift and then sets the hundred-eyed Argus to watch over it, whereupon enter Mercury in a quintessentially Ovidian amalgam of sweetness and brutality.

Mercury accepts with alacrity the assignment Jupiter gives him as a way of solving the dilemma:

> Now could no lenger Ioue abide his Lover so forlorne,
> And thereupon he cald his sonne that Maia had him borne,
> Commaunding Argus should be kild. He made no long abod,
> But tyde his feathers to his feete, and tooke his charmed rod.
> (With which he bringeth things a sleepe, and fetcheth soules
>   from Hell)
> And put his Hat upon his head: and when that all was well
> He leaped from his fathers towres, and downe to earth he
>   flue.
>
> (Golding, sig. C4)

Having laid aside cap and wings, and kept only his staff, Mercury in the guise of a goatherd plays a panpipe, and his music attracts Argus, who invites him to share the shade and pasture. With sundry talk and music Mercury does his best to lull Argus asleep (more humane than Ovid, Golding here has "Poore Argus," sig. C4v), to no avail until Argus inquires about his pipe.

Mercury then succeeds (unaccountably) in putting all Argus's hundred eyes to sleep with the brief, vivid, unsoporific story of Pan and Syrinx, ending with her transformation into the reeds with which Pan makes his pipe. For added insurance Mercury strokes all Argus's heavy eyes with his charmed rod, and then carries out his commission:

> Then with his Woodknife by and by he lightly to him stept,
> And lent him such a perlous blow, where as the shoulders
>   grue
> Unto the necke, that straight his heade quite from the bodie
>   flue.
> Then tombling downe the headlong hill his bloudie coarse he
>   sent,
> That all the way by which he rolde was stayned and besprent.
>   (Golding, sig. C5)

In Miller's translation Mercury uses a "hooked sword" (*Metamorphoses*, p. 53; "falcato . . . ense," l. 717) and sends the head rather than the body bleeding down the rocks. Still, Golding's most important alteration must be his "by and by he lightly to him stept" for Ovid's "nec mora" (l. 717; "forthwith," Miller, p. 53). Golding's adverb, with many of its rich semantic shadings brought into play by the context, is a brilliant stroke, for it shows the Ovidian Mercury at his most disquieting.

W H I L E it seems probable that Shakespeare had some acquaintance with Ovid's Mercury in the original Latin, and while he might also have known the god in the Latin of Plautus, Horace, and Virgil, he would have had more trouble with Apuleius, who wrote "in so darke and high a stile, and in so strange and absurd words, and in such new invented phrases, as hee seemed rather to set it forth to shew his magnificencie of prose, than to participate his doings to other" (Adlington, *Golden Asse*, sig. A4). But Adlington's popular translation, in three printings in the three decades before *Romeo and Juliet*, provides easy enough access.[14]

Mercury appears therein in three notable episodes. In the book's most popular, the inset story of Cupid and Psyche, at Jupiter's command Mercury in his office of herald aids Venus in her search for Psyche and then convenes the gods—"and if any of the celestiall powers did faile of appearance he would be condemned in ten thousand pounds: which sentence was such a terrour to all the goddesses, that the high Theatre was replenished" (sig. Q4v)—and escorts Psyche "into the Pallace of heaven" (sig. R1), where she is made immortal.

Later the judgment of Paris, one of the most popular subjects for Renaissance graphic portrayals of Mercury, is reenacted in a triumph:

> then came a young man a shepheard representing Paris, richly arrayed with vestments of Barbary, having a mitre of gold upon his head, and seeming as though he kept the goates. After him ensued another young man all naked, saving that his left shoulder was covered with a rich cloake, and his head shining with glistering haires, and hanging downe, through which you might perceive two little wings, whereby you might conjecture that he was Mercury, with his rod called Caduceus, he bare in his right hand an Apple of gold, and with a seemely gate went towards him that represented Paris, and . . . delivered him the Apple. (sig. 2E4v)

Here Mercury displays a kind of Ovidian heartlessness as, his youth and beauty emphasized,[15] he delivers the apple of discord to Paris. As will be seen below, this variant representation, with wings growing from the god's head instead of from his petasos, is not uncommon. It may express Mercury's cerebrality even more aptly than the standard representation.

Finally, in the procession honoring Isis, one of the initiates "held a tree of palme with leaves of gold, and the verge of Mercury" (Adlington, sig. 2G2v). The mortals are followed by a procession of gods in which Mercury appears as the dog-headed Anubis, one of the two Egyptian gods (the other being Thoth) with whom Mercury was identified from early times.[16] This final appearance in Apuleius invests Mercury with the pomp, exotic barbarity, and mystery of the Eastern religions.

IN the above-mentioned texts (and in many others as well, and in sculptures and pictorial representations, all beyond the scope of this study), Mercury assumes the character out of which postclassical versions of him evolve. In the texts examined, he is an exceedingly complex creature of disjunctions and contradictions. On the one hand he is Jupiter's herald, patron of merchants, an ancestor of Ulysses, and inventor of writing and mathematics—a culture hero and figure of rationality and urban civilization. On the other he is sender of dreams and border dweller, priapic herm and stone heap, patron of shepherds and father of the shepherds' god Pan,[17] trickster, and patron of thieves. He is at once a bearded patron of eloquence and a young golden-haired patron of gymnastics.[18] He may, as Martial (*Epigrams* 7.74) says, desire Paphie or be warm for Ganymede, but his eroticism transcends routine Olympian bisexuality. On the one hand, disturbing touches of misogyny color his heterosexual amours and, on the other, echoes of Ganymede in the ephebe subordinated to Jove may themselves disturb by virtue of the god's concomitant independence and autonomy. While among the Olympians he is uniquely tied to an office of service, unlike Iris he is no mere office personified. As herald he transports messages from gods to mortals, and souls from the land of the living to the world of the dead. More than any other Olympian he is a figure of helpfulness, companionship, and fraternality—with Jupiter, with Apollo, and with mortals—and yet he lies to and steals from his father and brother, and he punishes mortals peremptorily and severely with his own peculiar lightheartedness.

IN nearly every dimension but the chronological the medieval Mercury is more distant from Shakespeare than is the classical, and furthermore in late classical and medieval times the god situates himself in elaborate and competing structures of allegory, alchemy, and astrology well beyond the scope of the present study. Therefore a survey of the remainder of Mercury's itinerary to the Renaissance must stand in lieu of detailed attention to many textual specifics. But Mercury's appearance in Martianus Capella, whose "work may be likened to the neck of an hourglass through which the classical liberal arts trickled to the medieval world" (Stahl et al., *Martianus*, 1:ix), deserves notice since, while Shakespeare would probably not have known the work,[19] it was popular and influential, and it is in many respects representative of Mercury's medieval transformations.

In Martianus, *The Marriage of Philology and Mercury*, the fifth-century pedantic allegorical novel whose wide medieval popularity gives way to centuries of oblivion followed by widespread modern condemnation,[20] we find the classical god metamorphosing into his peculiarly attenuated or fragmented medieval embodiment. While he is the classical ephebe approaching manhood—

> his body, through the exercise of wrestling and constant running, glowed with masculine strength and bore the muscles of a youth perfectly developed. Already with the first beard on his cheeks, he could not continue to go about half naked, clad in nothing but a short cape covering only the top of his shoulders (Martianus, *Marriage*, p. 6)

—and the messenger of the gods, and is closely allied with his brother Apollo,[21] simultaneously or nearly so he is the Neoplatonic divine Mind or sacred Nous (p. 31), a planet with a known and fixed orbit (pp. 8, 15, 17), and the Egyptian god Thoth (pp. 35–36). Furthermore, in contrast to the classical Mercury's cavalier sexual impromptu, Martianus's Mercury dedicates himself to the institution of marriage and then goes looking for a fiancée (pp. 6–8), which bill the learned virgin Philology eventually fills.

According to recent commentary,

> The marriage of the soaring and subtle Mercury, dear to classical poets and satirists, to a medieval personification of musty handbook learning represents the decay of intellectual life in the West during the later centuries of the Roman Empire. Mercury's full circle is closed: In his earliest role, before assuming the graces of the Hermes of Greek poetry, Mercury was a trickster god of Italian marketplaces. He is here once again reduced to a bag of tricks—the rhetorical arts. (Stahl et al., *Martianus*, 1:231)

But dispersal accompanies the god's reduction. The system of allegory doubles and redoubles Mercury, and structurally similar correspondences come about through Martianus's "rich blend of faiths"

(Stahl et al., 1:87), including "astral religion ... Neopythagorean-ism, old Roman and Etruscan religious ideas, some Neoplatonic concepts, some Egyptian deities, more than a trace of Hermeti-cism" (Stahl et al., 1:83–84). Here there is space for only a glance at three of the vestments Mercury supplements his chlamys with for the long stroll from Martianus to Chaucer. Each in fact magnifies the associative resonances surrounding the classical god, while at the same time variously abstracting, reducing, and replacing the central figure.

Hermeticism. The hermeticism Stahl and others (see LeMoine, *Martianus*, p. 67n) find in Martianus derives of course from the *Corpus Hermeticum*, the body of assorted occult treatises dating from the third century A.D. whose putative author, Hermes Trisme-gistus, bears the name of—and is sometimes taken to be one and the same as (see Yates, *Study*, p. 85)—the Egyptian Thoth as more or less identified with Mercury. Through the Middle Ages these texts operate to associate Mercury with a Neoplatonic "religion of the world" (Yates, *Last Plays*, p. 90), with Eastern religious myster-ies, and (especially through the *Asclepius*) with magic. As trans-lated by Ficino at the behest of Cosimo de Medici, these works, still taken to be pre-Mosaic Egyptian texts, begin the second and more powerful phase of their influence, again in association with Neopla-tonism, in its own second, Renaissance, upsurge (see Seznec, Festu-gière, Yates, and others). Numerous commentators, including Yates in particular, have found influences of these works in Shakespeare, though none so far as I know has considered their influence on his idea of Mercury.

Astrology. Cumont, Seznec, and others recount the history of the association of preexisting gods with planets in Babylonia and later in Greece and Rome. Following Babylonian example, the Greeks learned to distinguish the planets from the fixed stars, and in the fifth century B.C. associated each planet with a Greek god. During the Alexandrian period, however, "the planetary lexicon be-comes extraordinarily confused. The planets change masters and their labels are correspondingly multiplied" (Seznec, *Survival*, p. 39). Greek astronomers then adopt names based entirely on the planets' physical characteristics, calling Mercury Στίλβων, the Bril-liant One.

Meanwhile, in the popular mind the associations between plan-ets and gods regularize. Then from the end of the Republic the designation *sidus* (or *stella*) *Mercurii* begins to be replaced by *Mercurius*, and the abbreviation becomes the name, establishing grounds for the late classical complete identification of the god with the planet and so helping to assure Mercury's survival:

> this process of "absorption" of the gods by the stars . . . finally resulted in assuring the gods of survival. One might indeed call it a piece of unhoped-for good luck on their side, for the old mythology had long been bankrupt and the Olympians had become mere phantoms. Now, however, a providential shelter is offered them . . . dethroned or about to be dethroned on earth, they are still masters of the celestial spheres, and men will not cease to invoke them and fear them. (Seznec, p. 42)

So Mercury takes his place in one of the great medieval systems of correspondences, that of astrology.

That system, pervasive in the Middle Ages and surviving well into the Renaissance (where of course it manifests itself importantly in Shakespeare's tragedy of star-crossed lovers), amplifies the received associations of Mercury with intelligence and learning, with eloquence, and with messages and guiding. At the same time it contributes to the medieval disintegration and dispersal of the classical figure, identifying him with the brilliant quick planet. The main significance for what happens when Mercury enters Shakespeare's love-tragedy would seem to be that through the god's medieval astrological transformations he acquires a dispersed power, an ability to influence from a distance, which acquired power he maintains then in his Renaissance reintegration (see Seznec, *Survival*, pp. 184–215).[22]

Alchemy. The most entirely medieval expansion and dispersal of the denotation of the god's name is its assignment to the metal. Through the late classical and early medieval periods there is considerable variation in assigned correspondences between metals and the seven planets, just as there had been earlier with the correspondences between gods and planets, although from Origen in the second century three equations remain constant. They are gold-sun, silver-moon, and lead-saturn. The three metals in question, the two noblest and one basest of the several lists, of course compose the caskets of *The Merchant of Venice*, which probably immediately follows *Romeo and Juliet*, and where some of the corpus of signification traced here recurs (see chap. 5). The planet Mercury was associated with both iron and the naturally occurring gold-silver alloy electrum before stabilizing around the seventh century in association with the metal it has since named in English and other European languages.

The stabilized equation of the planet Mercury with the metal mercury dates at least from the widely reproduced list of Stephanos of Alexandria (Crosland, *Studies*, p. 80). The metal does not appear in the earlier lists of Origen (second century A.D.) and Olympiodorus (sixth century A.D.), although the mining of cinnabar and extraction of mercury date from well before (Goldwater, *Mercury*, pp. 32–35, 49–50). The metal's nomenclature in the European languages is particularly interesting inasmuch as mercury is the only metal to which the name of the associated planet has extended in the way the gods' names earlier extended to the planets. The distinction reflects the "dominant role of 'mercury' in all of alchemy" (Goldwater, p. 25). And the metal's English nomenclature is interesting for the early establishment and long persistence of the synonym quicksilver, the term Shakespeare uses exclusively (though he would certainly have known the name mercury). Yet even quicksilver is sometimes used for a substance other than the metal, and Arab and European alchemists elaborated synonyms and secret names for the metal (Crosland, pp. 3–42).

The planet-god-metal correspondences show three variants in four historical stages in the European languages. For the two most familiar planets, whose recognition precedes everything else in the tabulation, all three names differ, so that we have the form *abc*:

planet	*god*	*metal*
sun	Apollo	gold
moon	Diana	silver

after these, the next correspondence to stabilize has an *aab* form:

Saturn	Saturn	lead

third in order of stabilization comes the unique *aaa* form:

Mercury	Mercury	mercury

the remaining three correspondences stabilize last, returning to the *aab* form:

Mars	Mars	iron
Venus	Venus	copper
Jupiter	Jupiter	tin

(The chronological order here is of course only the sequence of stabilization of all three terms of the equation, and some of the subsumed bipartite equations have other sequences. Equations of the first two terms in the fourth group, for instance, stabilize earlier than do the second and third terms in any group.)

Mercury's uniquely uniform nomenclature accords well with the fact that, while gold is the common aim in alchemy, mercury is central and preeminent for achieving that aim during the millennium from the fifth to the fifteenth century. "Mercury, either as quicksilver or as the metallic 'essence,' invariably appeared as a central figure" (Goldwater, *Mercury*, p. 25). Mercury's centrality derives from its liquidity (the characteristic Shakespeare highlights in his two references to the metal as quicksilver in *2 Henry 4* and *Hamlet*) and consequent ability to seem to dissolve other metals by forming alloys. Alchemical theory derives the centrality of mercury as a catalyst in the transmutation of baser metals into gold from Aristotle and other authorities, and holds that the constituents of all metals are mercury and sulphur (to which Paracelsus adds salt as a third essential constituent). Distinction is often made between the familiar metal and "our mercury" of the alchemists, a conveniently elusive substance that could at once be the same as and different from the metal.[23]

To look forward, all this suggests an alchemical underpinning for the action of *Romeo and Juliet*, where the titular heroes are transmuted into statues of "pure gold" (5.3.298)—in Brooke the tomb is of marble, and no statues are mentioned. And in that transmutation Mercutio plays a key catalytic role.[24]

THUS by the time Mercury reaches Chaucer his vigorous classical person and story have greatly attenuated. A ghost of his former self, Mercury thins and dwindles still further in the environment of Chaucer's earthiness and godliness. As McCall writes of Chaucer's gods in general, so with Mercury in particular, "When we . . . imagine backward and forward—to the statues of ancient Rome and Greece or to the reappearance . . . in later Renaissance and baroque art—the differences can overwhelm us" (McCall, *Gods*, p. 157). At least five of Chaucer's fourteen references to Mercury are clearly astrological (Dillon, *Dictionary*, p. 153), and with some of the others, for example, *Complaint of Mars* (ll. 113, 144), the planet is at least as much in view as the god. Wood notes that, "while Chaucer took the basic elements of his poem from Ovid, he cast them in a significant astrological form" (Wood, *Stars*, p. 115).

It is true that some traces of the classical Mercury appear in Chaucer. Troilus invokes him as psychopomp—

> "And, god Mercurye! of me now, woful wrecche,
> The soule gyde, and, whan the liste, it fecche!"
>   (*Troilus* 5.321–22)

—and the astrological analogue of the classical god's misogyny and antipathy to heterosexual love figures in the Wife of Bath's account of the opposition between the children of Mercury and those of Venus:

> Mercurie loveth wysdam and science,
> And Venus loveth ryot and dispence.
> And, for hire diverse disposicioun,
> Ech falleth in otheres exaltacioun.
>   (*Wife of Bath*, ll. 699–705)[25]

Even when Chaucer uses Mercury for a parodic "astrological embellishment" (Wood, *Stars*, p. 102)—

> Appollo whirleth up his chaar so hye,
> Til that the god Mercurius hous, the slye
>   (*Squire's Tale*, ll. 671–72)

—a touch of the god's character remains. It is only a touch though, and one may be tempted to see this moment, at which the tale breaks off without ending, as Mercury's medieval cul-de-sac.

Shakespeare in particular "made surprisingly little direct use of medieval writers, Chaucer included" (Reese, *Shakespeare*, p. 278). Surprisingly because "Shakespeare's mind was capacious and absorptive, and . . . he had a happy memory and a powerful digestion—or the fortunate gift of being able to recall at need almost anything that he had ever read or heard. Often this process may have been subconscious" (Reese, p. 275). It is rather in pre-Shakespearean Renaissance texts, especially those in English, that Mercury recovers the classical status of ground for the play of Shakespeare's absorptive and associative mind. He recovers that status partly by virtue of the frequency of his appearances, a frequency that makes the account of them here necessarily selective. The recovery also includes much of the classical god's complexity, peculiarity, and urgency, features made if anything more prominent by the broad range of medieval hermetic, astrological, and alchemical associations touched on above.

After his medieval dispersals, Mercury in the Renaissance recovers personhood; he becomes distinctly a person with personality and personalness. Seznec traces the disintegration and reintegration of the classical gods in pictorial representations through the Middle Ages and into the Renaissance, and he and others address and illustrate medieval transmutations of the classical Mercury into robed scribes, detached heads, figures whose "wings have so increased in size that they entirely cover the legs, and the chin and ears, and meet above the head to form a sort of crest" (Seznec, *Survival*, p. 181), in contrast to which stand most of the pictorial representations treated immediately below, where Mercury has full human, often nude, corporeality.

Yet even in these Renaissance pictorial representations Mercury sometimes appears with a kind of medieval or archaic or barbaric monstrosity, which indeed he, of the classical pantheon as it came to Shakespeare, seems most inclined to exhibit unabashedly. Particularly with some of Cartari's illustrations the god seems to say through Mercutio's visor, "What care I / What curious eye doth quote deformities?" (1.4.30–31).[26] Shakespeare's eye was curious and his visual memory excellent, so that some of the peculiarities in the pictures to follow may well have contributed to Mercutio.

Rather than leave the pre-Renaissance Mercury on the broken edge of *The Squire's Tale*, then, it seems more appropriate to end with a pair of his transitional appearances. The first is a combination of picture and text with both medieval and Renaissance elements. As with the preceding information about Mercury's medieval textual appearances, so here the claim is less about sources or resources than it is about the byways by which Mercury reaches his Renaissance embodiments. But with the second, in Henryson, the link with *Romeo and Juliet* may be more direct, given that *The Testament of Cresseid* appears in its first separate edition in 1593, and that within three or four years Shakespeare demonstrates knowledge of the poem in *Henry V* and *Twelfth Night*.

The woodcut accompanying the discussion of the "fixation" of Mercury in Nazari, *Della Tramutatione Metallica Sogni Tre*, 1572 (fig. 1), may put Shakespeareans in mind of Lavinia in *Titus Andronicus*, one of Shakespeare's characters who happens to be associated with Mercury, as we have seen. The mutilation is medieval in spirit and in fact illustrates one of the essentially medieval text's goals, the stabilizing or "fixing" of the fugitive metal as a stage on the way to the most fixed of metals, gold.[27] Yet the nudity, the *putto*'s face, the shading and the careful perspective all mark the picture as an unquestionably Renaissance production.

Contradictions and failures of congruence between text and illustration are of course very common in the first centuries of printing. They are not difficult to find in treatments of the classical gods, even though here they may be somewhat less common than generally since texts, especially mythographies, served not merely as occasions for illustration but also as guides to visual artists attempting to reconstruct the gods in the face of a scarcity of good visual models. All the same, with Nazari we find what seems a peculiarly Mercurial disjunction between illustration and text, an incongruity that recurs in some of the pictures treated in the next chapter. Of the illustrated statue Nazari (*Metallica*) writes:

> Questa (quantunque senza piedi, & membro genitale) all'ale pero del capello, & per il caduceo, connobbi ch'era la figura de Mercurio. (sig. B1v)
> [I knew that this (although without feet and genital member) was the figure of Mercury, because of his petasos and caduceus.][28]

There are actually several inconsistencies here—the caduceus missing from the picture, the missing hands missing from the text—but the key one concerns the god's penis, said to be absent in the text, and quite present in the illustration. As this particular ambivalence may suggest, in his Renaissance reintegration Mercury resumes a phallicity much like that of his classical embodiments, but one now deeply problematized. And as will be seen, the presence and absence of Mercutio's phallus index some of his uses to Shakespeare, as well as some of his uses in the culture Shakespeare delivers him to in 1595.

In contrast to Nazari's Mercury, the more medieval and astrological gods in Henryson's late-fifteenth-century portrayal of the coun-

1. The Fixation of Mercury; in Nazari, *Tramutatione*
(Rare Books and Manuscripts Division, New York Public Library,
Astor, Lenox and Tilden Foundations)

cil to determine Cresseid's fate are all clothed. In Cresseid's dream
Cupid summons the seven planets, who arrive in the order of their
spheres from Saturn down, so that Mercury arrives next to last,
before Lady Cynthia:

> With buik in hand than come Mercurius,
> Richt eloquent and full of rethorie,
> With polite termis and delicious,
> With pen and ink to report all reddie,
> Setting sangis and singand merilie;
> His hude was reid, heklit [fringed] atour his croun,
> Lyke to ane poeit of the auld fassoun.
>
> Boxis he bair with fine electuairis [medical conserves],
> And sugerit syropis for digestioun,
> Spycis belangand to the pothecairis,
> With mony hailsum sweit confectioun;
> Doctour in Phisick cled in ane skarlot goun,
> And furrit weill—as sic ane aucht to be—
> Honest and gude, and not ane word culd lie.
>
> (Henryson, *Testament*, ll. 239–52)

In this portrait there may be irony in attributing veracity to the
god of thieves and in the scarlet furred gown that shows how profitable the profession of medicine may be. Here the planet is com-
pounded with the god of eloquence and writing, and the Mercury-
Aesculapius figure of healing, and given the unusual attribute of
the merry songs. The portrait is supplemented a few lines later
with more about Mercury's "facound toung and termis exquisite"
(l. 268), and with what may be the sole surviving classical appurtenance in Mercury's tipping his "cap" (l. 271) to Cupid.

If Shakespeare knew the Henryson as Mercutio took shape, he
would surely have recalled the description of the seven planets,
"perhaps the most lively and arresting in English literature" (Stearns,
"Portraits," p. 911), and in particular that of Mercury, "one of Henryson's happiest creations" (p. 925), in which case Mercury's merry
songs in Henryson may well lie behind Mercutio's song, "An old
hare hoar." Furthermore, especially given Shakespeare's Mercury-
spice associative cluster, this Mercury's "Boxis . . . with . . . Spycis
belangand to the pothecairis" (ll. 246–48) may be involved in
Shakespeare's Apothecary of 5.1 (see below, chap. 5).

CHAPTER TWO.

RENAISSANCE PICTURES WITH TEXT

MERCURY returns in the Renaissance, along with other Olympians and assorted friends, throughout Europe (as demonstrated by Seznec and others), and in England in particular (as demonstrated by Purdon and others), in embodiments and portrayals far too numerous for complete documentation here. Rather the following pages are concerned only with those portions of the widening stream that might have flowed through the particular conduit of Shakespeare's mind to manifest themselves in the character of Mercutio. This is to say that I am concerned primarily with texts in English, or presumed to be available in England, before 1595, and even with these considerable selection is necessary. This chapter concerns pictorial representations, especially those associated with text or commentary, particularly in Cartari and in emblem books, while chapter 3 treats the god's important appearances in English texts alone.

The pictured gods survive and revive in the Renaissance, as Seznec demonstrates, largely through the richly fallible process of illustration, taken here most widely to mean the transference of textual description (often, as with the Cartari discussed below, of lost or otherwise unavailable ancient visual representations) into new visual representation. Some short circuits occur, as when a Hellenistic Hermes drawn by the antiquary and "Mercurialist" Cyriac of Ancona combines with appurtenances from the Mercury illustrating the mythographer Albricus, resulting in the Mercury of the *Tarocchi* of Mantegna (Seznec, *Survival*, pp. 199–201). Generally though the renaissance of the visually represented gods is from texts, including those treated above, many with new leases on life themselves. Such is the case even with many seemingly autonomous representations: in the broad sense just adumbrated, they illustrate texts.

In these translations from word into picture or sculpture Mercury appears too frequently for more than a glance here. He appears in textiles such as the Brussels Pannemaker tapestry showing Mercury and Herse (reproduced as the frontispiece to Candee, *Tapestry*), or the embroidery by Mary Queen of Scots—"of *Mercurius* charming *Argos*, with his hundred eyes, expressed by his *Caduceus*, two *Flutes*, and a Peacock, the word *Eloquentium tot lumina clausit*—" described by Jonson (*Works*, 1:208–9). He appears in frescoes such as that of Mercury and Psyche at the Farnesina in Rome, in reliefs and other architectural elements, in freestanding sculptures, and in still more paintings and prints. Among the most popular subjects are Mercury alone, often in series as a planetary deity or Olympian, and with mythographic appurtenances or the head of Argus, Mercury instructing Amor, Mercury with Cupid and Psyche, with the three Graces, with Argus and Io, with Minerva, with Aglauros, and perhaps above all Mercury in various stages of the judgment of Paris. Carracci, Cranach, Raphael, Raimondi, and Giulio Romano each shows Mercury in his *Judgment of Paris*.

The ancient cults of Mercury are reborn in the fervor of such "Mercurialists" as Cyriac of Ancona, who composed prayers to the god, and who copied a Hellenistic Mercury during travels in Greece. He later circulated the drawing among friends in Italy, where it influenced the Mantegna *Tarocchi* (Seznec, *Survival*, pp. 200–201),[1] and perhaps also provided the inverted tongues of flame on the chlamys of Botticelli's Mercury in the *Primavera* (Wind, *Mysteries*, p. 121n). The ancient cults were also reborn in the learned Neoplatonic hermeticism whose influences appear in some representations of the god, such as the Bonasone engravings for the *Emblems* of Bocchi discussed below. According to Wind (pp. 113–27), these same kinds of influences appear notably in the Botticelli *Primavera*.

Taking the part played by Mercury in that picture to be "the crux of any interpretation" (p. 121), Wind finds initially odd Mercury's disengagement from the Graces he normally leads. Acknowledging resonances between the inverted flames suggestive of death and the god's role of psychopomp, and between his heavenward gaze and his role as wind-god and skimmer of clouds, Wind (p. 122) yet holds that the most germane Mercurial role is that of mystagogue: "to humanists Mercury was above all the 'ingenious' god of the probing intellect, sacred to grammarians and metaphysicians, the patron of lettered inquiry and interpretation to which he had lent his very name (ἑρμηνεία), the revealer of secret or 'Hermetic' knowledge, of which his magical staff became a symbol." In this role, then, Botticelli's Mercury raises his eyes to contemplate intellectual beauty, while at the other side of the painting in a corresponding reverse movement, passion descends to earth from the beyond in the breath of the wind god Zephyr.

To elaborate for a moment on Wind, we may say that Mercury in his Renaissance pictorial and sculptural representations embodies kinds of impacted hermeneutical richness specific only to him. While as donor of the alphabet he is a patron of writing, as patron of lettered inquiry he is mystagogue of the text and patron of the interpretation of the written word. In particular he is patron of that interpretation here called illustration, that translation of textual information into visual representation through which all the pagan gods achieve their Renaissance reintegrations. Thus in a sense the pictured or sculpted Mercury represents textual-to-visual representation itself. To put the matter slightly differently, Mercury alone among the pictured and sculpted gods may be said to stand precisely for himself.

One group of painted and drawn Mercurys deserves special attention here. These are the representations of the god by the only visual artist Shakespeare names, Giulio Romano, "that rare Italian master" (*Winter's Tale* 5.2.96) said to be responsible for the "statue" of Hermione.[2] Pafford in his note on the passage suggests that "Shakespeare may have seen some of Julio's paintings, and Vasari's *Lives* in Italian." Of course the *Winter's Tale* reference by itself cannot place Shakespeare's knowledge of Giulio earlier than 1611, although Sells (*Influence*, pp. 193–94, 208) uses it in conjunction with the painting of Troy viewed by Lucrece to argue that the latter is based on Giulio's Troy frescoes in Mantua Shakespeare saw during a visit there in 1593. However, without adopting Sells's proposal one may still admit the possibility that Shakespeare knew something of Giulio's work by 1595, perhaps by report. He may in particular have known something of the nine or more Mercurys Hartt attributes to Giulio.[3] But the figures themselves are conventional, as with the drawing of Mars and Mercury (fig. 2), where the god is accoutred with chlamys, caduceus, and winged petasos and talaria, or the Mercury fresco in Giulio's own house in Mantua, with the

2. Mars and Mercury; Giulio Romano
(British Museum)

3. Mercury; Giulio Romano
(Mr. Luigi Risi; photograph, Frick Art Reference Library)

same accoutrements except the purse (fig. 3), so that I see no reason to give them any special weight in the composition of Shakespeare's Mercury.

In fact it seems probable that Giulio Romano relates to the Mercury-Mercutio axis less by his artistry than by his name. It would have fallen nicely to hand for a Shakespeare engaged in what was partly a reprise of *Romeo and Juliet* in a mellower key. The "piece many years in doing and now newly performed" (*Winter's Tale* 5.2.94–95) may be not only the "statue" but also *The Winter's Tale* itself. Furthermore the "many years in doing" could be the duration referred to in the next speech when Second Gentleman remarks that Paulina "hath privately . . . ever since the death of Hermione, visited that removed house"; that is, the sixteen years the Chorus slides over at the beginning of Act 4. Since imaginary artistic labors may be had for the asking, there seems no reason to stint; and the Chorus's "wide gap" may stretch precisely from 1595 to 1611 (see also Fineman, *Eye*, p. 307).

WHILE some continental works of visual art had found their way across the Channel into Shakespeare's England, as had reports and commentary, the best avenue into Shakespeare's consciousness for pictures of Mercury was probably via such illustrated printed books as the mythographies that served importantly for the Renaissance invasion of England by the gods. Seznec (*Survival*, pp. 312–15) summarizes and builds on the work of Bush, Schoell, and others, illustrating widespread English familiarity with mythographies of Boccaccio, Giraldi, Comes, Textor, and Cartari, with allusions and unacknowledged borrowings in works by Spenser, Marlowe, Chapman, and Marston. Purdon (*Mercury*, 1974) more recently surveys English Renaissance mythography, with extended treatments of Batman, *The Golden Booke of the Leaden Goddes* (1577), and Fraunce, *The Third Part of the Countesse of Pembroke's Yuychurch* (1592), among the mythographic works before *Romeo and Juliet*. Purdon (p. 145) enlarges interestingly on the nature of the specifically English fascination with mythography, arguing that one cause "is certainly that much of this mythic material . . . celebrated the power and ubiquity of sexuality. Mythological writing in England between 1580 and 1630 was avidly concerned with . . . especially those aspects of sexuality which found little hope of sanction in a narrow Christian morality. Though this mode was still Italian in fashion,

speech and colouring, for a brief period the English outdid Aretine."
One such unsanctioned aspect is of course the strong undercurrent
of homosexuality that runs through the figure of Mercury almost
from the beginning, and that powerfully animates Mercutio as well.

Of these mythographies the most popular was Vincenzo Cartari,
Le Imagini de i Dei de gli Antichi (1556, 1571, 1580, 1581, 1587,
etc.).[4] Purdon (p. 57) cites some of the "overwhelming" evidence
that the *Le Imagini* "was known, whether in Italian, French, or
Latin, by a wide circle of cultivated readers" in the Renaissance
even before the English adaptation by Linche, *The Fountaine of
Ancient Fiction*, 1599. While Seznec (*Survival*, p. 315) goes so far
as to mention "indications pointing to Shakespeare's having known
. . . Cartari," he reveals none of these indications other than a
doubtful claim by a Baconian.[5] But narrowly specific allusion is
hardly necessary to support the assumption that the work would
have crossed Shakespeare's path.

Its popularity derived importantly from the illustrations that accompany the text from 1571 and that migrate to later editions of
Giraldi and Comes and "contributed to the favour of those works,
especially in England, provincial as ever in this respect, and starved
for pictures" (Purdon, *Mercury*, p. 57). We may suppose that Shakespeare in particular would have been drawn to the engravings by
Zaltieri in the Venetian printings of Cartari's Italian text (*Le Imagini*, 1571, 1580, 1587) or the later woodcuts by Ferroverde in the
three 1581 editions from Lyon (being the Italian original and French
and Latin versions translated and augmented by Du Verdier) more
immediately than to the surrounding foreign text. Many of the illustrations are fairly riveting, as Purdon (p. 58) seems to acknowledge even in his protest, "What a collection of monsters stares at us
shamelessly from the pages."

And many of the pictures are of Mercury. He appears more often
than does Apollo, more often than any other major god with the
possible exception of Bacchus.[6] In Cartari's characteristically rambling chapter about Mercury, Peace, and Hercules entitled "Mercurio" (sig. Pp3v–Xx2; *Le Imagini* textual references are to the Venetian editions of 1571–80, the Zaltieri reproductions are from the
1580 printing of that edition, and the Ferroverde reproductions are
from the 1581 French edition), the god appears in his most familiar
form and most fully accoutred in the first illustration (sig. Pp4, fig.
4), where he appears with the goddess Peace. He holds the caduceus

4. Mercury with Peace; Zaltieri, in Cartari, *Imagini*
(Folger Shakespeare Library)

with entwined and knotted snakes (and without wings) and a purse. He wears the winged petasos and a chlamys over his shoulder (and nothing else); his heels are winged. He is accompanied by a goat and a cock.

Cartari says something, culled from classical and medieval sources, including some discussed above, about all these details.[7] They are all, according to Appian, the characteristic insignia ("insegna propria," sig. Pp4v) of the god. The caduceus is a symbol of peace because Mercury, having found two serpents fighting, threw between them the wand given him by Apollo, and so established concord. The purse indicates Mercury's concern with profit. Cartari quotes Virgil on the wand, talaria (absent though they be from the first illustration and some others), and wings. Mercury's feathers are for speed, because he is god of speech, and of commerce. The cock stands either for the vigilance of merchants or for the sleeplessness of the learned. The accompanying figure in this illustration is the goddess Peace with her own insignia, including the child Pluto, god of wealth.

Mercury appears rather similarly on the left in the illustration on signature Rr2v (fig. 5), although here he is without purse, goat, and cock, and the wings have migrated from his feet to the here unknotted caduceus. He makes a somewhat stranger figure here, as one of Zaltieri's starers—as if in consternation at some of the metamorphoses he must now undergo in the book's illustrations, beginning with the one on the right side of the same picture.

This figure illustrates a page-long discussion of the "Figura quadrata di Mercurio" (sig. Rr4–Rr4v). According to Pausanias, since Mercury invented letters, music, geometry, and gymnastics, and since in ancient times these four elements represented the cornerstones of physical and intellectual activity, it was customary to make his image on a quadrate pedestal installed in schools in certain parts of Arcadia. The account that follows (*Le Imagini*, sig. Rr3–Rr4) exemplifies Cartari's uncritical transmission of nonce explications and his routine citation of authority:

> Pausanias . . . describes him . . . dressed with a cape, [he] had neither legs nor feet, but was made as a small square column. . . . Galen depicts him young and handsome . . . with shining, sparkling eyes and places him on a square base. He who follows virtue . . . standing still and fixed [this a nonalchemical "fix-

5. Mercurys with Palestra; Zaltieri, in Cartari
(Folger Shakespeare Library)

ation"] . . . fears no injury from Fortune. Suidas writes that the square figure was given to Mercury because he spoke truthfully. He always stands firm and steadfast against anyone.[8]

Cartari says nothing about whether this Mercury's quadrate pedestal begins above or below his virile member, and, if anything, Zaltieri's engraving heightens the uncertainty of the organ's presence or absence. The girdling folds seem to cross just above what the corner of the chlamys seems nevertheless positioned to hide.

Ferroverde in the corresponding woodcut (sig. Ccc2v, fig. 6) lowers the curve of the girdling folds a bit on the quadrate Mercury's loins so that the end of the chlamys seems held more strategically, and the general effect is one of a certain salacious modesty. That effect seems peculiarly in keeping with Ferroverde's modification of Zaltieri's left-hand Mercury in the picture. There the god's male genitals have simply disappeared—there is hardly room for them in the shadow below the belly—and this Mercury in fact seems a bit of a transsexual, not only in the pubic region but also along the left profile of the torso and in the left breast.

Strategic folds of cloth are common as fig leaves, nor is censorship by simple deletion at any stage before or after the printing of illustrations especially rare. Furthermore, the concern here is neither with the dynamics of Ferroverde's psyche, nor even with the differences in levels and kinds of censorship between Venice and Lyon in the seventies and eighties, however interesting those subjects might be. Rather I wish to suggest that the evolution from figure 5 to figure 6 manifests much the same instability noted above with the alchemical illustration (fig. 1) and text, an instability more associated with Mercury than with any other god, and symptomatic of Renaissance discomfort and fascination with his newly problematic gender and sexuality. These Renaissance attitudes manifest themselves in strategies of both emphasis and denial of the god's phallicity. When the denial is accompanied with a degree of feminization, as with the Ferroverde left-hand god, one sort of homosexuality may be suggested. More often than not, however, the received body of story treated above makes Renaissance emphasis on the god's phallicity suggest not heterosexuality but a different sort of homosexuality. These factors seem especially important in the generation of Shakespeare's Mercutio, that most phallic of his characters, and they have also figured importantly in

6. Mercurys with Palestra; Ferroverde, in Cartari
(Folger Shakespeare Library)

the culture's subsequent processing of Mercutio (see chaps. 6 and 7).

The figure seated between the two Mercurys in the illustration under discussion is Palestra, or Gymnastics herself, one of the above-mentioned cornerstones of education. Cartari (*Le Imagini,* sig. Rr2–Rr3) writes of her: "Palestra . . . was the daughter of Mercury, and she was such that it could hardly be said whether she was male or female. At any rate, she had a smooth face and even though graceful she seemed to be more a boy than a girl. . . . the breasts were no larger than those of a delicate young man."[9] Although not much of the figure's grace remains in the Ferroverde, there (as in Zaltieri) Palestra looks in fact rather more female than male. But what is important is that, whether explicit in text or suggested in the illustration, the androgyny of Ferroverde's left-most Mercury appears also in the figure here closely associated with him.

If varying strategies of denial of gender appear in the Cartari Mercurys with Palestra, the three herms in the next Zaltieri illustration (sig. Rr3v, fig. 7) fairly sensationally exhibit the opposite strategy, that of emphasis. It is rendered doubly startling by its total absence from the immediately accompanying text on the facing page, where Cartari moves logically enough from the quadrate Mercury to the herms, citing several authorities including the Plutarch discussed above: "the Greeks often made the statue of Mercury square in shape, with only the head, without any limbs . . . which were called herms. . . . Cicero . . . says herms ornament all the academies. . . . The Athenians first made these statues . . . which could be called truncated, having no other extremity but the head" (sig. Rr4–Rr4v).[10] Cartari then proceeds to recount the legend of Mercury's bringing eloquence to humankind, thence to his sponsorship of merchants and scholars, whereupon he begins to discuss a different god altogether, Sleep (sig. Rr4v–Ss3), perhaps leaving the reader to wonder whether Cartari is following the example he later gives from Pausanias of the Corinthians' treatment of their bronze statue of Mercury—

> Di che ei tace la ragione aposta, come cosa misteriosa, e che non si possa ne si debba dire. (sig. Tt1)
> [As if it were a mysterious thing that cannot and should not be said, mention of it is purposely avoided.]

—and perhaps to turn back to the illustration to see whether the unmentioned parts really were there at all.

The problem is not that Cartari finds them unmentionable but rather that Zaltieri here illustrates noncontiguous portions of the rambling text. After some discussion of Sleep and dreams, Cartari breaks off to return to Mercury (sig. Ss3v), whom he discusses for a couple of pages before mentioning what appears eleven pages (and two illustrations) earlier in the Zaltieri engraving. Having recounted some intricate linkages of Mercury with the sun from Macrobius—Mercury represents the sun's speed, and his killing of many-eyed Argus is like the sun's dimming of stars at daybreak—Cartari continues,

> Oltre di ciò le figure quadrate di Mercurio, che haueuano il capo solo, & il membro uirile, mostrauano, che'l Sole è capo del mondo, e seminatore de tutte le cose. (sig. Tt1–Tt1v)
> [Besides this, the squared figures of Mercury with only the head and the male member showed that the sun was the head of the world and the originator of all things.]

Then, after still three more interpretations of the four corners of the herms' columns, Cartari (*Le Imagini*) adds,

> come scriue Herodoto, e gli Atheniese furono i primi che facessero, e mostrassero à gli altri di fare parimente le statoe di Mercurio col membro genitale dritto, forse perche dissero le favole, e lo riferisce Marco Tullio, che à lui si gonfiò, e drizzosi in quel modo per la voglia che gli venne de Proserpina la prima volta che la vide. (sig. Tt1v)
> [As Herodotus writes, the Athenians were the first to make and show others how to make statues of Mercury with his penis erect. Perhaps it was because it was told in legends and reported by Cicero that Mercury's desire for Proserpina gave him an erection the first time he saw her.]

Only here did Zaltieri find the appendages that easily divert attention from the beguilingly unconcerned faces above them in his engraving.

Some of the attention Mercury's genitals have drawn has understandably been disapproving. One of the Folger Library copies of the 1571 edition has the offending parts painted out, seemingly early in the book's history. Linche's 1599 unillustrated English ver-

7. Herms; Zaltieri, in Cartari
(Folger Shakespeare Library)

sion, *The Fountaine of Ancient Fiction*, elides the offending portion of the text. Ferroverde's corresponding woodcut (sig. Ccc3v, fig. 8) shows clear signs of second thoughts between the original and printed states. Since he has here kept the lighting from the conventional left but let the image reverse itself, the priapic herm would originally have been even more scandalous than in Zaltieri.

The next illustration in Cartari (*Le Imagini*, sig. Ss2v, fig. 9) is the most complex of the series on Mercury. One more herm appears, a bare quadrate roadside column topped by a three-headed god. At the base of the column is one of the stone heaps sacred to the cult of Mercury and probably serving originally as boundary markers, as well as a heap of first fruits of the season left for hungry travelers, as Cartari explains. The three heads might also have to do with travel, indicating the three ways one must choose from at a crossroads, or—this is one of Cartari's own frequent hermeneutic crossroads—they might show the great force of Mercury's eloquence (sig. Ss4).

A similar figure appears in French and Italian editions of Francesco Colonna's 1499 *Poliphili Hypnerotomachia*, both in the figure here reproduced from the French translation of 1546, *Discours du Songe de Poliphile* (sig. X1, fig. 10) and in illustrations of the triumph of the blindfolded Cupid on the two pages that follow. The god appears more recognizably elsewhere in the book's illustrations of an anecdote about Mercury's delivery of Cupid from Venus to Jupiter (sig. K5, fig. 11) and of a version of the birth of Bacchus (sig. K6v, fig. 12). While neither accompanying text identifies Mercury, for once the book's relentless mystification is mercifully transparent. The first figure is "vn messager aiant aëlles aus piedz" (sig. K5), and the second "vn ieune ho[m]me aiant aelles aus piedz & en sceptre entortillé de deux serpe[n]s" (sig. K6v). The English *Hypnerotomachia: The Strife of Loue in a Dreame*, London, 1592, is much the same. Yet the ithyphallic herm of figure 10, even though bareheaded and not identified in any way in the illustrated text, clearly is an analogue of the Cartari herms.[11]

To return to figure 9, two of the other Mercurys illustrate accounts introduced by Cartari with the statement that in ancient times Mercury was a patron of shepherds ("hauesse cura de pastori," sig. Ss4) and that are based on descriptions from Pausanias of statues of the god. The armed Mercury in the center of the illustration carries a ram and brandishes the scimitar with which he killed

8. Herms; Ferroverde, in Cartari
(Folger Shakespeare Library)

9. Mercurys, herm, Anubis; Zaltieri, in Cartari
(Folger Shakespeare Library)

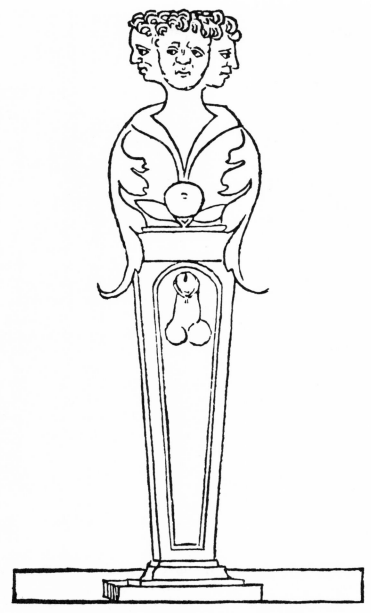

10. Herm; in Colonna, *Hypnerotomachia*
(Department of Rare Books, William R. Perkins Library, Duke University)

11. Mercury with Cupid; in Colonna
(Folger Shakespeare Library)

Argus. He wears the winged ankle bands that are Zaltieri's talaria with this and the left-hand figure here and again later in signature Xx3. The left-hand Mercury, in petasos and chlamys, also carries a ram. "Another statue was kept by the Tanagrei, a people from Beotia. This had a ram around its neck because it is said that Mercury ended a terrible plague by walking around the walls of the city that way. So when that town celebrated the feast of Mercury, a handsome young man circled the city walls with a lamb hung around his neck" (Cartari, *Le Imagini*, sig. Tt1).[12] Given the suggestive resonances with *Romeo and Juliet* in this association of Mercury, city walls, voyages, and plague, we may pause for a moment to touch on another set of resonances between the play and both Pausanian Mercurys in figure 9.

The Nurse calls Juliet by the pet name "lamb" twice (1.3.3, 4.5.2). She also tells Juliet that Romeo is gentle as a lamb (2.5.44), to which Juliet as in reply, in her first outburst at the Nurse's bad news, calls Romeo a "wolvish-ravening lamb" (3.2.76). Furthermore, as Gibbons suggests, there may be another lamb in the date of Juliet's birth, Lammas Eve: "the Nurse may . . . make the popular, fallacious assumption that *Lammas* derives from Lamb and Mass" (1.3.15n). This little flock, all Shakespeare's addition, seems to be a spin-off of the Mercurial transmutation of Brooke's Mercutio into Shakespeare's. The only place in Brooke where Juliet is said

12. Mercury with infant Bacchus; in Colonna
(Folger Shakespeare Library)

to be like a lamb—indeed the only appearance of the word in the poem—is in the handful of lines about Mercutio among the bashful maids, "Even as a Lyon . . . emong the lambes" (l. 257). Thus, while Shakespeare erases Brooke's Mercutio-Juliet interaction, it leaves echoes in the play's lambs. Hence one may say that Mercutio's ex- foliation in Shakespeare is a determinant not only of Romeo's char- acterization but also of Juliet's. Mercury in his role of patron of shepherds also figures in two reprises of Mercutio, Phebe's "Dead shepherd" in *As You Like It* (discussed in chap. 5) and Autolycus, the thief at the sheep-shearing festival in *The Winter's Tale*.

Without his caduceus the fourth personage in figure 9 might not be recognizable as Mercury. He is Anubis, the Egyptian Mercury from Martianus:

> con capo di cane per mostrare la sagacità che da Mercurio ci viene, conciosia che altro animale non si troui quasi piu sagace del cane. (*Le Imagini*, sig. Tt2)
> [with a dog's head to show the sagacity that comes from Mer- cury, because no other animal is more sagacious than the dog.]

Cartari goes on to explain that Anubis's canine head derives from his doglike loyalty to his father Osiris. The Mercury-Anubis con- nection leaves traces elsewhere in the Renaissance, as in the *Songe de Poliphile* illustration, figure 10, or in the initial in an edition of Martial from around 1470 that is discussed and reproduced in Armstrong (*Painters*, pp. 69, 105, illus. 14), showing the dog-headed god identified by an inscription simply as "Mercvrivs," with caduceus, wings at wrists as well as at heels and back, and the tortoiseshell lyre (fig. 13). Without dwelling on the matter we may recognize that, given Shakespeare's own apparent attitude to man's best friend, Mercury's canine connections would have given him negative overtones that may be active in Mercutio's two mentions of dogs in 3.1, his mock-accusation of Benvolio for quarreling with a man "because he hath wakened thy dog that hath lain asleep in the sun" (ll. 25–26) and his dying "Zounds, a dog, a rat, a mouse, a cat, to scratch a man to death" (ll. 101–2)—and also, more subtly, in the interchange between Romeo and the Nurse about " 'R' . . . the dog's name" (2.5.205–6) and in Romeo's near-echo of Mercutio in his talk of "every cat and dog / And little mouse" (3.3.30–31).

The number and complexity of Cartari's roadside Mercurys in figure 9 may suggest the importance of the site for Renaissance conceptions of the god. Only the first of the other Cartari Mercurys (fig. 4) appears in quite so geographically specified a setting, and there Peace's posture does less to suggest travel than does Anubis's here. Even the three heads of the herm in figure 9, as will be remembered, may signify roadways. This site, resonant with Mercury's role as ruler of border regions and wildernesses as well as of his role as guide—of travelers, of dreams, of dead souls—is, as we are about to see, where he also appears most frequently in the emblem books.

Mercury appears twice more in his own person in the illustrations in *Le Imagini de i Dei de gli Antichi* of Cartari. In the company of Minerva (sig. Xx3) and the Graces (sig. Aaaa2v) he looks most like himself, without physical aberration and for the first time with all four accoutrements: petasos, caduceus, talaria, and chlamys, a corner of which a convenient breeze has blown across his genitals in the first illustration, while his pose hides them in the second. Never mind that one of the pictures grows out of Cartari's discussion of the barbaric late-composite Hermathena—in the last pictures Zaltieri rewards Mercury for the preceding transmutations with orthodoxy.

IN the emblem books[13] Mercury appears in guises and situations largely derived from classical texts and the mythographies, and he

13. Mercury-Anubis; in Venetian Martial
(Bibliothèque Mazarine)

appears not infrequently. He may in fact be said to preside over the entire genre because of his patronage of hermeneutics, and also because Alciati, the author of the first and most famous of the emblem books, came to have as his own motto "Caduceum Mercurie," with the symbol reproduced from his *Emblematum Libellus* (1534, sig. B3v) of the petasos, caduceus, and cornucopias.[14] Here, after briefly considering eight varied representations of the god from emblem books, I look more closely at a ninth, the *in trivio* Mercury of the crossroads as he appears in four versions in three emblem books.

In emblem books as in mythographies Mercury occasionally appears in Olympian synods, as in Nicolaus Reusner's *Emblemata*, 1581 (sig. E1v, fig. 14). Here the only easily identifiable gods are Jove and Mercury, and Mercury holds an intermediate position between Jove and the arc of other gods. Thus the emblem's *pictura* gives Mercury a fairly exact visual structural analogue of the isolation with Jove and the light quasifraternal subordination to him remarked above, especially in Ovid's story of the visit to Baucis and Philemon. Reusner also has an *in trivio* Mercury discussed below, and the *subscriptio* of Book 1, Emblem 25 (sig. H2v), links Mercury and Bacchus.

In Guillaume de La Perrierre, *La Morosophie*, 1553, Mercury appears first as both planetary deity and patron of learning in the conventional analogy of planets and ages (cf. Ralegh, *History*, 1.2.5). After an emblem of a child led by the inconstant moon, in the *pictura* of the second emblem (sig. B6v–B7, fig. 15) a conventionally accoutred Mercury leads a boy. The *subscriptio* both in Latin and in French explains that after age seven, when he becomes capable of being taught, the boy is led by Mercury because he is the patron of all learning ("Car tous artz ont de luy fondement prins," sig. B7).[15] Later, in Perrierre's Emblem 89 (sig. N5v–N6, fig. 16), Mercury without talaria follows Phoebus:

> Co[m]e Phoebus prés de soy ha Mercure,
> Lequel le suyt, ou qu'il face son cours:
> Tous Roys aussi doiuent auoir la cure
> D'entretenir gens doctes à leurs courz
> (sig. N6)
> [As Phoebus has Mercury near him,
> Following him in his course,
> So kings should take care
> To have learned people at their courts.]

In this unusual case of Mercury's following rather than leading we find much the same neat amalgamation of planet and Olympian as in Perrierre's first Mercury, and the same association with learning.

In addition to Mercury's conventional appurtenances many other of the features and details noted above appear in emblem-book representations. In Geoffrey Whitney, *A Choice of Emblemes*, 1586, Mercury tuning a lute (sig. M2v, fig. 17) recalls the seated Mercury-Anubis with tortoiseshell lyre. In the *Emblemata* of Hadrianus Ju-

14. Synod of gods; in Reusner, *Emblemata*
(Folger Shakespeare Library)

nius (1565), Mercury as a pair of Siamese twins (sig. B2, fig. 18), said
in the *subscriptio* to be dissimilar but not noticeably so in the
plate, recalls Cartari's three-headed herm as well perhaps as his
other herms and his quadrate Mercury. Visual echoes with Cartari
also appear in the more arcane Mercurys of Achille Bocchi, *Symbolicae Quaestiones*, 1574. As *divinus amator* (sig. Tt4v, fig. 19) the
Mercury walking on flames holds a palm branch with the caduceus,
as does Cartari's Mercury-Anubis. The gesture of his left hand,
which may suggest a kind of musing, seems in fact to be a version
of that of the other most often reproduced Bocchi Mercury.[16]

Bocchi 64 (sig. Ss1v, fig. 20), like the Mercurys just discussed, has
a visual echo in Cartari, though not with Cartari's Mercurys. It
deserves mention because it is often reproduced and discussed, and
because it bears importantly on the subject of Mercury's eloquence.
The god holds his finger to his lips in the gesture of the god of
silence, Harpocrates, which Cartari reports from Apuleius and Martianus (sig. Zz3v)—"la sua statoa . . . era di giouinetto, che se te-
neua il dito alla bocca, come si fa quando si mostra altrui con cenno

15. Mercury leading a boy; in La Perrierre, *Morosophie*
(Folger Shakespeare Library)

16. Mercury following Phoebus; in La Perrierre
(Folger Shakespeare Library)

17. Mercury tuning a lyre; in Whitney, *Emblemes*
(Folger Shakespeare Library)

che taccia" [his statue . . . was of a boy holding his finger to his mouth as a sign for silence]—and which Zaltieri illustrates (sig. Zz4). The gesture itself, deriving from an early Greek misinterpretation of Egyptian representations of the infant Horus sucking his finger (Seznec, *Survival*, p. 296), is of considerable pragmatic and hermeneutic interest, especially when transferred from the god of silence to the god of eloquence. While it can, as Cartari states, signal to others that they should keep silent, it does so by a special rationale of imitation: you do as I am doing (or at least achieve the same effect). With this meaning, the gesture may also carry the added signal, "and listen to what I am about to say."

So understood, the gesture would be not paradoxical but rather precisely appropriate for the god of eloquence. It would also be of

18. Twinned Mercurys; in Hadrianus Junius, *Emblemata*
(Department of Rare Books, William R. Perkins Library, Duke University)

particular relevance and moment for a writer of drama, the one
literary genre in which this sort of silence is structural (Porter,
Drama, pp. 176–77). On the other hand the signal's referent may be
not the audience's behavior but the signaler's: I will keep silent (as
Wind, *Mysteries*, p. 12n, reads it). The inscription over the figure,
"The One remains in itself," would accord well with such a meaning (whereas the lower inscription, "Talk on the one hand often
brings perception, but being silent never does," is problematical
with either reading of the signal).[17]

BUT the emblem-book Mercury most likely to have been familiar
to Shakespeare is that *in trivio*, "at a crossroads" (though only a
single road is usually visible), Mercury as the traveler's guide. He

19. Mercury walking on flames; in Bocchi, *Quaestiones*
(Folger Shakespeare Library)

20. Harpocratic Mercury; in Bocchi
(Department of Rare Books, William R. Perkins Library, Duke University)

appears so first in the emblem books in Alciati, *Emblematum Libellus* (1534 ed., sig. F1, fig. 21). The road is busy if the tumulus of stones left by travelers is any indication, for they completely hide this Mercury from the waist down so that we cannot see what the *subscriptio* tells us, that he is a herm: "Trunca Dei effigies, pectore facta tenus." The finger that covers the god's lips in Bocchi here points out the right way, and the caduceus serves as a pointer too. Because of Mercury's posture, and because no other figures are present, the reader becomes the summoned, directed traveler, and the picture has a peculiar immediacy. The emblem's motto, "Quá Dii uocant eundum," interestingly replaces the god's directing with a summoning. The *subscriptio* moves from a description of the scene (ll. 1–3) through an immediate explication—"suspende uiator / Serta Deo, rectum qui tibi monstrat iter" (ll. 3–4)—to the generalized moral that we are all at crossroads and would take the wrong path without God's help.[18]

Fifteen years later in Alciati, *Diverse Imprese* .... (Lyon, 1549), in the emblem "Che l'huomo dee indrizzarsi, doue è chiamato da Iddio" (sig. A5, fig. 22), essentially the same picture appears. Here, however, a bodily complete Mercury is starting to be visible behind the tumulus, and the most notable developments in the *subscriptio* are the reduction and simplification both of the explication-become-exhortation, "Bada / Tu" (ll. 3–4) and of the description of the statue—"Posta è la Imagin de Mercurio" (l. 3)—with no suggestion that it is a herm. The transformation continues with this emblem in later emblem books until Mercury appears as himself down to talaria on a roadside with scarcely a pebble in sight.[19]

In Nicolaus Reusner, *Emblemata* (1581), Emblem 24, "Multa multum legenda," a *pictura* (sig. H1v, fig. 23) based on the Alciati *in trivio* Mercurys, combines with a *subscriptio* (sig. H2) influenced by mythography that elaborates on the gifts the god may bestow. In the *pictura*, as with Alciati, Mercury occupies the left foreground of the picture. He is armed (as in Cartari, sig. Ss2v) and kneels in a posture taken from the later editions of Alciati (and perhaps ultimately derived from the tumulus of stones in the early Alciati). He is pointing out the path, not to the reader now but to the burdened traveler approaching in the middle distance, and perhaps also to the two figures just visible on a hill in the background. The *subscriptio* makes Mercury the patron of a life of learning, and thus responsible

21. Mercury *in trivio;* in Alciati, *Emblematum*
(Folger Shakespeare Library)

for the benefits such a life provides, without making particular reference to the crossroads setting.[20]

Finally we may consider the roadside Mercury from Geoffrey Whitney, *A Choice of Emblemes,* 1586. Whitney reattaches Alciati's original Latin motto to yet another version of the familiar *pictura* (sig. A1v, fig. 24), and gives it some prominence as the second emblem in his collection. Mercury is again on the left, seated now,

22. Mercury *in trivio;* in Alciati, *Imprese*
(Folger Shakespeare Library)

and a pair of travelers appears on the right. Whitney's *subscriptio* describes the setting as a junction of "diuers wayes" (l. 2), and mentions Mercury only briefly, "Mercurius then, the perfect path did showe" (l. 3), without suggesting that the figure we see in the picture is of anything other than the god himself. Compare Alciati "effigies" (*Emblematum,* 1534) and "Imagin" (*Diverse,* 1549) with Reusner, for whom the point is moot since he doesn't speak so directly of his *pictura.*

THE simplicity and rightness that Mercury may seem from our vantage to have in the *picturae* of the later emblem books and later

23. Mercury *in trivio*; in Reusner, *Emblemata*
(Folger Shakespeare Library)

Cartari illustrations could mislead us into supposing that Mercury's significances there are equally simple, right, and legible, or at least that with the recovery of something approaching Mercury's classical appearance comes a simple recovery of his classical significance. But none of this is the case. As we have seen, Mercury's range of classical significances is far too complex for any recovery to be simple. Mercury survives by participating in the medieval panoply of correspondences and so takes on unpredictable new significances, as with his central position in alchemy. And, as the pictures with text examined in this chapter may indicate, Renaissance pictorial representations of Mercury are always potentially resonant with the entirety of his history at the same time that, as always happens, unpredictable new historical factors—mercantile capitalism, the celebration of sexuality—manifest themselves in the god's

24. Mercury *in trivio;* in Whitney, *Emblemes*
(Department of Rare Books, William R. Perkins Library, Duke University)

evolution. Therefore even Zaltieri's last Cartari illustrations, and even Whitney's picture, may carry the semiotic richness of the earlier pictures and history, a richness amplified in Elizabethan textual representations of the god, and thus ready to be touched into resonance in 1595 by Brooke's word "Mercutio."

CHAPTER THREE.

ELIZABETHAN TEXTS TO 1595

As with the pictorial-textual Mercury so too, or more so, with the purely textual in English: thick as the stars, Mercurys inlay the Renaissance to 1595 and after. The example of a single text from near the time of *Romeo and Juliet*, which Shakespeare was familiar enough with for an echo of it to appear in the play, may demonstrate how large a complete catalog of Renaissance references to the god would have to be (and how little feasible before such time as we have all our texts machine-readable).

The work in question is John Eliot's *Ortho-epia Gallica: Eliots Fruits for the French* (1593), a language manual consisting of brief dialogues in French and English on facing pages and a saucy introductory letter "To the Learned Professors of the French Tongue, in the Famous City of London." The dialogues, far from being learned (though with the occasional flourish of knowledge of the titles of books), are set in the daily life of contemporary London—"The Vprising in the Morning," "The Exchange," "The Drunken Mens Banket"—and constitute a sort of Berlitz course in conversational French. The work's one reference to "our mercury," one to Hermes Trismegistus, and three directly to Mercury in just under two hundred pages may provide a fair sample of Mercury's Renaissance textual frequency. These particular references furthermore bear on the question of Mercutio's mercuriality because Shakespeare knew the Eliot by 1595 since echoes of it appear in the aubade of *Romeo and Juliet* 3.5 (see Lever, "Fruits").

Eliot's mention of Hermes Trismegistus (sig. L1v) and that of "the mercurie of the Philosophers" (sig. X4) both occur in discussions of the occult sciences, the former in the "Drunken Mens Banket," the latter in the final dialogue, "The Conclusion of the Parlement of Pratlers." One of the banqueters boasts, "I haue no lesse studied Magicke, Negromancie, Alchimie, the Caballisticke science and Geomancie, then the Philosophie of Hermes Trismegistus." Later, one of the prattlers lists names for the philosopher's stone: "Tis called humane blood, the water of life, the dragon, the crow, the Elixir, the mercurie of the Philosophers." He goes on to tell some of the properties of the substance, such as its ability to transmute metals, including ordinary "quick-siluer," into pure gold.

In the transmutation of Brooke's rudimentary Mercutio into Shakespeare's spellbinder, these passages may have served to strengthen associations between the name on the one hand and, on the other, a complex of ideas of magic, mystery, and transformation. The crow of the second passage would also have had a particular personal associative resonance for Shakespeare, one heightened by the mention of crows earlier in the same dialogue—in a passage with echoes in *King Lear* (see Porter, "More Echoes")—because of Greene's 1592 "upstart crow" derogation of Shakespeare in *Groatsworth of Wit* (discussed below, chap. 5).

In the address to the reader introducing his pronunciation guide to French vowels, Eliot says that his rules will be "as Mercuries finger to direct thee in thy progresse of learning" (*Gallica*, sig. C1). This familiar *in trivio* Mercury then leads to the observation that the reader will need a hundred eyes like Argus to observe the rules well. A reader with only two eyes may note in the passage a somewhat unusual word of Mercutio's: "See here then the Atomes of the French tongue" (cf. "little atomi," *Romeo* 1.4.57).

Eliot's two other direct references to Mercury occur in nearly identical adieus, the one to the learned professors of French in the introductory letter—"I pray the God *AEsculapius* patron of Phisitions, *Mercurie* the God of cunning, and *Dis* the father of French crowns, in santy long time to conserue your Signiories" (sig. A4v) —and the other at the end of the dialogue "The Slasher": "I pray the god Mercurie, with Dis the father of crownes, in saunty long time to conserue your seigniorie" (sig. R4). Since the "cunning" of the first passage seems to be the possibly disreputable cleverness needed to acquire enough crowns for a life of ease, this Mercury seems patron of thieves as much as of merchants. Either would be glad of the added patronage of the god of riches, Dis.

There is reason to believe that in Shakespeare's reading of these passages Dis's other role as god of the underworld may have been present and so brought Mercury's role as psychopomp into play. Apparently the shadowy god's two disparate roles derive from the early classical location of the realm of the dead under the earth, the source of agricultural wealth (see Harvey, *Companion*, s.v.). Of the god's several names (including Orcus and Hades) Shakespeare uses only three, and does so in such a way as to suggest that he thinks of them as applying to distinct gods. For the god of wealth he invariably uses the name Plutus (*Caesar, Troilus, All's Well, Timon*), whereas for the god of the underworld he uses Pluto (*Lucrece, Titus, 2 Henry 4, Troilus, Coriolanus*), and later Dis (*Winter's Tale, Tempest*). Although all this evidence postdates 1595, in one case it carries more weight than may be apparent at first. While Pafford observes (*Winter's Tale*, p. xxxiv) that *The Winter's Tale* Dis passage seems to derive from Ovid, Lever's notation of Eliot as a possible source for *The Winter's Tale* 4.3.9 ("Fruits," p. 82) suggests that Eliot's Mercury-linked Dis may also figure in the name's appearance in Shakespeare.

The other personage Eliot links with Mercury, "the God *Aesculapius* patron of Phisitions," has a story Shakespeare could have known from Ovid, *Metamorphoses* 2.542ff., Fraunce, *The Third Part of the Countesse of Pembroke's Yuychurch*, sig. I4v, K3, and elsewhere, and the story has a history that could have come to Shakespeare directly or otherwise through various conduits including the *Asclepius*. The classical Asclepius-Aesculapius learned medicine from the centaur Chiron and became patron of a cult where sacred snakes and dogs were kept, and where patients came to be cured in sleep or by means revealed in dreams (see Harvey, *Companion*, s.v.). In the hermetic *Asclepius* Hermes Trismegistus describes the magic by which Egyptian priests animated statues of gods (see Yates, *Bruno*, pp. 5, 12, and *Last Plays*, pp. 90–91).

Both story and history have numerous points of contact with Mercury, including extension of ownership of the caduceus to Aesculapius, whence its representation of medicine, and early Renaissance illustrators portray both figures as scholars or scribes (see Armstrong, *Painters*, pp. 70–71). In the context of Eliot's adieu, Aesculapius's function is clear enough. On the surface he takes part in a threefold wish for health, cleverness, and riches, while just beneath the surface Eliot's attitude is less benign to the learned professors whose market his book aims to corner a share of. Medicine implies illness, and of course "French crownes" names the illness treated with mercury that Eliot is wishing on the professors. The general Mercury-Aesculapius link, then, associating Mercury with magic and with medicine, operates in *Romeo and Juliet* to bring Mercutio into the orbits of Friar Laurence's herbs and potion and Romeo's apothecary shop and poison, while Eliot's particular use of the link, insofar as operative, would seem mainly to contribute to Mercutio's attitude toward his friend's love as a malady.

As this brief discussion of the five[1] appearances of Mercury in Eliot suggests, no catalogue raisonné of all the textual Mercurys likely to have fallen under Shakespeare's eye by 1595 is feasible at present. However, as the discussion may also suggest, such comprehensiveness might not be appropriate anyway, given the finite if large number of significant attributes and associations of the god and the cumulative nature of the present study. Mercury's association with Aesculapius is the only entirely new information about him that a survey of Eliot brings into view.

T H E English mythographers Batman and Fraunce together provide something like the official Elizabethan Mercury. Stephen Batman's treatment in *The Golden Booke of the Leaden Goddes* (1577) is succinct enough to quote in full:

> MERCVRIVUS.
> Mercurie was portraicted with winges at head and feete, wearing an Hat of white & blacke colloures: A Fawlchon by his side, in one hande a Scepter, & in the other a Pype, on the one side stode a Cocke and a Ramme, and close by his side a Fylcher or Cutpurse, and headlesse Argus.

> Signification.
> By Mercurie Marchauntes be ment. His wynges at head & feete betoken the expedition of Marchau[n]tes, which to gett worldly pelfe, post through all corners of the World: the whyte & blacke coloured Hat, signifieth their subtilty, which for greediness of gaine, spare not to face white for blacke, & blacke for white. By his Fawlchon is signified, goodes gotten by violence, when subtiltie cannot comprehend. His Mace is a token of Peace, but the knot with two serpentes, clasping ech other aboute the sayde Scepter, doth intimate that no promise must be broken. His Pype resembleth Eloquence, which refresheth the mynde, as Harmony doth the eares.

> The Cocke is sayde to be the best obseruer of tymes and seasons, warning Marchantes and trauelers, to forsake no opportunity. The Ramme is a resemblau[n]ce of hys offyce, be-

cause the Poets fayne Mercurie, to be Embassadoure of the
Gods: all are obedient to hym, as the Flockes of shepe, are to
the Ramme: the figured Cutpurse, is a proofe that Mercurie
was a thiefe: and Headlesse Argus, is a witnesse, that one
Plague, bewrayes a thousand euilles. (sig. A4–A4v)

Here Batman recapitulates familiar information from a number of
sources, particularly Ovid. Along with conventional readings—the
caduceus, the pipe—we have more ingenious moralizing, as with
the serpentine knot. Most conspicuous, however, is Batman's nearly single-minded emphasis on Mercury's associations with merchants. Here is the Mercury of Eliot's language manual and, in fact,
this emphasis figures in the god's evolution generally in the new
mercantile culture of the West, perhaps nowhere more notably than
in England.

Abraham Fraunce, in *The Third Part of the Countesse of Pembroke's Yuychurch* (1592), retells the story of Mercury, Argus, and
Io, following Ovid more closely and at greater length than Batman,
and also moralizing at greater length. Mercury puts Argus to sleep
rather more credibly than in Golding—

> Now *Mercury* sits on a mountaine
> Hard by *Argus* side, and tells him there, of a purpose,
> This tale, and that tale . . .
> And each tale had a song, and euery song had a piping.
> (sig. D2v)

—and then promptly beheads him. Fraunce recounts the ethical
moralization of Natalis Comes, making Mercury figure the "celestiall and heauenly power in Man, called reason" (sig. D3v), which
suppresses the choler figured by Argus, and he quotes Pontano, a
contemporary (see Allen, *Mysteriously Meant*, p. 187), to the effect
that the episode represents the sun's extinguishing of the stars.

After mentioning Mercury in passing as Jupiter's opposite to Juno's Iris (sig. E2), and showing "light-footed *Mercurie*" (sig. G1v)
delivering one of Jupiter's messages, Fraunce then relates the story
of the theft of Apollo's cattle. He gives Mercury in disguise some
lines of rustic dialect probably based on Golding and calls the god
"*Ioues* Pretty Page, fine-filcher" (sig. K3) and "*Nuntio*" (sig. K3v).
As does Ovid, Fraunce follows this tale with that of Aglauros and
Herse. As Ovid does not, Fraunce then subjoins the story of the

birth of Autolycus.² The moralization of these tales is Fraunce's fullest of Mercury.

After telling of the god's office of messenger, and listing and moralizing standard accoutrements (sig. K3v–K4), Fraunce continues in an astrological vein in signature K4: "if he [Mercury] be predominant, he afordeth eloquence, elegancy, learning, and especially mathematicall knowledge. If he looke on *Ioue* luckily, he giveth skill in Philosophical & Theological speculations: if on *Mars* happily, he maketh good physitians, if unhappily, he maketh the[m] either bad Physitians, or starke theeues. . . . *Mercury* therefore is a plaine turnecoate, good with good, bad with bad." Fraunce goes on to relate that while "Such as be Mercuriall" are seldom rich, they may find ways to enrich themselves out of the chests of princes, and when caught can "smooth up al by facility of discourse." But Mercury's reconciliation and exchange of gifts with Apollo figures the "union of Iovial intelligence with Mercuriall eloquence, the only flower of Kings courts, and felicity of commonwealths" (sig. K4). While Mercury's term of that union continues to be associated with him, Jove's term slides Mercury's way in the following pages. Almost immediately Mercury is said to signify "the sensible part proceeding from the brayne" versus Apollo, with the "vital and quickening vertue comming from the heart," and Neptune, with the liver's nourishing power (sig. L1). And Mercury leads the Graces because good turns require "wisdome and discretion figured by *Mercury*" (sig. M3v); and "*Venus* is all for the body, and *Mercury* onely for the minde" (sig. N4).

A T an opposite extreme from the weighty mythographies that could have conducted Mercury to Shakespeare stands a body of popular or ephemeral works that could have served the same purpose, such as Barnabe Riche's *Dialogue, betwene Mercury and an English Souldier*, 1574. Confessing that he has "done as the Jay, who decked her selfe with the fethers of other Byrds, to the ende, she might seeme to be the more glorious" (sig. A3), Riche tells how, out for a stroll in the pastures he hears sweet music and lies under a tree to listen, whereupon "as Cyllemus [for Cyllenius] mery pipe, brought Ergus to a nodding nappe" (sig. A1v), so with him. He has a dream-vision in which Mercury first appears with a message from the other gods (sig. A5) and then engages the narrator in a Socratic dialogue about the profession of soldiering. Later, at the court of Venus, the narrator sees an arras on which are depicted love stories, including that of Mercury and Herse, and metamorphoses "for . . . better speede" in love, including Mercury's into a goat.

Riche's minor work is still substantial enough for inclusion as a principal publication of 1574 in *Annals of English Literature 1475–1950* (Ghosh and Withycombe, revised, 1961). Mercury appears as well in other minor works listed there, such as the anonymous *Rare Triumphs* (1589) and William Vallans, *A Tale of Two Swans* (1590), and also in numerous others, such as Thomas Salter, *The Mirror of Modestie* (1579), that are still less learned than the mythographies.

Between these extremes stands that large body of "literary" texts certainly or most probably known to Shakespeare. In these works too Mercury appears so frequently as to necessitate selection. Discussed below are examples of two versions of the god densely packed with significance for the English Renaissance to 1595 and in particular for Shakespeare's dramatizing of Brooke.

The Heraldic and Hierophantic Mercury

IN Elizabethan literary texts Mercury seems to appear most often as herald and patron of eloquence: carrying messages for Jupiter or other gods, summoning divine colloquies, and bringing concord. He appears so in Gascoigne (*Kenelworth*, 1587), in Peele, *The Araygnement of Paris* (1584), for instance, and in Lyly's *The Woman in the Moone* (1593 according to Harbage and Schoenbaum, *Drama*). The last sonnet to an individual god in the sequence of James VI of Scotland, *The Essayes of a Prentise, in the Divine Art of Poesie* (1585), presents the same image of Mercury, as do Marlowe and Nashe in *The Tragedy of Dido, Queene of Carthage* (1594; see Marlowe, *Complete Works*), and (by implication) engraved on the casket Henry II sends Rosamond in Daniel, *The Complaint of Rosamond* (1592).[3]

At the same time, and especially in the early 1590s as Yates, Schrickx, Brooks-Davies, Nohrnberg, and others have noted, literary London witnesses an upsurge in appearances of Mercury in what may be called the darker side of his verbal proficiency, those roles associated with the hermetic tradition and with magic. This Mercury appears in particular writers associated with the "school of night," with the Greene-Nashe-Harvey quarrel, and also, as

Brooks-Davies has shown, in *The Faerie Queene*, including the first three books published before 1590, even though Mercury does not appear as a character until the seventh book.

In *A Pleasant Comedy, Called Summers Last Will and Testament* (1600, but composed some years before), Nashe heaps scorn reminiscent of Eliot's for the professors not only on the heads of adepts of arcana (sig. GIv) but also on their tutelary deity:

> *Hermes*, secretarie to the Gods,
> Or *Hermes Trismegistus*, as some will,
> Wearie with grauing in blind characters,
> And figures of familiar beasts and plants,
> Inuented letters to write lies withall.
> (sig. F4v)

On the other hand Harvey, the primary target of Nashe's scorn, is pleased to parade a bit of Mercurial learning in a countersalvo: "The Aegyptian Mercury would prouide to plant his foote vpon a square; and his Image in Athens was quadrangular, whatsoeuer was the figure of his hatt: and although he were sometime a Ball of Fortune, (who can assure himselfe of Fortune?) yet was he neuer a wheele of folly, or an eele of Ely" (*Supererogation*, 1593, sig. C3–C3v).[4] Nashe's and Harvey's esoteric scribal Mercury thus wears one of the god's major guises, descended, as we have seen, from classical times through Martianus Capella and early Renaissance hermeticism. In *The Faerie Queene* he wears a graver and more serious version of this guise, with its attendant thaumaturgy made manifest.

Douglas Brooks-Davies (*Monarch*, 1983) explores in his introduction and first chapter Spenser's use in *The Faerie Queene* of the angelic and hermetic Mercury as "a type of the sovereign herself" (p. 2), unfolding at some length the implications of the Palmer's staff—

> Of that same wood it fram'd was cunningly,
>> Of which *Caduceus* whilome was made,
>> Caduceus the rod of *Mercury*,
>> With which he wonts the *Stygian* realmes inuade,
>> Through ghastly horrour, and eternall shade;
>> Th'infernall feends with it he can asswage,

> And *Orcus* tame, whom nothing can perswade,
> And rule the *Furyes*, when they most do rage:
> Such vertue in his staffe had eke this Palmer sage.
>
> (2.12.41)

—as well as those of Cambina's rod—

> In her right hand a rod of peace shee bore,
> About the which two Serpents weren wound,
> Entrayled mutually in louely lore,
> And by the tailes together firmely bound,
> And both were with one oliue garland crownd,
> Like to the rod which *Maias* sonne doth wield,
> Wherewith the hellish fiends he doth confound.
>
> (4.3.42)

While the second passage (quoted in full here as a guide to the first, and by way of clarifying the hermeneutic weight Brooks-Davies brings to bear on the first) postdates *Romeo and Juliet*, the first antedates it and was very probably known to Shakespeare.

The Palmer has just held "His mighty staffe, that could all charmes defeat" over the horde of wild beasts threatening him and Guyon outside the Bower of Bliss and turned their ferocity to fear, so that the staff serves as both magic wand and scepter. The power of the caduceus of the next stanza is over one particular class of monster, the chthonic, and the god wielding it, apart from the trace of his cunning transferred to the workmanship of the caduceus, is the uncanny Horatian Mercury of the underworld.

Mercury is also, Brooks-Davies shows, associated in Spenser's web of analogies not only with the Palmer but also with Moses and Aaron via his caduceus and the serpent rods of *Exodus* 4 and 7, with the philosopher's stone, with notions of Brunian Hermetic reform brought to Elizabeth by John Dee, and especially with Merlin (*Monarch*, pp. 14–50). Brooks-Davies finds such widespread traces of the resultant figure of magical sovereignty that, given the poetics of *The Faerie Queene*, the "point seems inescapable: the teleology of Book III . . . is towards Mercury. . . . Book III is Mercury's" (p. 46). One need not be quite so taken by the point as Brooks-Davies to agree that Mercurian resonances in the first three books of *The Faerie Queene* extend well beyond the two caduceus stanzas. Nohrn-

berg (who has many more fish to fry) acknowledges that, while
Spenser is "decidedly Apollonian," he is also "a Hermetic poet"
(*Analogy*, p. 730).[5]

The Mercury of *The Faerie Queene* would, it is safe to assume,
have colored Shakespeare's perception of the appearances of the god
in those small poems in the weakness of their first spring, "The
Ruines of Time" and *Mother Hubberds Tale*, in *Complaints*, 1591.
Both are impressive. In the last stanza before the envoy of "The
Ruines of Time" the speaker has a final vision:

> Lastly I saw an Arke of purest golde
> Vpon a brazen pillour standing hie,
> Which th'ashes seem'd of some great Prince to hold.
>
> (sig. D4)

Heaven and earth dispute who should keep Sidney's remains until a
kind of angel of last things appears:

> At last me seem'd wing footed *Mercurie*,
> From heauen descending to appease their strife,
> The Arke did beare with him aboue the skie.
>
> (sig. D4v)

This angel-Mercury, a Christianized psychopomp, partakes of the
tradition of hermetic hermeneutics by virtue of his textual locus.
The poem's speaker, having in "frosen horror" puzzled over the
wailing lady's "doubtful speach, / Whose meaning much I labored
foorth to wreste" (sig. D1), sees a sequence of visions "by demonstration me to teach" that amount to hieroglyphics or emblem
picturae of which Mercury with the ark of gold is the culmination.

Commentators agree that the caveat of the speaker of *Mother
Hubberds Tale* (sig. L3v), "Base is the style, and matter meane
withall," must be taken with a grain of salt, and the style rises well
above the good old woman's honest mirth for the episode of Mercury's witnessing of the wrongs in the kingdom of animals and his
rousing and reproaching of the lion. This herald and intelligence
agent is Spenser's least hermetic and most classical Mercury, with
his Virgilian descent from heaven—

> streight with his azure wings he cleau'd
> The liquid clowdes, and lucid firmament;
> Ne staid, till that he came with steep descent

Vnto the place, where his prescript did showe.
There stouping like an arrowe from a bowe,
He soft arriued on the grassie plaine,
And fairly paced forth.

(sig. Q2v)

—his Homeric and Virgilian berating, "Arise, and doo thy selfe re-
deeme from shame" (sig. Q3v), his Homeric ability to pass invisible
among a dangerous throng, and the Horatian severity and uncanniness of "his dreadfull hat" and caduceus (sig. Q3). As it happens,
more than any of Spenser's other Mercurys this one also shows
traces of the second group of literary Mercurys to be treated here, as
with "that faire face . . . Which wonts to . . . beautefie the shinie
firmament" (sig. Q2v).

The Erotic Mercury

IN a sometimes tense and disjunctive complementarity with the
Mercury Fraunce calls "onely for the minde" stands an altogether
corporeal and indeed essentially phallic Mercury delivered to the
Renaissance primarily by Ovid. Given England's scarcity of good
pictures—no *Primavera* there—it is paradoxically in text that the
physically beautiful Mercury appears most readily in Renaissance
England, as in the Spenser just quoted.

We may sense some of the erotic prettiness of the Mercury played
by a boy in Churchyard (*Entertainment*, 1578, sig. C4) who arrives
in a coach

> couered with Birdes, and naked Sprites hanging by the heeles in
> the aire and cloudes . . . as though by some thunder cracke they
> had been shaken and tormented, yet stayed by power deuine
> in their places. . . . [Out stepped] MERCVRIE himself in blew
> Satin lined with cloth of gold, his garments cutte and slasshed
> on the finest manner, a peaked hatte of the same coloure, as
> though it should cutte and seuer the winde asunder, and on
> the same a payre of wings, and wings on his heeles likewise.
> And on his golden rodde were little wings also, about the
> which rodde, were two wriggling or scrawling Serpentes, which
> seemed to haue life when the rodde was moued or shaken.

The boy's boldness made Elizabeth smile when he approached her and delivered his speech. Another probably somewhat erotic Mercury was that played by the page in the entertainment described in Goldwel (*Declaration*, 1581, sig. B6–B7) who gives assurance that Desire's children will not succeed in their assault on the fortress of beauty.

Several factors combine to make the Renaissance Mercury's physical attractiveness more erotic than Apollo's, and to make Mercury therefore, more than any other adult Olympian (Ganymede being a special case), carry some of the current of homoeroticism that sweeps through the nineties, animating not only Barnfield's *The Tears of an Affectionate Shepherd Sick of Love* (1594) and *Cynthia. With Certain Sonnets* (1595) but also, notably, the Ovidian epyllions of Marlowe, Shakespeare, and others. In such descriptions as this from Gascoigne (*Kenelworth*, 1587),

> That tatling traytor *Mercurie*
>   who hopes to get the gole,
> By curious filed speech,
>   abusing you by arte . . .
> You know that in his tongue
>   consistes his cheefest might.
>   (sig. C1v),

and from Wilson (*Coblers Prophesie*, 1594),

> Fresh Mayas sonne, fine witcrafts greatest God,
> Herrald of heauen, soule charming Mercurie
>   (sig. A3),

Mercury's eloquence and charm eroticize his measure of physical beauty. In addition, the prominence in the 1590s of Ganymede as an object of sexual desire activates some of the always latent Mercurial sexual attractiveness deriving from the fact that he alone of the adult male Olympians shares Ganymede's status as servitor of Jupiter.

As for the sexual attraction Mercury himself feels, it is ambivalent and problematic. His desire is heterosexual in the occasional reference to Aglauros or in the Mercury episode of *Hero and Leander*. On the other hand, in Peele, *The Araygnement of Paris* (1584), for the Children of the Chapel the god may evince a touch of homosexual susceptibility. At the arraignment, having heard of Paris's beauty (sig. C3v), Mercury alone among the thirteen assembled gods and goddesses acknowledges it directly: "I have not seene a more alluring boy" (sig. D2v). Furthermore, while Mercury's traditional opposition to Venus may be invoked with the heraldic and hierophantic Mercury "onely for the minde," that same opposition may also figure in the peculiar dialectic of the phallic Mercury.

The last quotation is from Fraunce (*Yuychurch*, sig. N4), and its almost entirely subversive context illustrates some of the logic by which the antivenereal Mercury may prove other than of the mind: "If . . . at any mans birth, there be a coniunction of *Venus* and *Mercurie*, it maketh him neither man nor woman, both woman and man, giuen to inordinate and vnnaturall lust. . . . For these two planets are so repugnant, that they can neuer be well conioyned; sith *Venus* is all for the body, and *Mercury* onely for the minde." The very "repugnance" of the two planets seems physical. Furthermore, the star-crossed man's maleness would seem to associate with the male planet-god and his femaleness with the female, so that Mercury becomes associated not with mind but with the male body's gender. The "inordinate and vnnatural lust," then, could seem attributable to Mercury's influence as well as to Venus's and, as at present, a natural reading for "unnatural" would be "homosexual." In such a context the astrological "coniunction" and "conioyned" sound sexual; indeed, after the passing salute to the mind, Fraunce returns the reader to the body with a piece of apocryphal physiology recounting where Mercury's semen engendered Hermaphroditus in Venus's womb.[6]

The use of mercury in the tubs also establishes an antivenereal and erotic, or at least genital, set of resonances for Mercury. Recommendations of mercuric compounds or of elemental mercury in the treatment of the French disease begin to appear in print with Schelli[n]g (*Malas Morbum*, ca. 1490) and grow in frequency past 1595. Through the sixteenth century and well after mercury is the treatment of choice, administered orally, in ointments, and in vapor in the tubs, with the only serious rival medicament being the New World wood guaiac (see Goldwater, *Mercury*, pp. 215–30). Thus pharmacology recapitulates mythology: just as the god cures the amorous infatuations of heroes with his remonstrances, so the element cures the *lues venerea* with its dangerous ministrations.[7]

KEY conduits for the erotic Mercury to Shakespeare in 1595 are the god's appearances in Marlowe and Greene, especially his two major appearances, in *Hero and Leander* (Marlowe, *Poems*) and *The Tragedy of Dido, Queene of Carthage* (Marlowe, *Complete Works*).[8] In both of these eroticized renditions of familiar love stories with tragic endings the god's role is surprising and memorable.

In the Dido play Marlowe elaborates importantly and tellingly on the basic Homeric-Virgilian story of Mercury come to call the hero away from his venereal entanglements. The appearance in the opening scene of the sleep-inducing god himself asleep seems unprecedented and may be Marlowe's invention, although the allegorical principle involved is as common as can be. Mercury's presence in the scene is of still greater interest inasmuch as he is almost entirely supernumerary: he provides only the feather plucked from his wing and an occasion for one of Jupiter's protestations of love for Ganymede, and he speaks not a word when Jupiter wakes him and sends him off with a message. Mercury's gratuitousness in the scene then draws attention to him, and Shakespeare reading or seeing the scene would probably have associated Mercury with the particular eroticism of Jupiter dandling Ganymede upon his knee. Indeed a natural first or subliminal reading for the scene would be to take all the action, including Venus's interruption of the idyll, as a dream of Mercury's.

This remarkable opening scene colors later mentions and appearances of Mercury in the play. It gives an added twist to the irony of Dido's naming Mercury in her reply to Aeneas's restiveness:

> Now lookes *Aeneas* like immortall *Jove*,
> O where is *Ganimed* to hold his cup,
> And *Mercury* to flye for what he calls?
> (ll. 45–47)

The opening scene also resounds in Mercury's bringing Ascanius with him in his monitory appearance to Aeneas (5.1), another of Marlowe's elaborations on the received story.

In the Mercury episode of the highly eroticized *Hero and Leander* (1.386–482) the god is both subject and object of heterosexual desire. Enamored of the proud shepherdess, he first attempts to have his way with her by the application of caduceus, pipe, smooth speech, and finally force until he is induced to relent, seemingly by her readiness to call for help, whereupon he accepts and accomplishes the task she imposes of stealing some of Jove's nectar for her. The poem makes no further mention of the shepherdess as Mercury moves into a rapid sequence of punishment and revenge with his father, a crucial component of which is the assistance Cupid provides by wounding the Fates with love for Mercury.

The Fates' love occasions Marlowe's only mention of Mercury's beauty when they "At his faire feathered feet, the engins layd, / Which th'earth from ougly *Chaos* den up-wayd" (ll. 449–50). They allow Mercury to depose his father in favor of Saturn for a brief return of the golden age, cut short because this very Marlovian Mercury "recklesse of his promise, did despise / The love of th'everlasting Destinies" (ll. 461–62). In response the Fates restore Jove to Olympus and punish Mercury with the decree "That he and *Povertie* should alwaies kis" (l. 470), so that the first sestiad ends with a Mercury modulated away from the erotic altogether and into the hermetic and scribal figure discussed above.

As is generally remarked, this episode in *Hero and Leander* is striking by its very intrusiveness, and it seems likely that Shakespeare would have mused over it as other readers have done. If so, he would have been aware at some level that the episode's seemingly disproportionate length is a function of the complexity of Marlowe's agenda. Included, it would seem, is the introduction of Mercury as a cause of tragedy in this story of heterosexual love. Where in *The Tragedy of Dido* he is the immediate cause, he is here closer to an ultimate cause, for behind the wrath the Fates show Cupid upon his appeal on behalf of Hero and Leander (1.379–84) stands Mercury. And, while Marlowe boldly trades on his own sexual orientation in the Neptune episode of the second sestiad, it is Mercury he would most seem to have identified with in the first.[9]

One further component of Shakespeare's received Mercury, which may finally color the god of the mind as much as the god of the body, comes from Robert Greene. In Greene's *Planetomachia*, 1585 (sig. B2), Jupiter characterizes Mercury at length and quite unfavorably: "And you Mercurie, pollicies sleights, faire promises & small performance, causing men by your variable impression to flatter friend or foe, to sweare in mouth, and forsweare in hart, to beare two faces under a hood, to carry a Lamb in his shield, and a Tygre in his bosome: with the one hand to present spice, and with the other hemlock." Then, in *A Briefe Apologie of the Sacred Science of*

Astronomie, which is bound with *Planetomachia,* Greene explains that "Antolycus" (*sic*) was not really Mercury's son, but "Given to deceipt and robberie through the malignant influence of Mercurie" (sig. A3v). Unfavorable representations of the god are not unprecedented, but this seems unusually energetic and, given its author, is of particular relevance to Shakespeare at the time of *Romeo and Juliet* since it has much the same tone as Greene's posthumous attack on Shakespeare and Marlowe.

S U C H then are some of the probable outlines of Shakespeare's Mercury in 1595, a figure weighted with complex significances that have evolved through his history and that are implicated in such new cultural factors as mercantile capitalism and the celebration of mind and body. This Mercury grounds and fuels the detonation by which Brooke's trace character flowers into Shakespeare's memorable subversive Mercutio. Of course "Shakespeare's Mercury" elides considerable mediation: the figure in question is the Mercury of our (or my) Shakespeare, and the mediation does not stop there. But all this is well enough known to stand as a given in the pages that follow. Much of the constant implicit reference to Mercury must also stand as a given, even in the next three chapters, for which he provides the large division of topics treated: first, Mercutio's eloquence and liminality, then his significance in the dialectic of Shakespeare's negotiations with the memory of Marlowe and with the notion of literary proprietorship, and finally what Mercutio reveals about Shakespearean gender, friendship, and sexuality.

PART TWO.

SHAKESPEARE'S MERCUTIO

SHAKESPEARE'S Mercutio, the subject of the following three chapters, deserves some preliminary explication. The phrase designates something that can only be approximated more or less plausibly; i.e., the character as he signifies for his creator at his creation. Even if Shakespeare were immediate, and even if Mercutio's significance for him could in principle be stated in a finite number of words, still the impenetrability of minds would rule out certain and complete recovery of Shakespeare's Mercutio. Nevertheless, as has been persuasively argued in much of the large body of relevant theoretical critical commentary of the part two decades (and as has been generally assumed throughout the history of the species), it is in practice possible to know something about other minds. About Shakespeare in particular it is generally accepted that we know a great deal about his mind, including things he himself was not conscious of. Beyond the certainties of nineteenth-century idealism and early twentieth-century positivism, and beyond the certainties of late middle-twentieth-century structuralism and deconstructionism, lies a hard-won beachhead of knowledge about Shakespeare's mind in its historical moment. This truth needs repeating if only because careers have been built on its denial. But my concern here is not to enter lists. Rather let me say a word more about what a subject like Shakespeare's Mercutio seems to involve in the late 1980s.

As we know, the notion of dramatic character in Shakespeare studies has often been problematic and has served as a proving ground for successive approaches. Such continues to be the case. Although in 1976 Honigmann (*Tragedies*, p. 4) could write, "now that the historical dust has settled . . . we may guardedly speak of Shakespeare's characters as life-like," there still seems to be a bit of dust in the air. While some recent critical approaches, such as those of pragmaticist, psychoanalytic, and feminist criticism, have had a good deal to say about those entities we call dramatic characters and take their primacy and accessibility more or less for granted, other recent approaches have kept largely silent on the subject of fictional, including dramatic, character, or have shown themselves openly hostile to the notion on ideological grounds. Critical opposition to the discussion of fictional character comes from several quarters. Some of it has structuralist roots, as Culler (*Poetics*, p. 230)—speaking of the novel—notes: "Although for many readers character serves as the major totalizing force in fiction . . . a structuralist approach has tended to explain this as an ideological prejudice. . . . This notion of character, structuralists would say, is a myth." Other biases against the maintenance of character in critical terminology grow out of Marx and still others out of Derrida, Barthes, and Foucault. Here are more lists I wish to avoid, but these variously compelling lines of attack on the discussion of such entities as Mercutio must be acknowledged.

As will have been noticed, I have not yet mentioned what by common consent is currently the most vigorous school of Shakespeare study, the new historicism. There, while character is not foregrounded as in psychoanalytic criticism, still it is generally accepted as a given. The present syncretic study, then, may take some authorization not only from the prominence of the notion of dramatic character in feminist, psychoanalytic, pragmaticist, and other current approaches to Shakespeare but also from the general acceptance of the category in the new historicism. At the same time the several lines of attack on the notion of dramatic character may justify the following caveats about the present study.

First, while the preceding part of this study has been diachronic, the following three chapters are generally synchronic in spirit. The pragmatic analysis of chapter 4 in particular is grounded in the sort of structuralist linguistic differential approach Sturrock (*Structuralism*, p. 11) describes: "The value of a character in a play . . . is estimated by the same procedure as one might use to estimate the value of a word in a given language, by comparison . . . with the economy of the play itself, with the other characters it contains. The differences between characters are the clue to their dramatic significance." At the same time the Mercutio in view in the next three chapters is, insofar as possible, thoroughly historical. This is to say that his significances are very much of a time in economic and political history, including the history of sexuality.

Finally, a word about the divisional title for these three chapters: its first term may be assumed to be under erasure. For us, as for virtually all of the play's audience since 1595, "Shakespeare's" is automatically understood with "Mercutio." In chapter 7 I return to diachrony to address the subject of that Mercutio, through the four centuries of his life to date. The following three chapters, however, concern the Mercutio who appears as it were unattributed in Shakespeare's mind.

CHAPTER FOUR.

ELOQUENCE AND LIMINALITY

Glossing Mercutio's Speech Acts

As Mercutio crosses the threshold from Brooke into Shakespeare he acquires not only a brother, a friendship, and a death but also a distinctively eloquent and vividly characteristic voice. To the extent that he stands outside the main plot, neither affecting it nor being affected by it until his death, mere language has a particular prominence with him. As is well known, Mercutio is a landmark in Shakespeare's early development of characterization in distinctive speech, and much of the impressionistic admiration (as well as some of the disapproval) he has elicited has been for his speech. Harbage (*Reader's Guide*, p. 145) speaks of his "matchless exercise in verbal cameo-cutting and imaginative fooling," Holland ("Shakespeare's Mercutio," pp. 118–19) of his "puns, rhymes, jokes, set-speeches, and other masks," and Snyder ("*Romeo*," p. 395) of the fact that "speech for him is a constant play on multiple possibilities: puns abound because two or three meanings are more fun than one." With pragmatic, or speech-act, analysis we may uncover some more of the nature of what Mercutio does with words.[1]

Pragmatics, the study of speech acts—of verbal action and "the relation between linguistic signs and their users" (Leech, *Explorations*, p. 2)—derives from the now classic first-generation investigations of J. L. Austin, and also of H. P. Grice and J. R. Searle, and has been extended, elaborated, and refined in a large number of second-generation studies—as early as 1978 Verschueren (*Bibliography*) lists over fifteen hundred. A speech act ("illocutionary act" in Austin's alternative terminology) is an act performed in speech, such as asserting, denying, naming, or thanking.

As Austin observes in his pioneering *How to Do Things with Words* (1962), speech acts may generally be inexplicit (i.e., have inexplicit illocutionary force), as when I say, "I wasn't there," or explicit (having explicit illocutionary force), as when I perform the same act explicitly by saying "I deny that I was there." In the latter case the act is called a "performative."[2] In addition to explicitness, many other features of speech acts have been studied, such as directedness, commitment on the speaker's part, and relative authority of speaker and hearer. Austin used such features as the basis for a taxonomy of illocutionary force dividing speech acts into five large families; a number of other taxonomies more or less resembling his have been proposed since.

The theory and study of speech acts has come to be called pragmatics, the term formed in parallel with the traditional levels of linguistic analysis, phonetics, syntactics, and semantics. Pragmatics includes not only the (taxonomic or other) study of discrete speech acts but also Gricean conversation analysis of strings of speech acts. Pragmatic conversation analysis concerns itself with global speech acts (composed of a number of separate illocutions), manifold speech acts (whose simultaneous discrete components may be directed to different hearers), and with such features of conversation as control and uptake. Pragmatic conversation analysis thus resembles sociolinguistic discourse analysis, and the two may be combined, as in Burton (*Discourse*, 1980).

The "pragmatic space" in which speech acts exist has for its dimensions the distinguishing features of the acts (see Leech, *Explorations*, p. 114). This space may be conceived of as absolute and Newtonian, but for a literary text, and especially for a play, it seems more reasonable to posit a relativistic space, one determined and successively modified by the speech acts it contains.

Many literary texts have by now been discussed or analyzed pragmatically. Speech acts in Shakespeare have been discussed by Fish and Porter, and in passing by Pratt, Elam, and Dubrow. The discussion here assumes those studies as part of its context, as it does the large evolving body of pragmatic theory, particularly of Austin, Searle, and Grice in the first generation and G. Leech, Bach and Harnish, and D. Burton in the second. Since pragmatic discriminations tend to be fine-grained, the first part of this chapter stays close to the text, especially Mercutio's four speaking scenes: 1.4, 2.1, 2.4, and 3.1. Therefore, in the next few pages in particular it may be useful to have a text of the play at hand.

THE servants in the opening scene of *Romeo and Juliet* establish the play's initial public, male, pragmatic space as one of edgy quarrelsomeness in which the salient kinds of speech acts are insults, challenges, and defiances, and in which the nicest calculations are carried out with respect to kind of illocution and degree of uptake—"take it in what sense thou wilt" (l. 25)—and directedness—"No sir, I do not bite my thumb at you, sir, but I bite my thumb, sir" (ll. 47–48).

This pragmatic space of Verona's streets undergoes two large modulations in the first scene. At the entrance of the Prince with his train (l. 78) the space grows heavily hierarchical and formal. All stand silent to hear the sentence of their prince, to which no reply is permissible. Then, after Escalus exits, the verbal action becomes comparatively intimate though still public in Benvolio's conversations with all three Montagues. By the end of the scene the play's dominant pragmatic space has been established. Under the variations lie obvious constants, such as the fact that virtually all of the action is performed by males more or less in public. The three varieties of this pragmatic space recur through the play, of course—the hierarchicalized one only at 3.1 and the last scene, but the other two repeatedly.

The play's other (and as it were tonic) main pragmatic space appears in the third scene. This is the withdrawn, private female and domestic space of the Capulet household, and of the marriage of Romeo and Juliet, which stands in a certain dialectical opposition to the dominant space. While my concern is not to treat what may be called Juliet's space at any length, it does figure as a determinant for what follows about the space that may be called Mercutio's. For, if Tybalt embodies the public world's narrow irritability, Paris its decorousness, Benvolio some of its fraternal support, and Romeo some of its honor, then that world's most illustrious representative is Mercutio. As ready as Tybalt to take offense, Mercutio seems more admirable inasmuch as the honor he dies defending is a friend's rather than his own. In the somewhat more retired space of his comradeship with Romeo and Benvolio, his high spirits make him generally more appealing than his friends. As embodied in speech acts the two sorts of behavior are closely related. Giving the lie, scorning, and mocking shade easily into friendlier kinds of jesting and ropery, and the preposition Sampson withdraws in his careful admission of thumb biting reappears naturally enough in Ro-

meo's characterization of Mercutio's speech action: "He jests at
scars that never felt a wound" (2.2.1).

Having been mentioned in the guest list in 1.2, Mercutio makes
his first appearance in 1.4 with Romeo and Benvolio immediately
before the festivities at the Capulet house. Benvolio, who has been
Romeo's confidant heretofore, now begins that recession by which
he eventually slips unheralded out of the play. Here he has four
speeches with a total of thirteen lines, one light chiding addressed
to Romeo and then another to Mercutio, and each of the two remaining speeches addressed to both of his companions.[3] Benvolio
thus provides a lightly ceremonial and retiring sanction for the
most vigorous friendship in the scene. His presence would matter
even if he had no lines. The first-person plurals of Romeo and
Mercutio include him in their reference, and some of what they say
may be understood as partly addressed to him. Even when one of
the two main speakers addresses the other by name—"Nay, gentle
Romeo, we must have you dance" (1.4.13), "Peace, peace, Mercutio, peace. / Thou talk'st of nothing" (ll. 95–96)—still what is said
seems to assume Benvolio as audience. Indeed it is of structural
significance that the parties to the most highly charged pair-bond
never appear alone together, while each does appear alone with
Benvolio (see below, chap. 6).

The spirited dialogue of Mercutio and Romeo in scene 4 sets
Mercutio's character and continues the characterization of Romeo
as it establishes a good deal of the dynamics of their relation for the
action to follow. Through the play of witty question, challenge, and
response weaves a pattern of answering imperatives—"*Rom.* Give
me a torch" (l. 11), "*Mer.* Give me a case" (l. 29)—and denials—
"*Mer.* Nay, gentle Romeo" (l. 13), "*Rom.* Nay, that's not so" (l. 44)—
that, together with the easy movement back and forth between
the pronouns of address "thou" and "you," establish an essential
equality and even fraternity between the two men.

Within that fraternity substantial differences appear. The basic
roles the two men play here in 1.4 and through 2.4, in scenes together and apart, exhibit many traces of Brooke's name's catalysis
of the god in Shakespeare's mind. In 1.4 Mercutio, through and
under the verbal play, delivers much the same exhortation and offer
of assistance as did Mercury to Odysseus and to Aeneas: end your
infatuation. The resonance with Virgil's Mercury in particular is

amplified by the "Rome" in Romeo, and fainter Trojan-Roman overtones sound in the names Paris and Juliet (see Cheney, *"Romei"*).

These basic roles for the two friends mean that, through the badinage, Mercutio is essentially active and Romeo reactive or passive.
Mercutio's exhortation, "be rough with love" (l. 27), his essential
one and his weightiest here despite its contextual wit, embodies
the hortatory mode characteristic here and below of Mercutio's address to his friend. Playful as these direct or indirect exhortations
are—"Nay, gentle Romeo, we must have you dance" (l. 13); "borrow
Cupid's wings / And soar with them above a common bound" (ll.
17–18); "Prick love for pricking" (l. 28); "Take our good meaning"
(l. 46)—and each perhaps of negligible importance alone, together
they contribute an urgent pressure to everything Mercutio says. Romeo by contrast characteristically replies that he is unable to comply with his friend's exhortations—he won't dance, don't ask him—
and his most urgent words, "Peace, peace, Mercutio, peace" (l. 95),
urge not action but its cessation.

Mercutio himself is rough with love in this scene, virtually
equating it with excrement (l. 42). Here as later his opposition is
only to love and not at all to sexuality, he being one of Shakespeare's most engagingly bawdy characters. The servingmen at the
beginning of 1.1 have engaged in some rough bawdy, and in 1.3 the
Nurse has introduced a lighter touch of bawdy into the female conversation, but the conversation between Romeo and Benvolio before 1.4 has been chaste as the fair Rosaline, with indeed only a
single direct reference to sexuality despite the fact that nearly all
their talk is of young women.[4] But here, in reply to Romeo's "Under
love's heavy burden do I sink" (l. 22), Mercutio begins to administer
the moly of bawdy: "And, to sink in it, should you burden love—
/ Too great oppression for a tender thing" (ll. 23–24). Mercutio continues with the bawdy language here and in the next two scenes,
making it usually, as in its introduction, a kind of witty play into
which he has some success drawing both his friends.

Another of Mercutio's salient characteristics, named memorably
twice after his death (3.1.120, 163) but apparent almost from his
first words, is a certain impatient scornfulness. In 1.4 it shows in
his dismissive "What care I / What curious eye doth quote deformities?" (ll. 30–31) and in the irreverence of his talk about love. There
is an air of dismissal also about Mercutio's change of subject at

l. 29. Soon after the three companions enter, discussing the speech they will not have delivered, Romeo brings the conversation around to his own love, the subject of his and Mercutio's first wit-sally. Then at l. 29, in the middle of one of his own speeches, Mercutio in effect concludes discussion of Romeo's lovesickness by asking for a visor. Benvolio seconds the change of subject (ll. 33–34), but Romeo must talk more of his distress, whereupon Mercutio delivers a light rebuke, "Tut" (l. 40), and a particularly unattractive figure for Romeo's predicament (ll. 40–43).

Roughly the middle third of the scene consists of Mercutio's longest single speech, a key one for his characterization as is generally acknowledged. It is also a key for some of the significances to be developed here. I return to it in the following pages, but some initial points may be made immediately.

Inasmuch as the Queen Mab speech is prompted by Romeo's mention of his dream and is itself both about dreams and dream-like, it may be that behind the fairies' midwife stands the classical deliverer of dreams. Inasmuch as this uncanny speech seems to catch everyone including the speaker unaware, it may be that what we have is a kind of possession of Mercutio by the god. Or, to put the matter differently, it may be that here the god looms through the man. If so, the face he presents is more disturbing than in the first part of the scene. And in the chill forebodings that darken the end of the scene there may be traces of Mercury's role as psychopomp. Indeed parts of the speech itself may come from beyond the grave inasmuch as Shakespeare seems possibly to have added to it after writing Mercutio's death (see Thomas, "Queen Mab").

The first touch of foreboding appears in the interchange leading into the speech, where Romeo gives his undisclosed dream as the reason "'tis no wit" to go to the masque. There may be a touch of disdainful fastidiousness in Mercutio's "Why, may one ask?" (l. 49), an interrogative embedded in an interrogative, with the distance and formality of the pronoun echoing similar qualities in the "sir" five lines earlier. The half-line with which Mercutio checks Romeo's recounting of his dream, "And so did I [dream]" (l. 50), then becomes the more decisive by virtue of its pronoun, as does his next, "That dreamers often lie" (l. 51), by virture of its rhyme.

The Queen Mab speech itself is notable as an example of failure to observe several of the conversational maxims that fall under

Grice's ("Conversation," pp. 45–46) "cooperative principle": "Make your conversational contribution such as is required, at the stage at which it occurs, by the accepted purpose or direction of the talk-exchange in which you are engaged." In particular Mercutio here infringes on the maxims of quality, "Try to make your contribution one that is true," relation, "Be relevant," and manner, "Be brief (avoid unnecessary prolixity)." Mercutio's conspicuous flouting of these maxims raises the possibility of what Grice calls "conversational implicature," the conveyance of unstated information by exploiting infringements of the cooperative principle (see Grice, "Conversation," and Bach & Harnish, *Communication*, pp. 165–72). The possibility seems especially worth considering in the context of talk about what pragmaticists term speaker-meaning (versus utterance-meaning) in Mercutio's "I mean sir" (l. 44) and "Take our good meaning" (l. 46) with Romeo's follow-up "And we mean" (l. 48).

The speech does seem to carry Gricean implicatures that can in principle be worked out. I return to the task below, but already a part of the implicated message has been broached. For Mercutio here is doing what he did less spectacularly above at l. 29: he is changing the subject away from Romeo's woes. A part of what the speech implicates, then, would seem to be something like "Please stop crying out loud, for crying out loud," at least in its beginning. As the speech continues, Mercutio seems carried away by it, so that Romeo's interruption (addressing Mercutio by name for the first time, as if to call him to himself) is like the breaking of a rapture. And whatever conversational implicature was present appears lost on Romeo as he says "Thou talk'st of nothing" (l. 96).[5]

Mercutio assents "True, I talk of dreams" in a remarkable speech, his last in the scene. Echoes of Mercury appear in the final four lines about the wind as well as in the mention of dreams. The cold hands Shakespeare found in Brooke have here been transmuted into the frozen bosom of the north. There is a bit of an echo of

> O'er ladies' lips, who straight on kisses dream
> Which oft the angry Mab with blisters plagues
> Because their lips with sweetmeats tainted are
>   (ll. 74–76)

in

                          the wind, who woos
            Even now the frozen bosom of the north
            And, being anger'd, puffs away
                              (ll. 100–102),

which increases Mercutio's association with a dangerous supernatural or inhuman vindictiveness that may itself derive partly from
Mercury. And in the entire speech, with its "vain fantasy, / Which
is as thin of substance as the air" and of the wind that "puffs away
from thence," there is a strong suggestion of Mercury's disappear-
ance after his first meeting with Aeneas ("From lookers eyesight
too thinnes he vannished ayrye," Stanyhurst, *Aeneis*, sig. L2v). Well
might Romeo's mind misgive some consequence hanging in the
stars.

WHILE Mercutio speaks of language or speech rather often, and
mentions several specific speech acts, he performs only three speech
acts explicitly, as performatives.[6] Two of these, "I tell ye" (2.4.111)
and "I warrant" (3.1.100), serve for passing emphasis, but the third
receives considerable emphasis itself. This is the conjuring he performs in jest in his second scene, 2.1. There, when Mercutio and
Benvolio enter looking for Romeo, and Benvolio urges "Call, good
Mercutio" (l. 5), Mercutio bursts out with one of his typical verbal
extravagances, first naming the act, "Nay, I'll conjure too" (l. 6),
then performing it inexplicitly, "Romeo! Humours! Madman! Passion! Lover! / Appear thou" (ll. 7–8), and then, when the act proves
unsuccessful or "unhappy" in Austin's term ("He heareth not, he
stirreth not, he moveth not," l. 15), naming the act again, "the ape
is dead and I must conjure him" (l. 16), and performing it again, this
time explicitly in a performative:

            I conjure thee by Rosaline's bright eyes,
            By her high forehead . . .
            That . . . thou appear to us.
                              (ll. 16–21)

Benvolio interjects, "And if he hear thee, thou wilt anger him" (l.
22)—and of course the withdrawn Romeo does overhear—and Mercutio in reply names his act thrice more, twice with the same
name, "conjur'd" and "conjure," and once with the phrase "My
invocation" (ll. 26, 29, 27).

As Gibbons points out, with the ritual of conjuration there is a possibly unique conjunction of naming and summoning, the two primary kinds of speech act called calling: "Mercutio burlesques the ritual summoning of a spirit by calling its different names; when the right one is spoken the spirit, it is supposed, will appear and speak" (p. 124n). Hence Mercutio here puts his distinctive stamp, jesting and supernatural, on two of the play's main bodies of speech act.

The importance of naming is generally acknowledged, the lovers being star-crossed first and primarily in their names Montague and Capulet,[7] and name-calling acting as a fuse for Verona's disorders. Mercutio's quinquepartite nomenclature of Romeo, then, is a direct anticipation of Juliet's "wherefore art thou Romeo?" of a mere sixty-eight lines later, also overheard by the man in question. But calling as summoning also figures importantly in the play at large, including stage directions,[8] and it figures in the way Juliet's balcony scene answers this scene of Mercutio's. Mercutio's Mercurian message is that Romeo should stay with, or come back to, the world of male comradeship. In 2.1, with that world represented onstage by Mercutio and Benvolio, Romeo overhears Mercutio summon him and does not comply. In 2.2, after overhearing Juliet offer herself to him in apostrophe, he does come forward. The play seems both to authorize and to regret Romeo's choice as its disastrous consequences unfold.

Those consequences seem to be enfolded in the very nature of Mercutio's performative conjuration. In 1.4 Mercutio has already shown himself something of a conjurer as he invokes Queen Mab for his friends. And just as there his "fragile constructions . . . cannot altogether conceal . . . a destructive, arbitrarily malicious 'animus'" (Snow, "Language," p. 191n13), so here a fair amount of aggression is apparent beneath the high jinks. In Benvolio's opinion Mercutio's jesting mention of Rosaline's "quivering thigh, / And the demesnes that there adjacent lie" (ll. 19–20) will anger Romeo if he hears. Mercutio, pleading innocuousness in reply, proceeds still further with the bawdy and personal. Romeo does overhear and, so far as we can tell, Benvolio's prediction proves inaccurate, but the scene invites us to consider whether that prediction might not have been more on target had Mercutio made light with Juliet's name instead of with Rosaline's. In any case a flickering Mercurian aggressiveness animates not only Mercutio's references to Rosaline but also his treating the flesh-and-blood Romeo as a spirit to be invoked: "The ape is dead and I must conjure him" (l. 16).

After the balcony scene[9] and Romeo's morning meeting with Friar Laurence, Mercutio and Benvolio enter at 2.4. Mercutio is still asking where the devil this Romeo should be. Here in particular Mercutio anticipates Hotspur whose scorn of the perfumed lord sent by Henry to demand prisoners (*1 Henry 4* 1.3.45–65) echoes Mercutio's scorn of Tybalt's fighting by the book. When Mercutio has divined that Tybalt's letter to Romeo is a challenge, and Benvolio has opined that Romeo will answer it, Mercutio's "Any man that can write may answer a letter" (l. 10) makes a pragmatic joke reprised in Hotspur's witty mistaking of Glendower's boast about calling spirits (*1 Henry 4* 3.1.50–52; see Porter, *Drama*, p. 58). As Gibbons notes, by "answer it" Benvolio means "accept the challenge," while Mercutio pretends to take him to mean "reply to the letter." Mercutio thus adopts as a ploy the behavior Romeo in 1.4 and Benvolio seemingly in the next line exhibit inadvertently toward him; that is, not taking the speaker's good meaning. The good meaning of Mercutio's willful misprision here would seem to be to call Romeo's valor into question, as he does more directly in his next speech (where once again in Mercutio's ominous jesting the lovesick friend has died).[10]

After some seventeen lines of Mercutio's witty denigration of Tybalt's fencing and speech, Romeo enters for the wild-goose chase of wit with Mercutio who, supposing his moly or some other to have cured his friend, ends the sally with a good-hearted congratulatory welcome back into the fraternity, coupled with another of his vigorously unattractive figures for love:

> Why, is not this better now than groaning for love? Now art
> thou sociable, now art thou Romeo; now art thou what thou
> art, by art as well as by nature. For this drivelling love is like a
> great natural that runs lolling up and down to hide his bauble
> in a hole. (ll. 88–93)

The ironies are rich. Far from being cured, Romeo is more deeply in love than before, betrothed, and with arrangements made for the secret marriage. And then far from groaning or driveling, he is inspirited enough by the secret match with Juliet to cry a match (l. 70) with Mercutio in the wit-capping. These ironies seem to me to work for the most part to build and enlarge our sympathy for Mer-

cutio in his welcome to Romeo. As we watch the addressee hang
back from any immediate reply, while Benvolio interjects "Stop
there, stop there" (l. 94), on which Mercutio seizes for a bit of
largely phallic bawdy wit-capping with him, we may also—depending on how Romeo's silence is performed—feel some rueful sympathy for him in the awkwardness of the moment.

The entrance of the Nurse and Peter in 2.4 provides more silence
for Romeo, while Mercutio jests with the Nurse. She stands as
something of a female analogue to him, as is generally recognized,
and as is suggested in the echo of Mercutio's earlier request for a
visor to hide his own visage in his remark to Peter about the fan,
"Good Peter, to hide her face, for her fan's the fairer face" (ll. 106–
7).[11] After the rapid interplay that follows, containing Mercutio's
memorable figure for the hour, his mockery of the Nurse's errone-
ous taking of Romeo's words to her, and his singing, he exits with
Benvolio.

There follows the play's most extended discussion of Mercutio's
speech, three speeches by Romeo and the Nurse with codas of a
kind in Peter's "I saw no man use you at his pleasure" (l. 154) and
the Nurse's second "Scurvy knave" (l. 159). The denigration in
what Romeo says,

A gentleman . . . that loves to hear himself talk, and will speak
more in a minute than he will stand to in a month (ll. 144–46),

seems designed to smooth ruffled feathers, but it may also contain a
grain of truth. The length of the Queen Mab speech, for instance,
could be taken as supporting evidence for the first clause, which
seems indeed to have been used as a warrant for some performances
of the entire role, such as Barrymore's in the 1936 film (see below,
chap. 7). Still, Mercutio's pleasure in the wild-goose chase of wit
with Romeo seems as much at his friend's talk as at his own, so
that Romeo's slight here may seem unfair and ungenerous.

Romeo's second and more surprising clause exhibits the momentarily pervasive bawdiness Mercutio has left in his wake. Romeo's
bawdy seems conscious, and Gibbons assures us that Peter's is also
(pp. 152–53n), although I see no reason it has to be. As for the
Nurse, while Gibbons is surely right that "she *unintentionally* expresses indecencies through unfortunate choice of words" (p. 147n),
he seems inconsistent in rejecting her "And he stand to [anything
against me]" from Quarto 1, which could be said as innocently as

"suffer every knave to use me at his pleasure." The Nurse has a further bit of unwitting bawdy here that depends directly on Mercutio. The vexation comes from him in her "I am so vexed that every part about me quivers" (ll. 158–59), and so too does the bawdy deriving from her unknowing echo of his conjuring by Rosaline's "quivering thigh, / And the demesnes that there adjacent lie" (2.1.19–20). The echo is the more conspicuous given that "quiver" is infrequent in Shakespeare, appearing only once in each of four other plays and *The Rape of Lucrece*.

The Nurse instigates the interchange by asking Mercutio's identity for the second time in the scene. Earlier when she asks the man himself, Romeo replies riddlingly, giving her only the first syllable of the name she asks for, "One . . . that God hath made, himself to mar" (ll. 114–15) and she, as if she can almost hear the name herself, repeats "By my troth it is well said; 'for himself to mar'" (l. 116). Now, asking again (and again in vain) for the man's identity, she herself uses the syllable, "I pray you, sir, what saucy merchant was this?" (l. 142), unwittingly giving Mercutio another light trace of the patron god of merchants.

MERCUTIO leaves ribaldry aside in his final scene (3.1), but not witty jesting. In his mockery of Benvolio for a quarrelsomeness they both know is more rightly attributable to Mercutio himself, in all his play with Tybalt's name and with his own mortal wound, we see the same sensibility as in his preceding scene, and similar verbal action. There are echoes from earlier scenes as well. The dismissive "What care I / What curious eye doth quote deformities" from his first scene here echoes first in his reply to Benvolio's announcement of the advent of the Capulets, "By my heel, I care not" (l. 36) and "Men's eyes were made to look, and let them gaze" (l. 53). Mercutio's oath, sworn by a part of his body peculiarly charged by his resonances with Mercury, is a scornful capping of Benvolio's "By my head." Mercutio's next oath, "Zounds" (l. 48), is far more impassioned, and with the same oath in his dying words (l. 101) he reaches "a peak of tension" (Shirley, *Swearing*, p. 101) in a sequence of oaths stretching back through all four of his speaking scenes.

In this last of Mercutio's scenes his speech acts constitute four large movements with an intermission in the middle. After the initial characterization of Benvolio as a quarreler (ll. 1–36) comes

Mercutio's first interchange with Tybalt (ll. 37–58), in which he vents some of the scorn for the man we have seen him express earlier to Benvolio. The fiery Tybalt, as is generally noticed, exercises restraint as Mercutio guys and challenges in speech bristling with imperatives—"Couple," (l. 39), "make" (l. 40), "look" (l. 46), "go" (l. 57), and first-person pronouns (ll. 39, 45, 46, 47, 54[2], 56)— in twelve lines that, in the context of Mercutio's first twenty-five lines to Benvolio with no imperatives and only four first-person pronouns,[12] manifest the aggressiveness Tybalt brings out in Mercutio.

Mercutio's aggressiveness of course has a strong phallic component deriving from his previous bawdiness and from the play's other sword-phallus linkages, as well as more distantly from Mercury's phallicism. Zeffirelli, as may be remembered, embodies some of this in the staging of Mercutio's "Here's my fiddlestick" (see below, chap. 7). There may even be a subtextual image of the phallic roadside herm in the combination of Mercutio's fiddlestick with Benvolio's "We talk here in the public haunt of men. . . . Here all eyes gaze on us" (ll. 49–52) and Mercutio's "Men's eyes were made to look, and let them gaze. / I will not budge for no man's pleasure, I" (ll. 53–54).

Pragmatically the most interesting moment in this part of the scene may be the transition from Mercutio's "Could you not take some occasion [for blows] without giving?" (l. 43) to Tybalt's reply, "Mercutio, thou consortest with Romeo" (l. 44). For one thing, Tybalt here shows that he knows Mercutio by name. More importantly, the force of what he says is open to interpretation to an unusual degree. While he could be answering Mercutio's question indirectly, he could also be returning to the subject of the "word with one of you" (l. 38) he requests at the beginning of the interchange; that is, presumably Romeo's whereabouts.

After the intermission of Romeo's appearance and Tybalt's challenge with Romeo's refusal to take it up, Mercutio in his third large pragmatic movement of the scene delivers his disapproval of Romeo's pacifism in the first words he speaks, "O calm, dishonourable, vile submission" (l. 72). If they are addressed to Romeo they are Mercutio's only words to him in this part of the scene, even though Romeo pleads, "Gentle Mercutio, put thy rapier up" (l. 83), and then exhorts both him and Tybalt to forbear and twice calls them both by name. Mercutio ignores his friend, addressing first one challenge and then a longer and more insulting one to the reluctant Tybalt, and then inviting the swordplay to begin.

T H E first sentence of the fourth and final movement of Mercutio's speech action, "I am hurt" (l. 91), has a brevity uncharacteristic of him, which may show his pain or his quickly dawning cognizance of the severity of the wound. And the brevity, together with the naked simplicity of the language and the absence of any vocative indicator, makes the sentence look as if Mercutio may be talking to himself as much as to anyone else.

Immediately—and the immediacy manifests much about the workings of Mercutio's mind here—he addresses Romeo, for the first time since "vile submission," with his malediction. Three more times in the lines that follow, including his final words in the play, Mercutio makes the same transition, from the gravity of his own condition to the curse. The repetition makes the retributive nature of the curse very clear, and Mercutio's uncanniness and access to the supernatural make his curse alone, even without his death, seem to draw down the consequence yet hanging in the stars. After the first utterance of the malediction Mercutio returns to the subject of his wound, now taking cognizance of its mortality, "I am sped." Then in "Is he gone, and hath nothing?" he addresses a third subject to which he also returns, Tybalt.

The initial incredulity of Benvolio and Romeo heightens audience sympathy for Mercutio and may help create an effect of clairvoyance for everything he has said and done in the play. The incredulity may create sympathy for Benvolio and Romeo as well, with its suggestion of a childlike inability to believe the worst. Benvolio's near-quotation, "What, art thou hurt?" in particular may produce that effect, and its intimate pronoun serves as a foil for the relentless new distance in the "you" with which Mercutio addresses Romeo, in the maledictions and also at lines 99, 104, and 105.

Mercutio addresses one further subject in addition to the main ones as he breaks off his fulminations against Tybalt to ask Romeo "why the devil came you between us? I was hurt under your arm" (ll. 104–5), recounting the action prescribed in the unusually detailed stage direction *"Tybalt under Romeo's arm thrusts Mercutio in"* (l. 89, in Q1 only), and strongly suggesting that Romeo is to blame for Tybalt's blow having hit home. Romeo's reply, "I thought all for the best" (l. 106), depending on how it is delivered may have some of the same childlike air as Benvolio's last question. However much or little explanation, excuse, or self-justification is given to the line, it seems addressed to Mercutio, and at least in part an answer to his question. Yet Mercutio seems not to take Romeo's statement as meriting any acknowledgement at all as he addresses his next words to Benvolio by name, "Help me into some house . . . Or I shall faint" (ll. 107–8). The meanings of "house" in ll. 107 and 108 are so different that the chime, if noticed, may seem the sort of homonymy we routinely ignore. It functions, though, to suggest that such shelter and safety as exists in Verona is in bourgeois familial structures, out of the reach of a figure like Mercutio.

In his last words Mercutio does finally address Romeo, with the curse, followed by an explicit assignment of blame for his death to the Montagues and Capulets—"your houses, / They have made worm's meat of me" (ll. 108–9)—a reaffirmation of the mortality of the wound and finally a contracted version of the curse, "Your houses!" (l. 110).

Almost immediately the chronic reporter Benvolio recounts these events with some elaborations and discrepancies. There may be an echo of Brooke in the hand with which, Benvolio says, Mercutio has beat cold death aside. Benvolio's quotation of Romeo (l. 167) is inaccurate (see Burckhardt, *Meanings*, pp. 162–63, for other such inaccuracies), but he describes the key tableau faithfully:

> Romeo . . .
> . . . 'twixt them rushes; underneath whose arm
> An envious thrust from Tybalt hit the life
> Of stout Mercutio.
>
> (ll. 166–71)

Thus for the third time the play emphasizes Romeo's immediate part in Mercutio's death.

MERCUTIO'S speech acts, then, constitute a characteristic manifold in significant contrast with that constituted by the speech acts of such other characters as Romeo and Benvolio, and full of resonances with Shakespeare's received Mercury. In the pragmatic space as it develops around Mercutio, Romeo describes his own situation and laments it, begs off dancing and play with words and swords but takes part in the latter two in response to Mercutio and Mercutio's death, protests the love he bears the furious Tybalt, and, with Juliet, wonders at her beauty and vows his love to her. All the while Benvolio notably reports what has happened, and also manifests his good wishes in mild suggestions to attend the festivity or to retire from the hot street.

Mercutio's speech acts differ eloquently. He urges, exhorts, and prods his friends, in jest and in earnest. He turns aside from the matter at hand in riddles he knows the answers to and also in the oracular account of Queen Mab that carries him away. He invokes Romeo, shrugs off the regard of others, challenges Romeo and Benvolio in jest and to wit-combat and Tybalt in earnest to mortal swordplay, and finally curses his friend and his friend's love. Mercutio's essential subtextual address is to Romeo, and it is a Mercurian summoning away from love to the fellowship of men, guarded with warnings of the consequences of not heeding. Although Mercutio stays in the dark about precisely why his friend shrugs off the summons, he dies with accurate enough knowledge that the ancient grudge has been complicated by love across the lines. And Mercutio's malediction, extending to the love as to the grudge, and past Rosaline to Juliet, punishes all.

"above a common bound"

AFTER Mercutio's last exit assisted by Benvolio Romeo speaks immediately of him in soliloquy, giving him the first three of the series of encomiums in obsequy that extends through the remainder of the scene:

> This gentleman, the Prince's near ally,
> My very friend, hath got this mortal hurt
> In my behalf.
>
> (3.1.111–13)

So begins what may be called Mercutio's exit limen, or threshold; that is, the space between his last appearance onstage and the last direct references to him in the play, at 5.3.75.[13] It answers his entrance limen, the space between the first reference to him, when he is named with his brother Valentine in the guest list at 1.2.68, and his first appearance onstage at 1.4. S.D., but it contains almost the entire second half of the play, with several important references to him beginning with this one, as well as other sorts of echo. Indeed as an exit limen for so important a character Mercutio's seems unprecedented in Shakespeare. It also, by the way, seems paralleled only by the titular hero's exit threshold in *Julius Caesar*, unless we include thresholds extending across more than one play, as with Richard's in the Lancastrian plays. The play with the most similar structure is, not surprisingly, *The Winter's Tale*, where Mercutio's exit limen is reprised in a happier key by the offstage "death" and long absence from the play's action of Hermione, in whose name we glimpse the same god as in Mercutio's. Since that liminal god himself presides over boundaries and thresholds, it is peculiarly and deeply right that Mercutio's exit limen should be so long, or, to put it slightly differently, that his vigorous presence in the first half of the play should be answered by as long an absence. That absence itself grows vigorous by virtue of Romeo's seemingly gratuitous mention of Mercutio in the play's last scene, and for other reasons that will be touched on below, so that in fact Mercutio has a kind of immanence through the second half of the play. The effect begins with the exit of the mortally wounded Mercutio aided by Benvolio, which shares some of the uncanniness of Mercury's abrupt disappearances "too thinnes . . . ayrye" as in Stanyhurst's *Aeneis*.

Romeo continues, in the soliloquy that becomes apostrophe, to exhibit the changed perception of his position in the state of affairs, a changed perception brought about by Mercutio's death-in-progress. His reputation is stained with Tybalt's "slander" and

> O sweet Juliet,
> Thy beauty hath made me effeminate
> And in my temper soften'd valour's steel.
>
> (ll. 115–17)

This strikingly sexist account of the effect of female beauty could almost have come from Mercutio himself.

Benvolio the reporter then enters with the news of what has happened offstage, beginning with the half-line that has introduced Juliet's balcony soliloquy shortly before:

O Romeo, Romeo, brave Mercutio is dead,
That gallant spirit hath aspir'd the clouds
Which too untimely here did scorn the earth.
(ll. 118–20)

Other features link the two moments, including a trace of the Mercury-angel wind-god "inter terram et caelum currens." It appears in Romeo's apostrophe to Juliet as "angel . . . winged messenger" (2.2.26–28), and here it recurs in the second and third lines, especially the second with its three wind images and the powerful phonetic chime between two of them. That chime sets up a phonetic resonance for "scorn," here first attributed to Mercutio—heretofore in the play scorn has been named only by Tybalt, and erroneously attributed to Romeo. Mercury however has displayed scorn repeatedly, indeed more clearly than aspiration. As discussed below in chapter 5 the image of aspiring the clouds, and even the word aspire, manifest Mercutio's Marlovianness. Here we may note a certain amount of apotheosis in Benvolio's account, to which his encomiums "brave" and "gallant" contribute.[14]

Benvolio's report is amplified in the remainder of the scene: in Romeo's "Mercutio slain" (l. 124) and his "Mercutio's soul / Is but a little way above our heads" (ll. 128–29); in the Citizen's "he that kill'd Mercutio? / Tybalt, that murderer" (l. 139); in Benvolio's own "brave," (l. 147), "bold" (l. 161), and "stout" (l. 171), and his new information that Mercutio is the Prince's kinsman (l. 147); in the Prince's own two references (ll. 184, 191), especially his second, "My blood for your rude brawls doth lie a-bleeding" (which like the Citizen's remark works to exonerate Mercutio); and in Montague's "Romeo . . . was Mercutio's friend" (l. 186).

This amplification keeps Mercutio very much present in the mind of the audience through the eighty-eight lines of the scene that follow his final exit, and so prepares for his continuing subliminal presence through most of the rest of the play. When Romeo in the Capulet tomb identifies the man he has killed as "Mercutio's kinsman" (5.3.75), the reference seems not gratuitous; rather it comes with a kind of naturalness or even inevitability, invoking a presence already immanent among the present and imminent corpses, a presence reactivated seven lines before by the "conjuration."

That presence is immanent because we miss Mercutio; we want him in the final scene, more perhaps than we want the actually present and named Paris and Tybalt, more than we want the other major absent characters, Benvolio and the Nurse (whose absence goes unmarked by any reference to either of them and may go unremarked by an audience), and certainly more than we want Lady Montague, the only other absent character referred to.[15] The explicit references just discussed have kept the absent Mercutio present in our minds, and so have other sorts of echo, such as the phonetic echo in the line with which the Prince closes Mercutio's death scene, "Mercy but murders" (l. 99). And we may see a trace of Mercutio in 4.2. When Capulet begins the scene by handing a guest list to a servant with the command "So many guests invite as here are writ" (4.2.1) he enacts a reprise of Mercutio's introduction into the play. Moments later Mercutio's shadow falls over Capulet's impulsive and disastrous decision to advance the marriage day from Thursday to Wednesday—*mercredi*, Mercury's day.

The aubade of Romeo and Juliet, 3.5, provides a good example of Mercutio's immanence. Juliet's claim that the daylight is a meteor exhaled by the sun to be a torchbearer (l. 14) recalls not only the wind and breath associated with Mercutio but also Romeo's denial of his friend's request, "Give me a torch, I am not for this ambling" (1.4.11). Mercutio also inheres in traces of the god Mercury who seems almost to hover over the scene, to effect the lovers' separation in one of the god's own liminal hours, the dawn, and to send the hero on the road. Traces of Mercury are associated with the lark and with the daylight. The lark is "herald" (l. 6) and it sings "harsh discords" (l. 28) with an echo of the words of Mercury at the end of *Love's Labour's Lost*, and the image of the severing clouds and day "tiptoe on the misty mountain tops" (l. 10) echoes Mercury's skimming the clouds and pausing on Mt. Atlas, as in *Aeneid* 4.

In addition to his posthumous presence in traces like these, Mercutio is immanent through his exit limen because his death occurs offstage. Any number of factors may have been involved in Shakespeare's decision to remove Mercutio's death from our view. It gives Romeo a moment alone onstage (except for servants) to deliver the soliloquy expressing his dawning awareness of the gravity of the situation. And then possibly the actor playing Mercutio needed to exit so that he could change and reenter thirty-two lines and a swordfight later as the Prince, in which case, by Meagher's ("Economy," pp. 8–10) principles of economy and recognition reference to Mercutio would inhere in everything the Prince does and says, including the last words of the play.[16]

Whatever its other effects, Mercutio's offstage death fixes Mercutio in a boundary region between life and death, or elevates him above that boundary. In all fictions including "reality" the more attractive a person the more likely we are somewhere in our minds to treat reports of his or her death as greatly exaggerated. Some genres accommodate real or apparent resurrection more readily than others. While resurrections and recoveries such as those of Philoclea (Sidney, *The New Arcadia*, pp. 485–88), Guyon, Arthur, and Amoret (Spenser, *The Faerie Queene*, 2.8, 3.5, and 3.12) are the staple of narrative romance, deaths in English Renaissance drama before 1595, in particular that written by Shakespeare, tend to be final. But Mercutio's peculiar offstage demise, coupled with his earlier access to the supernatural and the quality of the references to him and echoes of him through his exceptionally long exit limen, place his death under a kind of erasure, giving it an uncanny trace of Mercury's ascension from the earth to the vaulty heaven, or the whisper of a promise not fulfilled until the answering *The Winter's Tale*.

IN Mercutio's onstage presence too, before he crosses the mortal boundary into his long exit threshold, he embodies the liminality of the Mercury who presides over the wild border regions, the herm who stands by the roadside to guide a wayfarer or a *romeo*. Boundaries—that of the ancient feud, those of gender and generation, those between night and day and life and death—crisscross Mercutio's play, and much of its action transpires at such Mercurially liminal times and sites as dawn, the city walls, the garden and balcony, the interurban road, and the entrance to the tomb. Above all others Mercutio before his death manifests this liminality in his behavior, as when he turns aside from his companions as if rapt in his talk of dreams, fantasy, and the wind that, in Benvolio's words, "blows us from ourselves" (1.5.104).

Mercutio's social structures are themselves textbook examples of the liminal as expounded by Van Gennep, Turner, and others.[17] As with that stage in rites of passage and initiations when the initiates have left behind old social affiliations, and perhaps names, without yet having assumed new ones, so that they live together for a time outside the ordinary dwelling area, in radical equality and strong bondedness, so with the trio of Benvolio, Romeo, and Mercutio.

The avatar of this world is Mercutio. He summons Romeo back to it with his conjuration, and he works to hold both his friends in it with the verbal play he initiates and leads with both of them, and with his scorn of the love that ends in marriage and, in the Queen Mab speech, of adult occupations. But Mercutio's eloquence is for nought: Benvolio slips away, Romeo falls in love and marries, and the mortally wounded Mercutio is left to curse. As the form of his curse shows, a subtext of his concluding situation, at least in his understanding, is an *in trivio* Mercury without any *romei* to direct. They have all retreated to the shelter of their houses, which he curses for being houses. And since the Montagues and Capulets stand opposed, and since their opposition (combined with an individual attraction across the hostile boundary) is the cause of Mercutio's death, he has in a sense at last traded places with Romeo in the triad with Juliet. Now standing between them, Mercutio curses them and their houses because he is destroyed by them. Thus in Mercutio's final tragic configuration the liminal has become central, the god of the wild border region has become god of the agora.

The Historical Moment

THESE matters of eloquence and liminality, of locution and location, ramify massively in Shakespeare's 1595 London. Here, as with the two later chapter subdivisions titled identically, my aim is no more than to aerate a bit of accumulated sediment by suggesting some of the larger social, political, and cultural issues Shakespeare and his audience address consciously or not through the person of Mercutio.

Shakespeare's own career to 1595 had been governed by a rich interplay of periphery and center, and happy and unhappy eloquence. Whatever the lost years contain, during them if not before, the realm of discourse widened and Stratford, once securely central among its surrounding farms and villages, was displaced and revealed as comparatively peripheral to London. And yet as we all know from the subsequent career, and as indeed may be apparent in the works through *Romeo and Juliet*, the displacement was never unequivocal or irrevocable. Nor could it have been quite whole-hearted or guiltless. Nor are the movements at issue those of one man alone, but rather they are those of whole classes of the best and brightest provincials drawn to London, drawn away from lives mapped out for them by the dominant feudal order of the provinces, and drawn to more speculative futures by the emergent capitalism of the capital. In the comparative insulation of *Romeo and Juliet* Mercutio stands like a lightning rod for the social forces at play, and opposed charges run up and down him. From the provincial vantage he is the son become extravagant outsider, cursing the secure provincial houses by his very departure for a rented room in London; and he is also a kind of presiding spirit of the town center, with his bawdry and folklore and his life in the public haunt of men. From the vantage of the capital he consorts with sons of the bourgeoisie, entertaining them with his mercantile sauciness, but at the same time he is the kinsman of the County Paris and of the Prince, and so allied to the residual aristocratic social construct of honor. About this last allegiance, with Mercutio as later with Hotspur, Elizabethan social divisions and contradictions are especially apparent, as the play both necessitates the death and at the same time regrets and even in a sense denies it.

The primary effective means for Shakespeare's displacement of Stratford to the periphery seems to have been the eloquence of the playwright and narrative poet. As we know, while by 1595 he had achieved notable financial success with both sorts of writing, and recognition for both as well as (probably already) for his sonnets, internal strains, disjunctions, and contradictions in that success (variously exhibited in the changing tone of the dedications of the narrative poems, in the antitheatrical sonnets, and in the meta-drama of some of the plays) were reproducing similar stresses in the society at large, and were on the point of necessitating resolution.

That resolution, we know, would be the abandonment of nondra-matic verse and the decisive consolidation of interest and alle-giance in drama. But even without the hindsight of the later career it might be possible to see contradictions between nondramatic po-etry and drama, between patronage and the rewards of the market-place, between flattering the selected aristocrat and flattering the heterogeneous theatergoing public, in *Romeo and Juliet*, and to see portents of the resolution. Mercutio is surely dramatic to the lyric of the lovers. Carried away into his one extradramatic moment, the

Queen Mab speech, he seems to try to escape from it as it continues by subverting it from within, piling incongruity on incongruity and exhibiting a more and more alarming misogyny, as if gnashing his teeth and beating against the lines until Romeo rescues him. By contrast the lovers' lyricism gives even their "dramatic" interchanges with each other some of the stability of nondramatic verse. Their kind of eloquence culminates in the aureate immobility celebrated in the play's concluding lines. Mercutio's culminates in . . . what? Liminal persistence, a memory and a promise, the whisper of an increasing allegiance to the more marginal genre, the more questionable and ephemeral one that flies its flags in the margins of the city.

The city of London itself is liminal in a still widening realm of discourse. Hints along the way in the provincial schools could scarcely have prepared for the full weight of realizing in London that the center is elsewhere after all, the city of cities is in another country and irremediably anterior besides. Various kinds of frontal assault on the fact are possible, including the preliminary acknowledgement of setting one's first tragedy, *Titus Andronicus*, there. As we know, that strategy grows increasingly powerful—indeed preemptive—in the career after 1595. Still more powerful, it might be argued, is the more characteristic strategy of finding direction by indirection out, the liminal method. It works in *Romeo and Juliet* to suggest that there is life beyond Rome, a dramatic eloquence on the periphery.

"and a crow of iron"

I N the 1590 *The Faerie Queene* Spenser describes the horde of beasts threatening Guyon and the Palmer outside the Bower of Bliss, and so occasioning the Palmer's subduing them, with his staff made from the same wood as *"Caduceus* the rod of *Mercury"* (2.12.41.3), as follows:

> they came in vew of those wild beasts:
> Who all attonce, gaping full greedily,
> And rearing fiercely their vpstaring crests,
> Ran towards, to deuoure those vnexpected guests.
> (39.6–9)

Reading it, Shakespeare may have experienced a slight cognitive dissonance at the word "vpstaring." The word could mean "standing on end," and had been so used earlier in *The Faerie Queene* 1.9.22.3, and indeed had been so used with "crest" in Phaer's *Eneidos* (see *OED*, s.v.). On the other hand the visual component of "gaping" activates a disconcerting visual component in "vpstaring." It may then be that in his reading Shakespeare carried out the emendation Spenser himself would perform for the 1596 edition, to "vpstarting."

Assuming that Shakespeare read Marlowe's *Hero and Leander* (see *Poems*) in manuscript sometime before 1595,[1] we may assume he experienced a similar dissonance with the same word. In the second sestiad Neptune courts Leander with a tale

> How that a sheapheard sitting in a vale,
> Playd with a boy so faire and so kind,
> As for his love, both earth and heaven pyn'd;
> That of the cooling river durst not drinke,
> Least water-nymphs should pull him from the brinke.

And when hee sported in the fragrant lawnes,
Gote-footed Satyrs, and up-staring Fawnes,
Would steale him thence.

(2.194–201)

Here there seems to be no question of the meaning "standing on end," and the visual meaning is so incongruous that here too it seems possible (and in fact more likely than with the Spenser) that Shakespeare in his reading may have emended to "upstarting," the path favored by most editors and by *OED*, s.v. While Mercury is not mentioned here, theft is, and the passage is one of the most homoerotic of the poem.

Shakespeare himself had used the word "upstart" to mean something more like "arriviste" in *Henry VI, Part I* where Joan says of Lucy, "I think this upstart is old Talbot's ghost, / He speaks with such a proud commanding spirit" (4.7.87–88). Whatever the order of Shakespeare's possible reading the word in Spenser and Marlowe and his writing it into his play, his use of the word in context has resonances both Mercurian, with "ghost" and "spirit," and Marlovian, with Lucy's proud commanding Tamburlainian speech.

Probably by coincidence—the sort that would have left a trace in Shakespeare's unconscious whether or not he took conscious note of it—in 1592 what is probably the first published reference to Shakespeare also linked death, theft, Marlowe, and the word upstart. Shakespeare certainly seems to have taken conscious notice of Greene's (*Wit*, sig. F1) now familiar posthumous attack on Marlowe and on himself as "an vpstart Crow, beautified with our feathers, that with his *Tygers hart wrapt in a Players hyde*, supposes he is as well able to bombast out a blanke verse as the best of you: and beeing an absolute *Iohannes fac totum*, is in his owne conceit the onely Shake-scene in a countrey." As Chettle in the same year seems clearly to indicate, Shakespeare made a prompt personal response to the attack, acting with the frank uprightness we think of as characterizing his personal affairs. But he seems also to have made an equally characteristic far more delayed and oblique aesthetic response, in which Mercutio plays a key role.[2]

Among the components of Greene's accusation, Shakespeare seems to have taken the charge of theft, or appropriation, or conversion, or what we call plagiarism, most seriously. What we know from other sources suggests that the charges of vaingloriousness and cruelty probably were too wide of the mark to stick. The charge of *arrivisme*, so far as it went, was exactly on target, and there was no way it could be immediately countered short of forging documents to manufacture an earlier success or a university education. But what we know of Shakespeare makes that charge seem unlikely to have rankled long, and it must have been assuaged soon enough by the continuing theatrical success, and by the success of the narrative poems of 1593 and 1594. The charge of literary theft, however, seems to have occasioned and perhaps required a much more considerable processing.

For a very long time we have known how regularly Shakespeare lifted plots from other texts. That knowledge is still growing, as is our more recent knowledge of other kinds of his dependence in stylistic and conceptual realms. Eliot, "Massinger," made the borrowing out to a virtue in 1920, and recent studies demonstrate with ever more precision the subtlety of homage and response in Renaissance textual appropriation.[3] There is no shortage of reminders that the array of laws and assumptions about textual proprietorship in which Shakespeare wrote differs from ours, and that he seems to have shown comparatively little interest in the printing of his own plays, nor to have in any way objected to the appearance of leaves from his notebook in the work of other dramatists.

But Greene's attack was genuine and bitter; coming out of a misery he partly blamed Shakespeare for, it had some of the authenticity of dying words, and the accusation of theft vented Greene's most personal grievance: *our* feathers. Feathers are money, or can be, in Shakespeare's competitive theater as in the present MLA. Shakespeare could have heard these notes, it would seem, despite Greene's unsavoriness, and he seems to have begun a long slow response that would extend through most of his career. Some of the unfinished business with Greene may account for some of the radical expansion Brooke's minor character happening to recall the god of thieves undergoes as he passes into Shakespeare, as well as the play's foregrounding of the subject of economics.[4] Mercutio and his surrounding play seem in fact the first major step in Shakespeare's reply to Greene's charge.

Not that Mercutio himself has anything directly to say about theft, nor much about money. In the Queen Mab speech he shows an aristocrat's condescending affection for tradespeople and laborers, making the joiner a squirrel or an old grub and the waggoner a small gray-coated gnat, in contrast to an equally aristocratic disdain for the economic motivations of the professionals, the lawyers dreaming of fees, the parson dreaming of another benefice, and the courtier dreaming of marketing his access to the royal ear. Tact may have required his omission of merchants from the catalog, given the probable source of the wealth of Benvolio's and Romeo's families; Mercury's patronage of merchants may also have figured in the omission.

In fact, the liminal society of fraternal equality Mercutio participates in with his friends excludes their class differences, at the same time that it allows Mercutio's misogyny to adopt an economic guise, as when he makes the Nurse out to be a trader in flesh and one spent in the trade (2.4.128, 137)—and we might find more of the same in the ballad of King Cophetua and the beggar maid (2.1.14). Within the band, it is only just before Mercutio's death that some class difference begins to show, as in Mercutio's adherence to a feudal code of honor, and in the offense he takes at the class insult to Romeo he attributes to Tybalt (3.1.55–58).

Mercutio's most interesting reference to money follows his greeting to Romeo in 2.4.44–45: "Signor Romeo, bonjour. There's a French salutation to your French slop." Whatever other reasons there may have been for costuming Romeo in slops, the word calls to Mercutio's mind another word, which he first masks with a synonyn:

Mer.   You gave us the counterfeit fairly last night.
Romeo. Good morrow to you both. What counterfeit did I give
            you?
Mer.   The slip sir, the slip.

(ll. 46–50)

This is Mercutio's nearest reference to theft, and in it Romeo's presence equals true value and his absence stolen value. The figure thus puts into monetary terms the struggle for Romeo being carried out between Juliet (or Rosaline, as Mercutio supposes) and Mercutio—terms Romeo adopts in his reply, "my business was great," and terms that understandably legitimize Romeo's allegiance to his friend and criminalize his allegiance to his fiancée.

This figure completes the economic version of a structure the play has already presented otherwise, as with the paired summonings of Romeo; that is, Mercutio : Romeo :: Romeo : Juliet. Most of the play's language of valuation is in Romeo's descriptions of Juliet, as has been widely noted. The most familiar instances are at the Capulet feast where to Romeo Juliet seems to hang upon the cheek of night "As a rich jewel in an Ethiop's ear— / Beauty too rich for use" (1.5.45–46), and there are many others. Of the ten appearances of the word "rich," for example, eight have directly to do with Juliet or her father "rich *Capulet*" (1.2.81, 2.3.54), and one of the others has to do with Juliet's surrogate predecessor Rosaline (1.1.213). In contrast, when Juliet expresses her love for Romeo there is virtually no such figurative language. Until Mercutio's death, then, a vector of increasing one-way valuation runs from Mercutio through Romeo to Juliet. The riches-beauty equation, so prominent in the Romeo-to-Juliet half of the vector, appears also as a trace in the Mercutio-Romeo half read backwards, in Mercutio's deprecation of his own face (1.4.29–32), and hence implicitly there also with the vector read forward—in the implicit suggestion of the possibility that beauty makes Romeo valuable to Mercutio.

Romeo actually is beautiful in Brooke. He attends the Capulet banquet disguised as a nymph, and his beauty is such "That Ladies thought the fayrest dames were fowle in his respect" (l. 178). Shakespeare's suppression of Romeo's beauty is a function of his expansion of Mercutio's character and role. Brooke's Romeo's explicit effeminate beauty could not survive alongside Shakespeare's phallic Mercutio striving to rouse Romeo's own phallicism.

In the play's one remaining appearance of "rich" the word is negated, as Romeo tells the Apothecary,

> Famine is in thy cheeks,
> Need and oppression starveth in thy eyes,
> Contempt and beggary hangs upon thy back.
> The world is not thy friend, nor the world's law;
> The world affords no law to make thee rich.
>   (5.1.69–73)

In these lines as in much else in the scene the miserable poverty of the Apothecary is very powerfully foregrounded, far more than in Brooke and far more than is needed to make his illegal sale of the poison plausible. In fact what we have here seems to be another of those ghosts or traces of Mercutio that recur through the second half of the play, effecting his malediction. The man's profession has links with Mercury through Aesculapius and with mercury as treatment for syphilis, and the man's own "overwhelming brows" (l. 39) echo the beetle brows of Mercutio's visor (1.4.32). Furthermore the presence of the subliminal Mercutio is strongly announced by Romeo's opening soliloquy about Mercurial sleep and dreams, by his echo (noted by Gibbons) of a line from *Hero and Leander* (l. 8), by the talk of news and letters (ll. 12, 13, 31), by the news of Juliet's "death," and by Romeo's request for ink and paper (l. 25). The emphasis on the Apothecary's poverty, then, serves a number of related ends. It invokes a moribund Mercutio bereft of a Romeo not his friend after all, a Mercutio unable to steal back Romeo from his plunge into heterosexual love, and therefore effecting the curse in Romeo's very visit to the Apothecary. At the same time Shakespeare processes the state out of which Greene launched his attack in the Apothecary's deathly poverty. While the forty ducats Romeo pays him thus serve as a symbolic restitution, and hence admission of guilt, the more important restitution is in the very presentation of the dire straits of the Apothecary and the recognition that his distress is a product of legal and social forces far beyond his control. This is perhaps the first serious step in a consideration of distribution and excess that extends through much of the career to come.[5]

Juliet, who never speaks with or of Mercutio, nor ever hears him spoken of, and whose only chance to see him is at the Capulet festivity where he is visored and she has eyes mainly for Romeo, nevertheless is herself visited with an ominous trace of Mercury the thief and psychopomp. Declaring her willingness to Friar Laurence to "undertake / A thing like death" (4.1.73–74), she invites him to bid her do any number of "Things that, to hear them told, have made me tremble" (l. 86), including "walk in thievish ways, or . . . lurk / Where serpents are" (ll. 79–80). The way she follows, as if directed by a malign roadside Mercury, leads to counterfeit and then real death in the last house, via the conversation (5.2) between the brothers John and Laurence, where we learn that because of plague on a house in Mantua a crucial message has gone awry.

As noted above, Mercutio's long exit limen ends with the speaking of his name in the last house by Romeo, and the appearance of Mercutio's name is heralded by Paris's "conjuration" a few lines before. A few lines earlier still we have yet another heralding, in Romeo's explanation to Balthasar that he intends to open and enter the Capulet tomb

> partly to behold my lady's face
> But chiefly to take thence from her dead finger
> A precious ring, a ring that I must use
> In dear employment.
>
> (5.3.29–32)

None of this is in Brooke. While to Romeo it is only a nonce false-
hood to cover his suicidal intent, for us it is one of those gratuitous
details a subliminal force impels. Here the force is Mercutio, un-
doing the marriage he couldn't prevent by making his friend that
peculiarly unsavory kind of thief, a grave robber.

About the Capulet tomb the crows gather. Where in Brooke Romeus's man waits at the tomb "With lanterne, and with instruments, to open Juliets toomme" (l. 2612), in Shakespeare, while the
"instruments" are so called once (5.3.199), they are specified in the
dialogue as "that mattock and the wrenching iron" (5.3.22) and in
Quarto 1 stage direction (21 S.D.) as *"a mattock and a crow of
iron."*[6] A similar situation occurs with Friar Laurence. While in
Brooke, "for the opening of the tombe, meete instrumentes he
bare" (l. 2694), in Shakespeare he asks, "Get me an iron crow and
bring it straight / Unto my cell" (5.2.21–22), and in Quarto 2–4,F,
a stage direction specifies *"Enter FRIAR with lantern, crow and
spade"* (5.3.120 S.D.).

These iron crows at the place of death at the end of the play echo
a trio of references to avian crows in the first act. Two of those
answer each other, as Benvolio's prediction that at the Capulet feast
"I will make thee think thy swan [Rosaline] a crow" (1.2.89) is
borne out literally, assuming Rosaline's presence at the feast, when
to Romeo "So shows a snowy dove trooping with crows / As yonder
lady [Juliet] o'er her fellows shows" (1.5.47–48). As is widely noted,
this carefully staged statement and response partakes both of the
play's pervasive imagery of light and dark and of the tendency toward oxymora especially marked in the first half. Additionally,
Brooke's lines about "Juliets snowish hand" (l. 260) and Mercutio's
icy hands (ll. 261–63) echo in the "snowy" dove Juliet is compared
to.

The third reference to crows in Act 1, however, seems more involved with the iron crows of Act 5. At the beginning of 1.4 when
the question of a prologue for the maskers is raised Benvolio (or
Mercutio) demurs:

We'll have no Cupid hoodwink'd with a scarf,
Bearing a Tartar's painted bow of lath,
Scaring the ladies like a crowkeeper.

(ll. 4–6)

As Armstrong (*Imagination*, pp. 18–24) has shown, this reference to crows is part of an image cluster the key term of which, the beetle, appears shortly after in Mercutio's line about his visor's beetle brows. In the immediate vicinity of these two, Armstrong notes other of the cluster's linked images—mice, night, and fairies. Unmentioned by him (perhaps because its explicit appearances are farther away) is another key term of the cluster, death, present in the soldier's dreams of cutting throats (l. 83) and more importantly in Mercutio's "elf-locks . . . Which, once untangled, much misfortune bodes" (l. 91) and Romeo's foreboding of his own untimely death (ll. 106–11).

The crows at the tomb, then, contribute to Mercutio's immanence there. In so doing, they also constitute part of Shakespeare's processing of Greene's charge. Having persisted and succeeded in the theater (with the attendant success in narrative poetry), Shakespeare in *Romeo and Juliet* opens a serious investigation of the fact of economic differences, lets the thief-god bloom into Mercutio, continues unabashedly to appropriate and transform feathers (and, at the level of plot, very nearly the whole bird) and so demonstrates that the upstart crow is made of iron.

The way these matters develop after *Romeo and Juliet* is beyond the scope of this study, but two stages in the development may be mentioned. In what is probably the next play, *The Merchant of Venice*, with Mercutio transformed into Antonio and Romeo into Bassanio, Shakespeare continues the consideration of competing demands of love and friendship (see below, chap. 6) and proceeds much farther in the consideration of wealth, poverty, mercantalism, and theft, with both the Apothecary's ducats and the stolen ring resounding through that play. Then in *The Winter's Tale*, which as we have seen answers *Romeo and Juliet* in many other ways as well, Shakespeare pays Greene the tribute of resuscitating his *Pandosto* by stealing from it. He revives the old charge too, and pleads guilty once again, with his invention of Autolycus littered under Mercury. At the same time he pays Greene the additional tribute of appropriating cony-catcher's tricks for Autolycus from

Greene's pamphlets. Still another tribute appears in the name Mamillius adopted from Greene's *Mamillia*—Shakespeare seems to have undertaken something of an omnibus review of Greene for *The Winter's Tale*. The circumstances suggest a glancing allusion to Greene's charge in Paulina's berating Leontes for casting Perdita "forth to crows" (3.2.191).[7]

The Historical Moment

THE laws and codes of property and propriety, the social fractures and structures, and the movements of power that show themselves through Mercutio and his play comprise an "episteme" (to use Foucault's term) that increasingly through the past two decades has seemed to grow both stranger and more immediate. Such is especially the case with matters involving the intersections of theater and the printing press with some of Mercury's spheres of influence: text, theft, and commerce. Some of my sense of that episteme will have been apparent in the preceding pages about literary appropriation, and more will be apparent in the following pages about how Shakespeare negotiates with the memory of the most significant artistic and commercial rival of the first years of his theatrical career, Christopher Marlowe. However, I want to pause here to lay open a bit more of how these matters look from my present vantage, and so make a bit more explicit some of what that vantage is by sketching a version of the production, reproduction, and consumption of plays in 1595 London.[8]

The early play-work of producing such a work as the play *Romeo and Juliet* consists of receiving and amplifying such signals as produce a Mercutio. Probably none of this labor feels like coney catching because the new possession seems a gift. Later, the procedure becomes verbal, and almost certainly scribal. Immediately the possibility of theft (in either direction) enters. One ought to have a care about one's foul papers and fair copy. The language, on the other hand, is the most public and inexhaustible of property, or seems so, and similarly for verbal works of the dead. As for the verbal work of one's recent or living peers, published whether by printing or by performance, its status is far more ambiguous. While modern copyright law doesn't begin until the eighteenth century, the word plagiarize, and hence the notion of a certain authorial property right, appears in Martial, was very soon to appear in English, and is clearly implicit in Greene's attack.

The Latin *plagiarus*, kidnapper, derives from *plaga*, a net (see *OED*, svv.). The English meaning of literary theft follows the transference exemplified in Martial 1.53.9, available in editions from Venice (1501) and London (1547). The transferred meaning appears in sixteenth-century French and in English during 1597–98. The earlier Latin meaning, which Cicero uses, occurs in English only from 1613 to 1706 and even then seems never to have held its own against the literary meaning. For the history of Anglophone copyright law see Kaplan (*View*, 1967), who tends like many earlier literary scholars to underestimate the Renaissance value of the author function: "claims of infringement were heard by the court of Assistants of the [Stationers'] Company . . . but the tendency to compromise was so strong that we get little impression of any prevailing notions of piracy or plagiarism. . . . while there was an idea of piracy of content which might reach beyond verbatim copying, we should not suppose that any abstruse or refined ideas of literary theft could have been entertained" (p. 5). Ex cathedra pronouncements about whether Shakespeare could entertain refined ideas ring notoriously hollow and, while notions of verbal piracy and plagiarism do not prevail in the law before the eighteenth century, they do figure in Elizabethan London, in a society increasingly cognizant of the "marketability of such skills" as writing (Whigam, *Ambition*, pp. 55–56). Of course an attack like Greene's could backfire. And, as participants in the Greene-Nashe-Harvey quarrel, the Marprelate controversy, and the wars of the theaters well knew, an attack could also prove profitable to both parties involved (see also White, *Plagiarism*; Orgel, "Plagiarist"; and Agnew, *Worlds*, p. 64). Best have a care then too about avoiding the grosser kinds of plagiarism as one performs the labor of writing the work.

The matter might end here but with Shakespeare it seems not to. Names are in the air on the Bankside and in the City, and the author function attaches more than is sometimes admitted not only to narrative poems in search of patronage but also to plays in search of paying audiences.[9] Making plays, one also begins to make a profitable name for oneself in London, with the continuing bankability of "Marlowe" always in view. We need adopt no naive *auteurisme* to recognize the recognition value Shakespeare could have seen in "Marlowe," and could have seen accruing to "Shakespeare." Nor,

incidentally, need we adopt Bloom's exemption of Shakespeare from
the stresses of posteriority and influence, at least not the Shakespeare of 1595 (Bloom, *Anxiety*, p. 11; see also Cohen, "Marlowe,"
p. 1). And those psychological stresses have a firmly materialist
base: a Theatre by any other name is the Rose, with Marlowe still
packing them in. Best play it fairly close to the vest then with one's
literary appropriations, as Shakespeare does, fashioning a self most
notable for its withdrawal or absence, and a "Shakespeare" in the
most complex of relations with Marlowe.

With plays as with narrative poems the product is produced for
consumption, but large differences inhere in that similarity. With
Shakespeare's narrative poems, as we know, the labor of production
seems all out of proportion to the payment from the publisher,
and could be so for a young man with a family to support, because
of the hope (perhaps partly attained) of far larger rewards from the
dedicatee or patron. In this essentially feudal arrangement a key
link, missing in earlier artist-patron arrangements, is the capitalist transaction between printer-publisher and customers, a transaction made possible essentially by the iterability of language and
instrumentally by the revolutionary technology of the printing
press. With publication of plays by performance the situation is
very nearly the reverse. While no new technology is involved, here
the operative economy is far more thoroughly capitalistic, especially when the work's author is a company shareholder.

The greater penetration of the capitalist mode into literary production with plays than with other literary forms shows in numerous ways, such as the greater frequency of multiple authorship, or
the evidence for revision in rehearsal prompted by marketplace
forces and probably done at the behest of the shareholders, as with
Mercutio's Queen Mab speech (see Thomas, "Queen Mab"). Evans
(*Signifying*, p. 213) writes that while the acting companies had the
status of feudal retainers in relation to the aristocratic patrons
whose support the law compelled them to seek, as companies
"jointly financed and managed they were in the vanguard of capitalist enterprise." The new technology of course may be applied in the
parasitic and sometimes antagonistic role of printing plays, and
here piracy, the largest-scale literary theft, is most likely, as with
the first printed *Romeo and Juliet* that would appear in two years.
The iterability of language continues, with plays as with narrative

poems, to enable the capitalist enterprise, but with plays the situation differs in two important respects.

While the publicity and iterability of language makes any verbal work potentially iterable and so marketable, drama alone among genres is essentially (re)producible, and essentially audience-directed, made exclusively for repeated mass distribution and collective consumption. When Benjamin ("Work," p. 226) writes that in the age of mechanical reproduction "To an ever greater degree the work of art reproduced becomes the work of art designed for reproducibility," he has in mind still photography as opposed to painting or cinema as opposed to staged drama. Useful as are most of the distinctions he draws between cinema and drama, this one is obfuscatory.

All plays are designed (some better than others) specifically for reproducibility in performance, as with composed texts in other performing arts, such as instrumental music, song, and dance, to mention three with examples set into *Romeo and Juliet*. While no two performances are identical, the play itself is reproducible in performance, and we give other names—masque, pageant, theatrical, performance piece—to playlike things that are less reiterable. Of course nondramatic poetry retains various traces of performability, but with drama iterative performability is an overriding design determinant. The case is much the same with a play's polyvalent audience-directedness, its design for simultaneous consumption by a large number of people. With plays, then, reproducibility and mass distributability in performance are constitutive.

Benjamin ("Work," p. 246n7) is accurate about films but off target about dramatic "literature" when he writes that "In the case of films, mechanical reproduction is not, as with literature and painting, an external condition for mass distribution. Mechanical reproduction is inherent in the very technique of film production. This technique not only permits in the most direct way but virtually causes mass distribution. . . . because the production of a film is so expensive." In fact, theatrical if not mechanical (re)production is inherent in the technique of authorial production of plays. Furthermore, while production costs for Shakespeare's plays in his time were small compared to today's movie production costs, they were far from negligible, including as they did the expense of the playhouse and the livelihoods of the actors and support personnel.

There is a reciprocal determination between plays being written on the one hand and companies and playhouses on the other, so that theatrical reproduction is anything but an external condition for mass distribution of plays.

Romeo and Juliet, then, because of the constitutive iterability it shares with such other verbal constructs as rituals and formal pledges, manifests traces of the probable origin of drama (and probably of all other "literature" as well) even as it also manifests the advance of the emergent capitalist mode of distribution: hierophant and saucy merchant inhabit the same body.

And then a play's constitutive iterability may give its language a peculiarly heightened textuality, even (even especially) in performance. Shakespeare seems to have recognized the effect as early as the stage emblem of Lavinia writing with her mouth, and he seems to keep it in view and maintain it with exceptional steadiness through his career to 1595 and after. The effect derives from the audience's awareness that the words it hears spoken have first been written, by author and copyist, and read, by those as well as by the actor. About the last, incidentally, it is tempting to see some metadrama in 1.2, where Capulet hands the guest over to an illiterate servant who could well have been acted by an illiterate player of bit parts—none of this business is in Brooke, so that the emphasis on reading is conspicuous. The mercurial writtenness of the words spoken in a play may be exploited by the author in various ways, including the profitable amplification of the author function, as with Marlowe and, far more indirectly, intensively, and unremittingly, with Shakespeare.

On the other hand the effect may also be exploited by pirates, as awareness of the spoken word's prior inscription may facilitate transcription. The first appearance of Mercutio's name, written and read before his actual appearance in *Romeo and Juliet*, makes resonant the *mark* in his name and associates him from the beginning with the writtenness of the play, and so with the attendant issues of proprietorship.[10]

Though acting companies working the provinces because of the plague might get away with piracy, in London piracy was the business of the printers and booksellers, who of course also published works to which they had title. Although either sort of publication of plays in print is parasitic on theatrical publication, such publication does rematerialize the play's textuality and so makes the play at last susceptible to mechanical reproduction and distribution to potentially larger masses than with theatrical publication. We may then wonder about the resultant effect on the writtenness of the play in performance. What we know about Shakespeare's diffidence about quarto publication suggests that for him such publication possibly drains away some of the performed play's valuable writtenness.

Play, plagiary, plague. In 1595 there was especial reason for the players to have a care for the ownership of their scripts as they attempted to resume full-scale operations after the severe plague of 1592–1594. One wonders at the emotions of the audience who came to the Theatre instead of the Rose and heard from Mercutio (himself a would-be Ciceronian plagiary, a man-stealer) "A plague o' both your houses."[11]

Shakespeare's Marlowe

IN Benvolio's announcement of Mercutio's death,

> That gallant spirit hath aspir'd the clouds
> Which too untimely here did scorn the earth
>
> (3.1.119–20),

a Marlovian note sounds that differs altogether from the echoes and traces of *Hero and Leander* treated above. Here, instead of the erotic or hermetic we have the clear sound of *Tamburlaine* (Marlowe, *Complete Works*, vol. 1). The image is that of the overreacher associated with both the Scythian shepherd and his creator. In fact the lines echo a particular image of Tamburlaine's from the second scene of Part 1. The immediate context is Tamburlaine's urging Theridamas to forsake Mycetes and ally with him, the long stirring speech ending

> Then shalt thou be Competitor with me,
> And sit with *Tamburlaine* in all his majestie
>
> (1.2.208–9),

to which Theridamas replies,

> Not *Hermes* prolocutor to the Gods,
> Could use perswasions more patheticall
>
> (ll. 210–11),

and swears allegiance. Tamburlaine responds with six lines to "*Theridamas* my friend" ending,

> Thus shall my heart be still combinde with thine,
> Untill our bodies turne to Elements:
> And both our soules aspire celestiall thrones
>   (ll. 235–37).

The echo of the last of these lines in Benvolio's announcement of Mercutio's death (remarked by Malone as cited by Gibbons in his note to the lines) also differs from the other traces of Marlowe in *Romeo and Juliet* already discussed here, as from Tamburlaine's use of the image, in being not only heroic but also retrospective and elegiac. Furthermore Benvolio's lines are distinctive by virtue of the degree to which Marlowe's appearance in them is abrupt, forthright, and extensive.

This authoritative Marlovianness suggests that in Benvolio's brief elegy for Mercutio Shakespeare performs an elegy for Marlowe, dead some two years, and hence that the fictional dramatic character serves in some ways as a simulacrum of the dead competitor. The likelihood increases given the phonetic similarity of Marlowe and Mercutio, which may indeed have figured in the way Brooke's insignificant character caught Shakespeare's attention. *Marlowe* was spelled variously, including *Marley*, so that it stands as a phonetic bridge between *Mercutio* and *Mercury*. In "To the Gentlemen Readers" (*Perimedes*, 1588) Greene puns on Marlowe-Merlin, thus making explicit another phonetic and conceptual link between Marlowe and Mercury-Mercutio. In the next few pages, then, I want to consider how Mercutio figures in the negotiations Shakespeare has under way in 1595 with his memory and conception of Marlowe.

These may be the murkiest waters of the present study. As Charney writes in 1979 ("Ring," p. 43), "The relations between these two great dramatic poets . . . have not yet been fully understood." Nor will they ever be. Still, we may understand their relations better, as I try to do in the following consideration of a subset of the general subject, that is, Shakespeare's Marlowe in *Romeo and Juliet*. First I consider some homologies besides the sexual (treated in chap. 6) and the phonetic between Marlowe and Mercutio, then how Mercutio functions in Shakespeare's negotiations with Marlowe, and finally I glance at earlier and later stages of a process that looks at once like assimilation and exorcism.[12]

MERCURY, we have seen, is at once bearded adult and youth. The same ambiguity appears selectively in *Romeo and Juliet*, with its opposition between "on the one hand, such 'young' characters as Romeo, Juliet, Benvolio, Tybalt, Petruchio, Paris, and *perhaps* Mercutio, and, on the other, such 'old' characters as Capulet, 2. Capulet, Montague, Montague's Wife, the Nurse, the Friar, and *perhaps* the Prince" (Hosley, "Children," p. 6, emphasis added). While Hosley's doubled hedge would accord nicely with a doubling of the roles, Mercutio's ambiguity of age differs from the Prince's. With the Prince there is no telling evidence beyond his official authority, and since the zero-degree case for authority is years he is usually cast old, although he may also easily be cast young, as in the Zeffirelli film. With Mercutio the ambiguity comes from the fact that while he associates with Romeo and Benvolio as a peer in the liminal bond, at the same time he speaks and acts with authority greater than theirs, and he is the Prince's kinsman.

The ambiguity of Mercutio's age is homologous with the chronological ambiguity deriving from the fact that on the one hand Marlowe and Shakespeare were born in the same year, Marlowe only two months before Shakespeare, and on the other Marlowe seems years older by virtue of his precocity and earlier achievement. Note that the location of the ambiguity depends on our vantage—from Marlowe's, Shakespeare is both contemporaneous and younger, and similarly from Mercutio's vantage with, say, Romeo. But in the case of the playwrights, for obvious reasons, we customarily view Marlowe from Shakespeare's vantage (as I do here), and for equally obvious, though different, reasons we customarily view Mercutio from Romeo's (as I try to avoid doing here). The appreciably anterior success of the almost exactly contemporary Marlowe, making him both twin and elder brother, stands as the main fact to be processed by the Shakespeare of 1595 and suggests metadramatic significance for the play's warnings against Romeo's rash haste. In fact Mercutio is far more rash and impulsive, and compared to him Romeo seems almost studied, at least in his dealings with Tybalt. But the metadramatic point is that Shakespeare in 1595 must still see himself as having some catching up to do.

In plot the most striking homology is between Mercutio's death and Marlowe's. In Brooke Mercutio has long been forgotten by the time of the skirmish that culminates in Romeo's killing Tybalt (ll. 961–1022). There a band of Capulets including "a yong man . . . that cliped was Tibalt" (ll. 963–65) meet a band of Montagues, Tybalt instigates a brawl, news of it spreads through the city to Romeo "walking with his frendes" (l. 994), he and his friends come to the site of the brawl, he tries to part the fray, entreating Tybalt to have done, Tybalt calls him "coward, traytor boy" (l. 1016) and attacks, and Romeo responds by killing his new cousin.

All this was in Shakespeare's mind in 1595, and had indeed been there since about the time of Marlowe's death, when some of Romeus's incidents reappear as Valentine's in *The Two Gentlemen of Verona*, and possibly before. During the two years between Marlowe's death and Shakespeare's return to Brooke for *Romeo and Juliet* the brawl in the streets of Verona seems to coalesce with the brawl in the Deptford house where Marlowe was killed. That coalescence, which may be either instrumental in Mercutio's Marlovianness or a function of it, then places Mercutio at the brawl and makes him its first casualty.

Mercutio's character resembles Marlowe's in rashness and scornfulness, and there may even be a trace of Marlowe's view of religion in Mercutio's anticlerical picture of the venal parson (1.4.79–81) and in his entirely secular and materialist preview of his own death. While, except for an occasional mordant and sardonic note, Mercutio's language does not appear especially Marlovian, the prominence of his conjuring may involve an echo of *Dr. Faustus*.

Still more such echoes and traces of the dead playwright in Mercutio might be cited, even though they risk seeming to be examples of that critical opportunism Levin (*Readings*, pp. 209–29) calls Fluellenism. One has to hold back from running the wildgoose chase with Marlowe's father's cobbling and Mercutio's and Romeo's badinage about shoes, 2.4.62–68, where no editor seems to have noticed that "Sure wit" (l. 63) is "shoer wit." And then it seems likely that, as Shakespeare brought Mercutio into his fatal fray, Brooke's lines (1019–20),

And then at Romeus hed, a blow he strake so hard,
That might have clove him to the brayne but for his cunning
    ward,

might have resonated with the

> mortal wound over his right eye of the depth of two inches & of
> the width of one inch (Hotson, *Death*, p. 33)

given Marlowe by Ingram Frizer, as described in the coroner's inquisition. Let me then mention further only the general political resemblance.

With surprisingly few adjustments Walter Cohen's ("Marlowe," p. 1) account of Marlowe's "incipiently bourgeois, iconoclastic, subversive stance" and "negativity" fits Mercutio very well. The adjustments have to be made in Cohen's notion of "incipiently bourgeois," which he contrasts with an "aristocratic and monarchical . . . response" he finds Marlowe eliciting from Shakespeare. But some adjustments need to be made in Cohen's account of the two playwrights' political stances anyway. While bourgeois elements are apparent in Marlowe, powerful antibourgeois elements complicate the picture. Marlowe like the Mercury of wild places ignores the institution of the bourgeois nuclear family, giving it none of the attention Shakespeare gives it regularly throughout his career, and notably in *Romeo and Juliet*. Going from shepherd to emperor Tamburlaine overleaps any incipient bourgeoisie, and the parallel with Marlowe's leap from shoemaker's son to university wit, master of the London stage, and hobnobber with aristocrats could hardly have been lost on the son of a leading citizen and former bailiff of Stratford, himself unable to secure aristocratic patronage in London. And then while Cohen is surely right that some of the complex subversion Greenblatt has found in Shakespeare is generated by his containment of Marlovian subversion, and some more to his "adherence to the . . . socially untenable conflation of monarchism and nationalism" (Cohen, p. 1), Shakespearean subversion has other geneses as well, notably including the kinds of protofeminism explored in numerous recent studies.

This complex of relations echoes in the respective stances of Mercutio and Romeo. Mercutio, through the *merx* in his name (amplified by the "rich Mercatio" of *Two Gentlemen* 1.2.12), exhibits bourgeois affinities that contradict his kinship with the Prince. As for Romeo, while his father is able to raise Juliet's statue in pure gold, bourgeois elements are far more apparent in rich Capulet with his busy household and marriage brokering, and Romeo has a Shakespearean sort of aristocratic orthodoxy in his support of the

Prince's edict against brawling. Despite these complexities the basic sort of relation Cohen finds between Marlowe and Shakespeare
is apparent between Mercutio and Romeo, with Mercutio aggres-
sively subversive, as well as ambiguously prior, and eliciting from
Romeo a response of attempted containment.

In the preceding paragraphs I have let the Mercutio-Marlowe link
generate a Romeo-Shakespeare link, as happens, I maintain, in the
play. Since the second link is a function of, and signifies primarily
in terms of, the first, the second is much the more evanescent.
Shakespeare's character, for instance, does not seem to show in Romeo the way Marlowe's does in Mercutio. Nevertheless the Romeo-
Shakespeare link does seem present, by virtue of the tendency embedded deep in Western (and perhaps all other) culture to identify
imaginer and primary imagined personage, and also by virtue of
Mercutio's Marlovianness. Marlowe after all works his way into
Romeo and Juliet because of his importance to Shakespeare—the
personage Mercutio figures is Shakespeare's Marlowe, and under
the circumstances a degree of figuration of Shakespeare would seem
morely likely than not. This Romeo-Shakespeare link seems furthermore to go some way toward explaining a pair of slight oddities
in the play. To arrive at those explanations I must now make the
most frankly speculative claim of this entire study.

Whatever the personal relations may have been between Marlowe
and Shakespeare, what we know of their professional rivalry and
the high degree of challenge and response, subversion and containment, and productive cross-fertilization in their work suggests that
a nearly universal psychological process would have been at work
in Shakespeare in 1595. Whether or not Marlowe had been Shakespeare's "very friend" (*Romeo* 3.1.112) or rival in love as on the
stage, it seems nearly certain that, whether or not the news of
Marlowe's death occasioned sorrow, that news would also have occasioned immediate gratification in Shakespeare. With the passage
of some time the gratification would then have occasioned guilt
and a need for atonement, and in such circumstances a common
enough mechanism is the irrational and unconscious assumption of
responsibility for the death. Romeo may bear some obvious enough
kinds of indirect responsibility for Mercutio's death, for not earlier
making Mercutio party to the reason for his mild responses to
Tybalt's taunts, and perhaps for some heedlessness in his attempt to
halt the sword fight. But the elaborate stage direction from the first

quarto *"Tybalt under Romeo's arm thrusts Mercutio in"* (3.1.89 S.D.), coupled with the emphasis at the end of Mercutio's penultimate speech, *"—why the devil came you between us? I was hurt under your arm"* (ll. 104–5), carries a strong if fleeting suggestion of authorization by Romeo for Mercutio's death, a death Shakespeare has added to the story and so bears his own peculiar responsibility for. We may thus have here a trace of Shakespeare's unconscious assumption of responsibility for Marlowe's death.

The other slight oddity in which the Mercutio-Marlowe's resultant Romeo-Shakespeare link seems at work is in Romeo's words to the Apothecary. As we have seen, this character bears certain traces of both Mercury and Mercutio, so that we might expect the Romeo-Shakespeare link to be activated in the scene. That link does seem to appear, more conscious and intentional than in the scene of Mercutio's death, and more muffled too, and now almost entirely without the irrational assumption of responsibility for the death, in Romeo's sympathy for the Apothecary, a sympathy quite absent in Brooke. This moment of imaginative identification and sympathy under duress is one of Romeo's finer in the play, and it looks forward to Lear's access of sympathy for the poor naked wretches of the world. The slight oddity here is in Romeo's somewhat gratuitous account of "the world," all added by Shakespeare. Upon the Apothecary's admission that he has the mortal drugs whose sale is a capital crime, Romeo exhorts him,

> The world is not thy friend, nor the world's law;
> The world affords no law to make thee rich;
> Then be not poor, but break it, and take this.
>
> (5.1.72–74)

Here, especially in 1.72, there seems to be a touch of elegiac recapitulation of Marlowe's sexual, theological, and political deviancy, in what doubles as an address to him. A few lines later in another seemingly gratuitous addition by Shakespeare Romeo speaks of the world again:

> There is thy gold—worse poison to men's souls,
> Doing more murder in this loathsome world
> Than these poor compounds that thou mayst not sell.
>
> (ll. 80–82)

Given the other traces of Marlowe in the scene, Romeo's "murder in this loathsome world" looks like a veiled revision of the official story that Frizer had killed Marlowe in self-defense.[13]

Some veiling would seem advisable for one's own protection, especially if in 1595 the possibility that the death was an assassination seems as real as it will later. But then pragmatic (in both senses) considerations may call for a certain veiling of all Mercutio's Marlovianness, since elegy and praise clearly meant to be so recognized always contain a recognizable and questionable element of self-interest. Furthermore, while some two years have passed since his death, Marlowe remains controversial. As with other controversial matters, a prudent discretion may seem the better part of valor.

Such considerations would seem involved in the fact that Shakespeare's Marlowe appears no more assertively than he does in *Romeo and Juliet*, and may also be involved in the triplicate signature Shakespeare inserts in the middle of Romeo's talk of the Apothecary and the world. As with the same word in the contemporary Sonnets, multiple games are in progress, but a single one, or at least the relevant subset, may be foregrounded by isolating certain phrases:

> *Apoth.* My poverty, but *not my will* consents.
> *Romeo.* I pay thy poverty and *not thy will.*
> *Apoth.* Put this in any liquid thing *you will.*
>   (ll. 75–77, emphasis added)

In the first emphasized words Shakespeare has his Marlowe through the Apothecary posit Shakespeare's independence of him, which independence Shakespeare affirms (though it will not be altogether realized for several years yet) through Romeo's variation on the phrase. Finally the Apothecary once more uses Shakespeare's name, in a perhaps wholly unconscious "tu, Brute."

As Kenneth Muir (*Sources*, p. 46) observes, in the last scenes of *Romeo and Juliet* Shakespeare "wrote the finest poetry which had yet been heard on the English stage; it was the first play in which he went beyond Marlowe; and in the characters of Mercutio and the Nurse he displayed for the first time his unequalled power for the dramatic presentation of character." As we have seen, Shakespeare gets beyond Marlowe by containing him, indeed by incorporating him and reenacting his death. But the process of exorcism and relinquishing is far from over by the end of *Romeo and Juliet*. Shakespeare's roughly concurrent rewriting of *Edward II* in *Richard II* also partakes of, and contributes to, his Marlowe. So too does his rewriting of *The Jew of Malta* in what is probably his next play, *The Merchant of Venice*. There the negotiations with Marlowe continue not only in the Shylock plot but also notably as a part of the issue of friendship versus love discussed in the next chapter, and particularly in the figure of the titular character, the melancholy *merx* left uncoupled at play's end.

The next major stage of the negotiations has been discussed by Garber ("Vision," p. 7), who suggests that "The conflict between . . . Hal and Hotspur, discloses a conflict between Shakespeare and Marlowe" and that we see "Hal's victory over Hotspur as a metaphor for Shakespeare's dramatic victory over Marlowe."[14] The irrational assumption of responsibility for Marlowe's death whose traces in *Romeo and Juliet* are for the most part so light as to look unconscious gets played out in full consciousness in *Henry IV, Part 1*, where the echo of Mercutio's "worm's meat" in Hotspur's and Hal's "food for . . . For worms" seems an acknowledgement of the subliminal fratricide in *Romeo and Juliet*. Hotspur also echoes the ambiguity of age we have seen in Mercury and Mercutio. As is well known, with respect to Hotspur's age Shakespeare departs from Holinshed, his primary source, and rather follows Daniel in giving Hotspur the unhistorical youthfulness that makes him Hal's fraternal rival.

Hotspur's death at Hal's hand seems to complete the process of incorporation and exorcism, and so to enable Shakespeare's most explicit reference to Marlowe, in *As You Like It* in Phebe's

> Dead shepherd, now I find thy saw of might,
> 'Who ever loved that loved not at first sight?'
> (3.5.80–81)

According to Reese (*Shakespeare*, p. 269), "The directness of the reference to Marlowe . . . startles by its unexpectedness." Maybe. But the directness also has a grace and ease earned through the long negotiation in which Mercutio plays his key part. And the affection apparent in the characterizations of Mercutio and Hotspur appears here too, in the directness, in the appellation, in the fact of quotation and the subject of the quotation, and perhaps also in giving to silly Phebe this reference to the mighty rival Greene had reached out of the grave to attack alongside Shakespeare.[15]

CHAPTER SIX.

FRIENDSHIP AND LOVE

The Historical Moment

MERCUTIO takes shape in Shakespeare's mind as a product of, and response to, a distinctive array of social forces determining the received entities of friendship and love. Some of Shakespeare's address to these matters is recognized in commentary on the scrutiny of social, particularly verbal, determinants on the emotion of love in *Romeo and Juliet* (see especially Kahn, "Age," 1980, and Snow, "Language," 1985). The subject is much larger, though, and furthermore our understanding of the historical moment changes, being itself historical. In particular, numerous commentators over the past two decades, from Michel Foucault to Lawrence Stone, have contributed to a revision of earlier essentialist views of psychological states and relations in favor of more thoroughly historicized notions of them.

Therefore a preliminary word about the affectional constitution of the moment seems in order (even though no more than a word is possible here), to situate the following treatment of Mercutio by making explicit some of the assumptions that underly it and sketching some of the historical topography. Neither of the terms in the title of this chapter is any more immediate for Shakespeare than for us, although there is reason to suppose that social changes underway in Shakespeare's moment create an effect of immediacy for both friendship and love. Sexuality, a third key term figuring in this chapter, is as complex and mediated as love and friendship. Unlike them it postdates Shakespeare; like them it serves here as an umbrella for a body of related phenomena.[1] Given the general subject of this study, the following pages primarily and almost exclusively concern the friendship of men with men, and the love of men for women. The sexuality in view is also male.

Ronald Sharp (*Friendship*, p. 7) writes, "Though I make no at-

tempt to be exhaustive in my treatment of the literature [of friend-
ship], I do deal with many of the major writers and works in this
tradition: Aristotle, Cicero, Shakespeare, Montaigne, Johnson, Austin, Thoreau, . . . Auden, Hellman, and Rich." While there is medieval friendship and commentary on it, some mentioned by Sharp (p.
162n20), still we find in the Middle Ages "almost no glorification of
friendship as a boon and privilege on this earth" (Mills, *Soul*, p. 17)
so that the long hiatus in Sharp's list between Cicero and Shakespeare feels immediately right. For in its broadest outlines the moment of *Romeo and Juliet* is the arrival in England of the renaissance of secularity, commerce, social mobility, and other social
forces tending to foreground nonhereditary interpersonal bonds by
giving them increasing consequentiality and putting them more at
risk. The profile of the tradition of the literature of love is lower in
classical times and much higher in the later Middle Ages, but here
too Shakespeare's moment is a watershed, one marked fifty years
ago as a division between "some five centuries of human experience, mostly painful" (Lewis, *Allegory*, p. 341) of courtly love, and
the succeeding centuries of "that romantic conception of marriage
which is the basis of all our love literature from Shakespeare to
Meredith" (p. 360). And the same social forces that give friendship
new prominence in the moment also figure in the new prominence
of the love that is realized and sanctioned in marriage.

Among innumerable factors giving the Renaissance in England
its distinctive national character, certain ones seem particularly to
figure in the constitution of affection. The emergent mercantilism
and incipient colonialism give a peculiar urgency to questions of
love and friendship by raising into prominence the kinds of distinctions between gift exchange and commodity exchange treated recently by Hyde (*The Gift*, 1983) and by Sharp (*Friendship*) in his
chapters on "Friendship as Gift Exchange" and "*The Merchant of
Venice*." The separation from the church of Rome, together with
distinctive features of the English law of inheritance, colors English
romantic love by making English marriage differ from its Continental analogue in ways currently most vigorously discussed in feminist treatments of Shakespeare such as Dusinberre, *Shakespeare
and the Nature of Women* (1975), and of literature of the period
such as Woodbridge, *Women* (1984). And the gender and marital
status of the English head of state figure pervasively if not always

calculably as determinants in the constitution of English Renaissance affection.

Two additional factors in the general moment of the English Renaissance seem particularly worth noting for their bearing on the unruly eroticism that is more or less manifest in love and more or less latent in friendship. The first is the already noted comparative dearth of pictures in England. It means that the English eye has far less instruction than the Continental in the appreciation of human physical beauty, of face and of unclothed body, and it may also mean that verbal descriptions of physical beauty need therefore to accomplish more in English than in other European languages. A second key factor in English Renaissance eroticism is the theatricality of the Renaissance in England. Here it is a question not only of the uniquely English Renaissance prominence and popularity of the literary genre of drama but also of such phenomena as the famous theatricality of Elizabeth's practice of rule. The recent "Shakespearean Revolution," to use Styan's phrase, in the direction of increased attention to questions of performance, has included valuable assessments, by Goldman and others, of the erotics of the theatrical situation of the actor's body performing for spectators. In the English Renaissance theater that erotics includes the deferrals and displacements imposed by prohibitions against female actors and against stage nudity.

If we narrow the focus to literary texts from 1595 and the few years immediately before, a number of other determinants on the affectional makeup of *Romeo and Juliet* stand forth. Some of these are familiar landmarks, such as the vogue of the erotic Ovidian epyllion, the traditions of Petrarchan love poetry, of the amatory sonnet sequence, and of the debate on the relative merits of love and friendship, and such specific texts as Shakespeare's own poems and plays, Sidney's *The New Arcadia*, Spenser's *The Faerie Queene* III, and his *Amoretti* and *Epithalamion*, both from 1595.

Somewhat less familiar, at least until recently, but coherent, prominent, and, as I shall argue, addressed and processed in *Romeo and Juliet*, particularly in the character of Mercutio, is the wave of homoerotic poetry in the first half of the 1590s. Conspicuous examples are Richard Barnfield's *The Tears of an Affectionate Shepherd Sick of Love, or The Complaint of Daphnis for the Love of Ganymede* (1594) and *Cynthia. With Certain Sonnets* (1595), "a cycle of twenty poems in which the older lover, Daphnis, woos his Ganymede in indubitably amorous terms" (Pequigney, *Love*, p. 65). The explicitness and exclusiveness of the homosexual orientation of Barnfield's poems apparently prompted objections in his time, and have doubtless caused some of the subsequent neglect of the poems, as claimed by Pequigney in his recent argument for an explicitly homosexual reading of *Sonnets* 1-126: "One might have thought that the other Elizabethan sequence that also treats of love for a youthful master-mistress would have received attention— even particular attention—in the vast output of the Shakespearean commentators. Instead, Barnfield is a dirty little skeleton to be kept in the closet, while insistent and exaggerated claims are advanced for the concept of 'Renaissance friendship'" (*Love*, p. 65).[2] But in the early 1590s Barnfield can only have been mildly objectionable, and only because of his single-mindedness. For his poems appear in the context of far more insistent homoeroticism in *Hero and Leander* and even *Venus and Adonis*, and possibly the *Sonnets* in ways suggested by Pequigney.

And then there is the general case of Marlowe's own assertive homosexuality, flaunted in the remark about tobacco and boys and repeatedly in his writing. Those commentators discussed above who have recently helped to open hitherto unacknowledged depths in the subject of the relations between Shakespeare and Marlowe, notably Brooke treating Marlowe as a provocative agent in early Shakespeare and Cohen discussing Marlovian subversion and Shakespearean containment, have not addressed the subversiveness of Marlowe's homosexuality and Shakespeare's response to that subversion. Yet regardless of the persuasiveness of Pequigney's claim that the *Sonnets* record a physically consummated homosexual episode in Shakespeare's life, a claim that seems tenable if weakened by some of Pequigney's strained argument, we may apply Brooke's ("Agent," p. 44) remark about Marlowe's political heterodoxy— "Marlowe seems to have been for Shakespeare . . . the inescapable creator of something initially alien which he could only assimilate with difficulty"—mutatis mutandis to Shakespeare's response to Marlowe's sexual heterodoxy. Mercutio's Mercurial phallicism thus serves in Shakespeare's negotiations with Marlowe's subversive sexuality, as I shall argue in the third part of this chapter. But first we turn to other conflicts in the affectional realm.

Friendship versus Love

SHAKESPEARE'S earlier Veronan-Brookean play makes his first major dramatic statement of the theme of rivalry between friendship and love. It is a major theme of the *Sonnets*, of course, and one Shakespeare returns to repeatedly in plays of all four genres in his career through *The Winter's Tale* (and which reappears in *The Two Noble Kinsmen*). Kahn ("Age," p. 104) calls it "a conflict between male friendship and marriage which runs throughout his [Shakespeare's] work." The second major dramatic statement of the theme, and a far clearer one than in *The Two Gentlemen of Verona*, is *Romeo and Juliet*, with the essential opposition being that between Romeo's friendship for Mercutio and his love for Juliet.

A number of recent commentators have noted the importance of this conflict in *Romeo and Juliet*. Janet Adelman, "Male Bonding in Shakespeare's Comedies," pp. 82–83, writes that

> when Shakespeare allows women to test the solidity of male bonds without *Much Ado*'s comic protection from harm, that testing issues in Macbeth's murder of Duncan at Lady Macbeth's instigation, in Coriolanus's ambiguous betrayal of Aufidius at his mother's request, and above all in *Hamlet*'s image of literal fratricide. . . . In fact *Romeo and Juliet* gives us a condensed but suggestive analogue for the turn of this fantasy material from comedy to tragedy. The play seems to begin securely in a comic realm. . . . The bantering love and competition between Romeo and Mercutio seems safely of this realm, even when it suggests the dissolution of friendship threatened by Romeo's . . . love of women. After one such wit combat, Mercutio claims Romeo as his own. . . . But Romeo is not Mercutio's; and the play turns . . . tragic at the moment that Romeo's new loyalty to women graphically destroys the old male bond. Mercutio's death signals the end of the comic realm.

I quote Adelman at some length here because her remarks seem fairly representative of current feminist and psychoanalytic thinking about the play, and because what she says seems true and useful as a starting point for a consideration of Mercutio's place in the conflict, but also because elsewhere in the same essay she indulges in a certain kind of psychosexual prescriptivism that is regrettably common in discussions such as hers, and that Shakespeare in fact seems to call into question by his creation of Mercutio.

That prescriptivism is of course the doctrine that heterosexual love ought to succeed homosexual bonding in the maturation of the individual and, more generally, that adult heterosexuality is superior to adult homosexuality. The doctrine, promulgated to Shakespeare most notably by the church, and to us most notably by the law and by the discourses deriving from Freud, results from the conversion of description into prescription by a hierarchical valuation of contingent facts, a canonization.[3] In Adelman's article the doctrine appears in such phrases as "the necessary sorting out into male and female that enables marriage" (p. 90), and (of *Winter's Tale*) "the necessarily disrupted homosexual union of the parents" (p. 92). The doctrine implicit in Adelman's "necessary" and "necessarily" is recognized and stated with approval by Kahn ("Age," pp. 104–5): "As Janet Adelman points out . . . same sex friendships in Shakespeare (as in the typical life cycle) are chronologically and psychologically prior to marriage."

Certainly the doctrine appears in Shakespeare, most conspicuously in the festive comedies with their celebrations of the pattern described by Adelman and Kahn, but elsewhere as well, and in particular in *Romeo and Juliet*. But as with other received ideas, as we have come to see, so with this psychosexual doctrine in Shakespeare—it is subjected to various sorts of question and subversion. Leaving aside for the moment the question of homosexual sexuality, we may then consider how Mercutio figures in the testing of that doctrine.

None of this is intended to suggest that Adelman, Kahn, and other feminist and psychoanalytic commentators fail to see Shakespearean tensions between friendship and love. In the essay under discussion Adelman (p. 97n6) accepts the part of Fiedler's account of Shakespeare's personal mythology that makes "not marriage but male friendship the redeeming sentimental relationship" (Fiedler, *Stranger*, p. 127); Kahn quoted above and other recent accounts also acknowledge this conflict.[4] The problem with these critics is rather the construction they put on the conflict. Because their vantage is more exclusively orthodox than is Shakespeare's, I maintain, they fail to take account of some of the kinds of weight Shakespeare grants the conflict, and they do less than justice to the kinds of claims Mercutio makes on Romeo and on us.

These critics recognize in *Romeo and Juliet*, as in *The Merchant of Venice* and elsewhere in Shakespeare, the "tug of war in which women and men compete—for the affections of men" (Kahn, "Age," p. 110). And they are aware that friendship and love determine each other in *Romeo and Juliet*, so that not merely aesthetically or structurally in terms of the particular work of art but also, as deeply as we can go into the cultural constitution of the relevant affectional differences, who Romeo and Juliet are and what they do is a function of who Mercutio is and what he does (as well as vice versa). But at the same time these critics carry and promulgate (as do we all) inadvertent traces of acculturated prescriptivism. According to Novy (*Argument*, p. 106), "Romeo's exclusion of Mercutio from his confidence suggests that his love of Juliet is not only a challenge to the feud but also a challenge to associations of masculinity and sexuality with violence." Half of Novy's last phrase is a throwaway: associations of masculinity with violence are probably specieswide, and in Shakespeare, including *Romeo and Juliet*, are smoked out and questioned in ways widely recognized and beyond the scope of the present study. But the other half of Novy's last phrase—"associations of . . . sexuality with violence"—demands more attention here, because while it masquerades grammatically as coordinate with the first, in fact the first subsumes it. That is, by "sexuality" Novy here means "male sexuality," and she thus uses "sexuality" as a term subordinated to and included within "masculinity."

We are not at an easy time. The foregoing notations of antifeminist residua in feminist critics mean only to flag sidetracks along the way to a feminist, humanist future. While Mercutio stands like an *in trivio* herm along our way to that future, his directions go unheeded and misinterpreted in production and in much criticism, including those works immediately in view here.

In those works a symptom of the failure to grant adequate moment to Mercutio's claims for the value of friendship is the consequent thinning and reduction of Mercutio himself. Reductive characterizations such as Dash (*Wooing*, p. 81), "Mercutio—the brash, imaginative male who, incidentally, denigrates women"—are familiar and hardly restricted to criticism of this century or to feminist criticism. In "Coming of Age in Verona" Kahn provides a more useful picture of the problems Mercutio presents to feminist and psychoanalytic study.

Kahn ("Age," p. 176) acknowledges the character's attractiveness for us, who "want . . . the death of Mercutio, that spirit of vital gaiety, revenged," and then proceeds to assign him a place in the following schema: "Among the young bloods serving as foils for Romeo, Benvolio represents the total sublimation of virile energy into peacemaking, agape instead of eros; Tybalt, such energy channeled directly and exclusively into aggression; and Mercutio, its attempted sublimation into fancy and wit." Apart from the nineteenth-century ring of "virile energy"—an authentic and perhaps inadvertent echo of Freud's own metaphors for mental processes —several other features of the remark deserve note. Why, for instance, isn't Benvolio's virile energy "channeled" into peacemaking as "directly" as Tybalt's into aggression? When we come to Mercutio he begins to work some havoc with Kahn's schema, the tidy "total" and "exclusively" of Benvolio's and Tybalt's assignments giving way to the "attempted" of Mercutio's. And just who is making the attempt, and how and why does it fail, we may wonder. And then what about friendship? Among these four outlets for virile energy (the fourth being Romeo's love for Juliet) the only remotely amiable one is Benvolio's pacifist agape, which is indeed remote from Mercutio's full-blooded friendship for Romeo.

Kahn certainly is right that Mercutio "would rather talk than love" (p. 177), but her account of what he says obscures the character as much as does her account of his virile energy. Here the spanner in the works is not psychological but rather feminist doctrine of a particular sort. Kahn's terms are slipperier than they might seem when she maintains that Mercutio "suggests" that feuding's psychological function is as a definition of manhood (p. 176). It seems doubtful that exactly this is what Kahn sees Mercutio as meaning to suggest to Romeo and Benvolio. She may rather mean that Mercutio through his wit expresses some approval of the feud to his friends, or at least acceptance, and links that attitude to his notion of manliness. Or she may mean that Shakespeare is making the suggestion to us through Mercutio. Or she may mean the impersonal "suggest," as when we say, "The sky suggests rain," in which case what she is really talking about is a suggestion of her own. Under any of these constructions (the list is not exhaustive) Kahn's point is tenable, although the exceptional sliding of signifiers hardly bodes well for our understanding of Mercutio. In fact, I suggest, the slipperiness is an index of the fact that Kahn is not so much attending to Mercutio as using him in support of dogma.

That situation is clearer, and the picture of Mercutio so clouded by dogma as to be untenable, in her "Love is only manly, he [Mercutio] hints, if it is aggressive and violent and consists of subjugating women, rather than being subjugated by them" (p. 176). The feminist stance is apparent, as are traces of a feminist dogma opposed to sexist patriarchy. The dogma in itself seems unexceptionable, and perhaps too the stance, but in the quoted sentence they clearly impede Kahn's understanding. Again we have the ambiguous attributive, "hints"—but is Mercutio one to hint? Kahn supports her claim with two examples of Mercutio's "hinting," his advice to Romeo to "be rough with love" (1.4.27–28), and his remark to Benvolio that Romeo "is already dead, stabbed with a white wench's black eye, run through the ear with a love song, the very pin of his heart cleft with the blind bow-boy's butt-shaft. And is he a man to encounter Tybalt?" (2.4.13–17). But in neither speech does Mercutio hint at the doctrine Kahn attributes to him. Neither there nor anywhere else does Mercutio hint at approval of "subjugating women." Neither there nor elsewhere does he hint that a particular kind of love is "manly"—as Kahn herself observes, "Mercutio mocks . . . all love" (p. 177).

Again, while Mercutio is not averse to fighting, Kahn's claim that he "would rather fight than talk" (p. 177) seems obviously false. The wrongheadedness Mercutio elicits from Kahn also manifests itself in numerous ways in her discussion of the Queen Mab speech. Mercutio "would like to think that women's powers, and desires for women, are as bodiless and inconsequential as the dreams to which they give rise, and to make us also think so he concludes his whole speech with the mock-drama of a courtship between the winds. For him the perfect image of nothingness is unresponsive and inconstant love between two bodies of air" (p. 177). None of this is accurate. The Queen Mab speech is not concluded at all since Romeo breaks into it, "Peace, peace, Mercutio, peace" (1.5.95), and it is not until Mercutio's next speech, one about the Queen Mab speech, that he mentions the inconstant wind. But there he does not speak of winds, or of love between them. He speaks of one wind, who woos first the frozen bosom of the north and then the dew-dropping south.

Kahn's otherwise admirable and helpful essay traduces Mercutio in these and other ways because he stands outside the feminist reflex division of men into those who wish to dominate women and those who are able to love them in a way characterized by mutuality. The real and subversive Mercutio, standing outside that division, tests it and its underlying assumptions. Similarly he tests the psychological dogma prescribing the supplanting of homosexual by heterosexual bonding. Too often critics adhering to either dogma or, like Kahn, to both, attempt ploys like Kahn's, attempting to contain Mercutio's subversion by radically rewriting him. "Ploys," though, is not meant to imply full consciousness on the critic's part. Kahn's self-contradiction about Mercutio and love, for instance, is too patent to be anything but guileless, and the fabricatedness of her Mercutio seems entirely unconscious.

Characteristically such critics are at pains to read Mercutio as a foil to Romeo, to make Mercutio into a case of arrested development that Romeo outgrows. And characteristically they devalue Mercutio, and devalue or ignore the claims of his friendship. While psychoanalytic and feminist critical stances increase the likelihood of such misreadings in ways described here, the play itself provides some grounds for the misreadings, as does what we know about Shakespeare's other plays. But audiences find Mercutio more attractive than Romeo not only because of Mercutio's own vitality but also because he uses it to elicit an answering vitality in Romeo, and because Mercutio is a better friend—more generous, more concerned with the other—than is Romeo. Prescriptivists find *The Merchant of Venice* and *The Winter's Tale* more amenable to citation without distortion, but even those plays keep something of an open mind about conflicting claims of friendship and love. The mind is most open of all in *Romeo and Juliet*, where Shakespeare's most significant and notable single alteration of the received version is his transformation of a canonical story of love into a story of rivalry between friendship and love.

"To raise a spirit"

THE Mercurial phallicity that Shakespeare could have known from Cartari or any number of the other sources noted above is present in *Romeo and Juliet* from the opening interchange between Sampson and Gregory with their talk of standing, being felt when standing, thrusting maids to the wall, being a pretty piece of flesh, drawing a tool, and having a naked weapon out. This is in fact the most relentlessly phallic opening in all of Shakespeare's plays, and in only a few passages from anywhere in his work is the notion of the phallus more prominent. The opening establishes the phallus as much as the feud as a major theme, and sets up those equations between phallus and weapon, and between male heterosexuality and the violent subjugation of women, that Kahn and others transfer to Mercutio. Gohlke (" 'I wooed thee,' " p. 152) holds that "the way in which heterosexual relations are imagined" in these lines manifests a vision of intercourse as murder and, more generally, a "masculine ethic ... which defines relations among men as intensely competitive, and relations with women as controlling and violent," which ethic, she argues, turns the play's incipient comedy to tragedy and is also instrumental in later tragedies.[5] Certainly such difficulties inform the opening interchanges, and in numerous ways the play that follows draws attention to costs exacted by the social institution of patriarchal sexism.

The play contains three additional notably phallic passages, in all of which the phallicity is still more concentrated and prominent than in the play's opening. All three are in Mercutio's speech: at his talk of sinking in love, pricks and pricking, and beating love down (1.4.23–28); at his long bawdy interchange with Benvolio about raising a spirit (2.1.23–32); and at his talk with Romeo and Benvolio, and then the Nurse, of love's bauble, of his own "tale," and of the prick of noon (2.4.91–99, 111–12). Given that in each passage it is Mercutio who introduces the phallicism and primarily sustains it, and given the proportional prominence of such talk in Mercutio's total of lines, he is easily, in terms of what he talks about, Shakespeare's most phallic character. And several points should be made immediately about the insistent references to the phallus that mark his eloquence like priapic herms.

While Mercutio's phallicity is as aggressive as the Capulet servants', his is in a thoroughly different key by virtue of his speech acts, his range of reference, and his speech situation. Sampson in effect boasts to Gregory of the tool with which he thrusts maids to the wall, but with Mercutio we find neither boasting nor envisioned male aggression toward women. Indeed he begins his first phallic passage with

> And, to sink in it, should you burden love—
> Too great oppression for a tender thing
>
>   (1.4.23–24),

a mock counsel to Romeo against love on the grounds that heterosexual intercourse per se is overly aggressive against women. The
roughness in the remainder of his counsel,

> If love be rough with you, be rough with love;
> Prick love for pricking and you beat love down
>
>   (ll. 27–28),

is directed not against women but against love, who has changed
gender from female to male in Romeo's intervening speech. We do
have a kind of Mercurially abrupt misogyny later in the scene in
the Queen Mab speech, in the representations of the maid with lazy
fingers and the ladies with tainted breaths, and the mention of foul
sluttish hairs, and in the portrayal of Mab herself as a hag. None of
this misogyny is phallic though, and the phallus is conspicuously
absent in the final image of the speech, of Queen Mab's pressing the
maids when they lie on their backs.

Nor do we find misogyny or particular aggressiveness toward
women in Mercutio's other concentrations of phallic speech.[6] Nor,
it may be worth noting, is Mercutio's disapproval of Romeo's infatuation and heterosexuality at all sternly prescriptive. Rather it is
genial and tolerant, and the increasingly sensual catalog of Rosaline's parts that introduces the second concentration of phallicism
is appreciative throughout, if streaked with sexism in the anatomi-
zation and in the word "demesnes" (2.1.20) deriving from Latin *do-
minus*, lord, and meaning "property" (see *OED*, s.v.). Furthermore
in an important respect Mercutio's phallic talk reverses Sampson's.
While Sampson talks boastfully and exclusively about his own
phallus, and induces the compliant though not entirely credulous
Gregory to talk about it too, only a portion of Mercutio's bawdy,
and that not boastful, is about his own "tale" (2.4.95–98). The other
phalli that come up more or less explicitly in his speech are love's
(1.4.28, 2.2.33, 2.4.91–93), noon's (2.4.111–12), a stranger's (2.1.23–
26), and Romeo's (1.4.28, 2.1.29, 38). Mercutio, that is, very readily
grants phallicity to others, notably including his friend Romeo.[7]

Mercutio's three references to his friend's phallus serve as an in-

dex of the sexual dynamics of the friendship. The quibbling figurativeness of

> If love be rough with you, be rough with love;
> Prick love for pricking and you beat love down

makes the sentence exceptionally resistant to close paraphrase.
Still, clearly the exhortation is antivenereal, like most of what
Mercutio says in the first part of the scene, and prophallic, so that
(being rough with the sentence) we might paraphrase it as "Use
your phallus against love." A lightened and, as it were, genially
resigned antivenerealism appears in the context of "in his mistress'
name / I conjure only but to raise up him," with its sensually appreciative but irreverent talk of Rosaline. The prophallicism, on the
other hand, is stronger and more apparent.

Furthermore Mercutio here exhibits an attitude toward Romeo's
phallus that is at once generous and interested. It is as if Mercutio
has a personal investment, as we say, in his friend's erection. The
nature of that investment might seem, on the basis of the line and a
half quoted here, to involve the idea of Mercutio's taking Rosaline's
place not only as conjurer but also as container of Romeo's phallus,
and it is true that Rosaline has receded from active participation
with the stranger, her circle around his spirit, to a mere deputizing
name at Mercutio's raising of Romeo.[8] But that fleeting, apparently
subliminal trace of sexual desire on Mercutio's part for Romeo,
which seems to reappear in Mercutio's image of biting Romeo by
the ear (2.4.77; see Gibbons's note), is preceded by the genially explicit talk of Rosaline as sexually active and attractive, and is followed shortly by the third reference to Romeo's phallus, in Mercutio's mock wish that Romeo were a "poperin pear," another image
that (like "raise up him") reduces the friend to his genitals, while
naming the phallus precisely for its use in heterosexual intercourse.

These references of Mercutio's to Romeo's phallus add up to a
highly Mercurial stance combining an opposition to love, an amiable erotic permissiveness, and a phallocentrism that admits traces
of homoeroticism. The stance, given Mercutio's other Mercurial
stances of herald and hierophant, and given his hortatory eloquence, amounts to a directive. Mercutio, that is, points like a
roadside herm to a fraternally bonded realm, with its attendant latent misogyny and homosexuality, and with its gratifications in-

cluding strong friendship and celebration of the phallus. It is a path
his friend the *romeo* never seems much tempted by. Romeo's repar-
tee with Mercutio never seems quite wholehearted, and when Mercutio shifts into the bawdy, while Benvolio plays along—"Thou
wouldst else have made thy tale large" (2.4.96)—Romeo hangs
back; and Romeo's love for Juliet is notably uncarnal and unphallic.
Certainly the play authorizes Romeo's choice of a direction other
than Mercutio's. The generally neglected point, though, is that
through Mercutio the play gives Romeo's love an opposition other
than and different in quality from the opposition of the feud. Where
Brooke's Romeus has merely a choice between love and family
honor, Mercutio gives Romeo a third choice. I want to conclude
this chapter on love and friendship, then, and these three chapters
looking at the Mercutio of 1595 from the vantage of the late 1980s,
with some further specification of the Mercurial and Marlovian
road not taken by Romeo.

Mercutio's service to Shakespeare—and this is to say, to Shakespeare's culture—as a means of processing the memory of Christopher Marlowe has of course its sexual dimension. We may describe
Marlowe's sexual stance in increasing degrees of provocativeness or
subversiveness as follows. He is intermittently misogynistic, as
for instance when he preceded the interchange discussed above between Tamburlaine and Theridamas with the interchange

> *Tech.* What now!—in love?
> *Tamb.* Techelles, women must be flattered:
>   But this is she with whom I am in love
>   (*Tamburlaine* 1, 1.2.106–8).

Marlowe's intermittent misogyny affronts Shakespeare's proto-feminism, but the affront is of a kind the culture supplies from many
quarters, and indeed of a kind we may find in Shakespeare himself.
The abrupt intermittent misogyny that Mercutio exhibits has been
discussed above. Marlowe's more insistent eroticism, the sensuality that seems pervasively incipient when not present, seems more
idiosyncratic and more subversive than his misogyny. Much of
Shakespeare's early career through *Romeo and Juliet* may be read in
terms of strategies for processing Marlovian sensuality. In Mercutio
some of that sensuality appears in some of his bawdy, especially his
anatomy of Rosaline, and some appears as if sublimated in the
minute particularities of the Queen Mab speech. Marlovian sensu-

ality undergoes a further sublimation, and a displacement of sorts, in the amorous figurativeness of Romeo and Juliet. But Marlowe's flaunted homoeroticism is surely the most provocative and subversive feature of his sexuality.

As is well known, Marlowe flaunts his minority sexual preference in the vivid homoeroticism of *Hero and Leander*, in the love of Edward and Gaveston, at various other points in his work, such as the opening scene of *Dido*, and reportedly in the remark about tobacco and boys.[9] The flaunting seems to serve Marlowe for several not entirely compatible ends, including self-promotion and self-destruction, and it is intended as, and is surely received as, a challenge. The challenge is general, to all of whatever individual sexual persuasion who condone heterosexual hegemony, but the challenge is also obviously weighted toward men, since not merely sexually but indeed quite generally Marlowe is very much more interested in men than in women.

While there is substantial agreement now with respect to these facts about Marlowe, Shakespeare's case seems less clear. Certainly he is far more interested in women generally than is Marlowe. Indeed as recent feminist studies have helped us to see, a good deal of fairly subversive proto-feminism animates Shakespeare's works. It also seems safe to read heterosexual desire in the biography, the *Sonnets*, and the plays, although no clear consensus is apparent about the degree and nature of that desire. There is still less consensus about the presence or absence of homosexual desire in Shakespeare. Here the key text is of course the *Sonnets*, the subject of Pequigney's *Such is My Love*, which provides a useful if tendentious survey of responses to the challenge of possible autobiographical homosexual content in the sonnets, and argues "(1) that the friendship treated in Sonnets 1–126 is decidedly amorous . . . the interaction between the friends being sexual in both orientation and practice; (2) that verbal data are clear and copious in detailing physical intimacies between them; (3) that the psychological dynamics . . . comply in large measure with . . . Freud's . . . discussions of homosexuality; and (4) that Shakespeare produced not only extraordinary amatory verse but the grand masterpiece of homoerotic poetry" (p. 1). Pequigney's often suggestive though less than entirely persuasive support for these claims would not be the last word on the subject even if it were much more persuasive, in part because the stakes are still high.[10]

The present study takes no stand about the *Sonnets*, nor does it assume or support any grander claim about Shakespeare's own sexual orientation than that he seems generally heterosexual, though far less prescriptively and possibly less exclusively so than commentators generally, and feminist and psychoanalytic commentators in particular, make him out to be. Mercutio as a processing of Marlowe exemplifies such a Shakespeare, because while Marlowe's sexual orientation is obviously not paraded, neither is it cancelled, denied, or ignored. Rather Shakespeare proceeds in ways Greenblatt and others have taught us to see him as a master of, admitting and incorporating the subversive element, to some extent containing it, and to some extent rendering it still more subversive.

Marlovian homosexuality resonates not only in the general prominence of phallic talk, and the warmth and urgency of Mercutio's friendship for Romeo, but also in several specific things he says: his mock threat to bite Romeo by the ear and his "conjure only but to raise up him" discussed above, and also at least two other of his bawdy remarks.

As noted, in the interchange between Mercutio and Romeo at 1.4.23–28, "love," referred to with only the genderless pronoun "it," effectively changes gender from female in Mercutio's

> And, to sink in it, should you burden love—
> Too great oppression for a tender thing

to male in Romeo's answering

> Is love a tender thing? It is too rough,
> Too rude, too boisterous, and it pricks like thorn.

Thus when Mercutio replies

> If love be rough with you, be rough with love;
> Prick love for pricking and you beat love down,

the action he advises is homosexual, whatever its nature.[11]

And then there is Mercutio's direct explicit reference to sodomy in

> O that she were
> An open-arse and thou a poperin pear!
> (2.1.37–38),

the only such, I believe, in the canon (though Pequigney, Colman, and others find what they take to be numerous indirect, inexplicit, and more entirely metaphorical ones).[12] Of course the sodomy is heterosexual, but its uniqueness in Shakespeare suggests that the image rises out of the system of substitutions and representations Mercutio partakes of. It is as if here Shakespeare has Mercutio wish for his friend heterosexual intercourse as it might easily have been imagined, in passing, by Marlowe.

The bibliographical and critical history of "open-arse" is a good yardstick for measuring Mercutio's changing phallic subversiveness and the changing containment it elicits, and so previewing the subject of the next chapter. Suggested by Farmer and Henley, *Slang and its Analogues* (1903; noted by Gibbons, s.v.), as the meaning of Quarto 2's "open, or," the word does not appear in printed texts of the play before Hosley's 1954 adoption of the reading.[13] Partridge in 1948, s.v. "et cetera," gives the then accepted lines received from Quarto 1 and Quarto 4,

> O, that she were
> An open *et-caetera*, and thou a poperin pear!

and glosses "et cetera" as pudend, so that he is spared acknowledging mention of even heterosexual sodomy, although he does note at the same entry that the medlar ("Now will he sit under a medlar tree," 2.1.34) is "slangily an *open arse*." Since Hosley, editors generally, including Wilson and Duthie, Williams, Spencer, Gibbons, and Evans—though not Hankins—accept "open-arse," but pass in silence over the extraordinariness of the implied act.

Colman, whose view of Mercutio in *The Dramatic Use of Bawdy in Shakespeare* (1974) is less doctrinaire than most of the feminist and psychoanalytic ones discussed above but still reductive,[14] quotes the lines with "open-arse," holding that Mercutio's mockery in them is "so gross as to be self-defeating," and then announces that "It is unlikely that Mercutios of Shakespeare's own day spoke the term 'open-arse' here, as both the Bad and Good quartos of *Romeo and Juliet* suppress it, and some such action as Benvolio's clapping his hand over Mercutio's mouth seems called for" (p. 69). Colman allows that Shakespeare's audience would divine the suppressed word, but he has no more to say about the image of sodomy than the rather prim observation, "Clearly, all that Romeo needs to do about so broad a sally is to keep out of the way and flatly disregard it." But the grounds presented for this ingenious rearguard censorship performed by an authority on Shakespearean bawdy writing well after "open-arse" proved the accepted reading, are in fact not quite the grounds Colman makes them out to be. While Quarto 1's "open *Et cetera*" suggests suppression, the Quarto 2 reading "open, or" is not, as Hosley and subsequent editors recognize, a suppression but rather a compositor's misreading or misunderstanding. The *er-ar* equation we have seen variously attending Mercutio plays a part again here, for it seems possible that what the compositor misread was "openers" or "open ers."

As with Mercutio's references to homosexual and heterosexual sodomy, so generally with his phallicity and even his physicality: in all these respects Shakespeare appears to be processing some of what is most disturbing in Marlowe. The processing is far from a sanitizing, even of poetic imagery, as witness the potentially grotesquely sodomic image of Mercutio's offer to Romeo:

> we'll draw thee from the mire
> Of—save your reverence—love, wherein thou stickest
> Up to the ears.
>
> (1.4.41–43)

Nor is the processing quite like any of the other sorts we can see in progress around 1595, condemnation, apology, outspoken praise, or dismissal.[15] Rather with Mercutio Shakespeare performs some containment, some incorporation, and some transmission of Marlovian corporeality, itself a notable instance of renascent classical physicality problematized by centuries of Christian transcendent doctrine. Although the scandalous phallus reappearing (and re-disappearing, as we have seen) in pictorial representations may not be presented directly to the theater audience's gaze, it like all other parts of the male body is always actually present, and not merely represented, on the Elizabethan stage. Mercutio's phallicity then resonates not merely with Marlovian corporeality but also with the scandalous, dangerous, and, in 1595, male corporeality of the theater. In directions marked out both by "phallogocentrism" and by "materialism," that corporeality is potentially subversive in Mercutio, as it was in Marlowe—and as it is elsewhere in Shakespeare, though in other ways and perhaps nowhere so much as in Mercutio.

For, as we know, Marlowe provides Shakespeare with directions he is unable to follow. But Shakespeare keeps and uses those directions, especially in Mercutio, where he conjures the god Mercury and also the raised spirit of Marlowe.

PART THREE.

MERCUTIO SINCE

Tʜᴇ subtitle of the present study might have been "His History, Drama, and History." For, having begun in Part One with a diachronic tracing of the road traveled by Mercury from prehistoric times to the Shakespeare of 1595, and having continued in Part Two with a synchronic treatment of Mercutio in his drama as a site, for Shakespeare and for his historical moment, of struggle and negotiation with a rich manifold of received notions—of kinds and uses of eloquence, of cultural liminality and centrality, of property, mercantilism, and theft, of Marlowe, rivalry, and fratricide, and of love, friendship, and sexuality—now in Part Three we return to diachrony for a consideration of Mercutio from 1595 to the present and beyond.

The kinds of history traced and considered in the two chapters of Part Three differ somewhat. Chapter 7 follows Mercutio's historical evolutions in adaptations, promptbooks, and performances. Here I am concerned particularly with Mercutio's role as an index of the changing character of the culture in which he participates. Finally in Chapter 8, "Mercutio's Shakespeare," I turn to a more theoretical and speculative sort of history, as I address the question of the kind of "Shakespeare" Mercutio points to.

CHAPTER SEVEN.

ADAPTATIONS, PROMPTBOOKS,

PERFORMANCES

I N the nearly four hundred years since Mercutio intruded himself
into Shakespeare's *Tragedy of Romeo and Juliet* he has played,
in the transmission, canonization, and institutionalizing of Shakespeare, a role whose significance is all out of proportion to the
number of lines his name precedes.[1] In part that role is a function
of Mercutio's own layered Mercuriality and Marlovianness, but it
also of course is a function of countless other factors in the historical continuum. That is to say that a "complete" account of Mercutio's transformations is no more possible—indeed no more imag-
inable—than a "complete" account of his genesis. At the same
time that the new historicism has enabled an increasingly sophisticated awareness of the importance of history, it has also forced an
increasing abandonment of naive belief in the possibility of completeness in the history of anything. Nevertheless, as with Mercutio's genetic significances, so here: his history can be traced, and
some of the significance of that history can be uncovered. The following pages, then, follow some of Mercutio's transformations in
the four variously overlapping realms of adaptations, promptbooks,
stage performances, and films. Given the character's subversiveness, it should come as no surprise that the history of his transformations is one of manifold strategies of preemption, containment,
and accommodation.

Adaptations, 1662–1773

Romeo and Juliet was the fourth (following *Hamlet, Twelfth Night,*
and a mangled *Measure for Measure*) Shakespeare revival by Sir
William D'Avenant's company in Lincoln's Inn Fields, a produc-

tion about which we have information from Pepys and from John Downes (see Odell, *Shakespeare*, 1:37; Spencer, *Improved*, pp. 73–74). Thomas Betterton, the leading man of the company, played Mercutio. On March 1, 1662, Pepys "saw *Romeo and Juliet* the first time it was ever acted," in what may have been an unaltered version (Spencer, p. 73), but when the same company revived the play it "was made . . . into a Tragi-comedy, by Mr. James Howard, he preserving Romeo and Juliet alive; so that when the Tragedy was Reviv'd again, 'twas Played Alternately, Tragical one day, and Tragicomical another; for several Days together" (Downes quoted in Spencer, pp. 72–73). Mercutio's (and perhaps Paris's) death would seem to have provided the tragical part of the tragicomedy, so that Mercutio would seem to have proved more indelibly death-marked than the lovers. At the same time, the genre instability hypothesized by Plautus's Mercury and notably present in Shakespeare's *Romeo and Juliet*, where it is associated particularly with Mercutio, here gains further ground.

ODELL (1:52) writes of Thomas Otway (*History*, 1680): "Otway had conceived the really astounding idea of grafting the romantic story of Romeo and Juliet on a situation involving strife between Marius and Sylla [from Plutarch's *Life of Marius*] . . . No amount of familiarity with the resulting work can quite dim one's astonishment at it. . . . it is hard to see how he ever came to join these two obviously repellent fables." Spencer (*Improved*, p. 296) also disapproves of "this abominable mixture of Roman and Renaissance."[2] Otway's play is no masterpiece, but it did have a long intermittent stage life, until 1727, and some of its innovations persist in eighteenth-century adaptations of *Romeo and Juliet*. Furthermore disapproval of the sort cited looks dated and even misguided now. Shakespeare's own plays are mixtures of Renaissance and Roman and, as we have seen, *Romeo and Juliet* in particular variously resonates with the idea of classical Rome, so that, far from being altogether unaccountable, Otway's transposition has a peculiar appropriateness. As will be seen, other features latent in Shakespeare manifest themselves in Otway, while others effectively undergo the reverse procedure by being suppressed.

The play opens as described by Spencer (p. 293), "with an agreement among the patricians, headed by Metellus (Capulet) to make

Sylla (Paris) consul instead of Marius (Montague). The latter . . . commands his son [Young Marius, Romeo], who loves Metellus's daughter Lavinia (Juliet), to renounce her. This act is Otway's own except for a brief dialogue in which Sulpitius (Mercutio) rallies Young Marius . . . on his love." From this opening situation the "unruly" (Warner, *Otway*, p. 102) action unfolds, setting the Elizabethan and Veronan love tragedy in the seemingly or genuinely chancier Restoration and Roman political universes.[3] Otway generally simplifies the Shakespearean part of the action, omitting the entire Rosaline complication, for instance. He has Lavinia awaken in the tomb after Young Marius has drunk the poison but before his death, so that the lovers may have an interchange immediately before dying; this innovation, a plot device used by Bandello but suppressed by Brooke, recurs in later adaptations.

With the Roman factional warfare on progress Otway has no need for Sulpitius to die midway through and so initiate tragedy. In fact he survives the young lovers and has the last words of the play proper. In the concluding moments a messenger brings the grief-stricken father Marius Senior the "most disastrous news" (sig. K1) that his enemy Sylla is marching on Rome, the city's rabble are in new rebellion, and Sulpitius is mortally wounded (sig. K1–K1v), whereupon Sulpitius and Granius and two guards enter, to overhear Marius's cautionary lament—"Be warn'd by me, ye Great ones . . . Ambition is a Lust that's never quencht"—and portrayal of himself as now "bound for the dark Land / Of loathsome Death" (sig. K1v). This prompts Sulpitius to proclaim "A Curse on all Repentance! how I hate it! / I'd rather hear a Dog howl than a Man whine," in which both the scorn and the canine imagery descend from Mercutio. Granius notices Sulpitius's wound—"I hope it is not much"— whereupon Sulpitius has the final speech, a truncated version of Mercutio's "deep as a well" speech, ending

> If I get a Monument, let this be my Epitaph:
> Sulpitius *lies here, that troublesome Slave,*
> *That sent many honester men to the Grave,*
> *And dy'd like a Fool when h'had liv'd like a Knave*
> (sig. K1v)

after which *Ex. omnes* ("And . . . time they did," snaps Spencer, p. 296). Thus the offstage death is conserved, though obviously it is not required here by any doubling, and in a sense Mercutio has shown himself capable of appropriating the monument of Romeo and Juliet.

A trace of the Mercutio-Romeo fraternal bond survives in Sulpitius's

> Is not this better now than whining love?
> Now thou again art *Marius*, son of Arms,
> Thy Father's Honour, and thy Friends Delight.
>
> (sig. E2)

For the most part, though, Otway's Sulpitius is a cohort, assistant, and friend of Marius Senior. Thus the persistent ambiguity about Mercutio's (like Mercury's) age here resolves in a Mercutio more of the parents' generation, and one whose relations with Marius Senior echoes Mercury's with Jupiter. Shakespeare's Mercutio-Romeo bond is displaced onto the bond between Marius Junior and Granius (Benvolio), which has become literal brotherhood. At the same time "Libertine *Sulpitius*" (sig. B2v) retains Mercutio's liminal fraternality, and indeed has it magnified in

> His Band of full six hundred *Roman* Knights,
> All in their youth, and pamper's high with Riot,
> Which he his Guard against the Senate calls;
> Tall wild young men, and fit for glorious Mischiefs.
>
> (sig. B2v)

Certain atavistic traces of Mercury latent in Mercutio manifest themselves in Sulpitius. He has a thirteen-line speech (sig. E1–E1v) far more explicitly and categorically misogynist than anything of Mercutio's. Later in the same scene, in his encounter with the Nurse, he calls himself "A Woman's man" (sig. E2), and envisions a bit of libertinage for himself that echoes Mercury's tumbling of the country maid, and other of the god's passing amours:

> Lead me amongst the Beauteous, where they run
> Wild in their Youth, and wanton to their Wildness,
> Where I may chuse the foremost of the Herd,
> And bear her trembling to some Bank, bedeckt
> With sweetest Flowers.

And in Sulpitius's allusion at the end of the speech,

> throw my inspir'd Arms about her,
> And press her till she thought her self more blest
> Than *Io* panting with the Joys of *Jove*,

we may see the beheader of Argus showing through just shy of explicitness. Hence the play's numerous references to beheading, and to people as heads, have a Mercurial resonance, as does the peculiar abruptness of Sulpitius's killing of Pompieus's son (sig. D4). And when Sulpitius gives an account of his recent activity "doing Mischief up and down the City" (sig. H1), a trace of the archaic trickster-god seems to surface.[4]

Sulpitius retains Mercutio's scorn of love, as in the lines quoted above about whining love, or in his "Pox o' this Love, this little Scarecrow Love / That frights Fools with his painted Bow of Lath" (sig. D1), transferred with some alteration to the garden scene (the Capulet ball having been omitted altogether). Otway retains some of Mercutio's wit, as in the concluding speech quoted above, and he adds a bit that seems entirely in character, as when, addressed by the Nurse as Gossip (good sib), in reply he calls her "my Sibyll" (sib ill, sig. E2). Nearly all of Mercutio's bawdy, however, has been either suppressed or otherwise bowdlerized. Two of Mercutio's bawdiest moments, the "raise a spirit" speech (2.1.23–29) and the interchange about his tale with Benvolio (3.4.94–99), collapse into Otway's chaste

> *Sulp.*   'Twould anger him
> To raise a Spirit in his Lady's Arms,
> Till she had laid and charm'd it down agen.
>
> .   .   .   .
>
> *Gran.*   Stop there . . . let's leave the Subject and its Slave.
>   (sig. D1)

This spirit raising is so drained of Mercurial phallicism that Otway can safely use it again shortly after, when Marius Junior tells his father "Y'have rais'd a Spirit in me prompts my Heart / To such a Work as Fame ne'r talkt of yet" (sig. E3–E3v).

Otway's cast list (sig. A4v) announces that, while Betterton took the role of Marius Senior, Sulpitius was played by "Mr. [Cave] Underhill." The "Epilogue / Spoke by Mrs. *Barry*, who acted *Lavinia*" (sig. K2), addressed to "you who here come wrapt in Cloaks, / Only for love of Underhill and Nurse Nokes,"[5] suggests that Mercutio's subversive appeal survived his transcription into the Sulpitius of Otway's Rome. Still, "Sulpitius" is not "Mercutio," and in the balcony scene when Mrs. Barry, for whom the playwright suffered an unrequited love, asks "O *Marius, Marius!* wherefore art thou *Marius?*" (sig. D1v), several sorts of answer come to mind. They include the possibility that in the complex economy of nomenclature in the play's transition to Otway, in which Shakespeare's "Romeo" shifts to "Rome," and his Veronan tragic heroine's name is replaced by that of his earlier Roman tragic heroine, the first syllable of "Mercutio" is redistributed between the father and son, gathering them under its sign. In a sense, then, here too we have a throwback, to the Mercurial dream of an exclusively male reproduction, for Otway has excised not only Rosaline but also Lady Montague and Lady Capulet from the story.

THEOPHILUS Cibber's *Romeo and Juliet*, performed in 1744 and printed in 1748, begins a slow textual progress from Otway back toward Shakespeare. The play has returned to Shakespeare's Verona and to action and language that is mostly his. Lady Capulet reappears, though not yet Lady Montague. Cibber inherits from Otway the strategy of his most prominent alterations of Shakespeare. At the beginning of the play Cibber like Otway omits the Rosaline complication, and he also inserts a history of Montague's having sought Juliet for a daughter-in-law, Otway's

> *Metell.*   This Monster *Marius*
> Ev'n now would wed his Family with mine
> And asks my Daughters for his hated Offspring
> (sig. B2v)[6]

reappearing in Cibber's

> *O. Cap. Mountague . . .*
> Wish'd his Son Romeo, and our Daughter, married.
> (sig. B1v)

And Cibber adopts verbatim Otway's final entombed conversation between the lovers, and most of the long speech Otway gives Lavinia after Marius Junior succumbs to the poison.[7]

Cibber's Mercutio returns to a basically Shakespearean place in the story. He kills no one, and Tybalt kills him midway through, so that he has none of the peculiar prominence and atavistic harsh-

ness that Otway gives him. But Cibber's Mercutio is still some distance from Shakespeare's, as a result of numerous local alterations,
especially cuts. Many of the cuts amount in effect to a bowdlerizing
inherited from Otway, and Cibber has gone still farther in that direction, suppressing the catalog of Romeo's love's parts, and all
mention of raising a spirit (which, as we have seen, is already
drained of explicit bawdry in Otway). It is true that Cibber's play
(like Otway's) is much shorter than Shakespeare's, but in Cibber the
abridgement seems especially extreme with Mercutio.

Cibber's Mercutio is closest to Shakespeare's in his death scene,
3.1 as in Shakespeare, adopted with only a few cuts from Shakespeare. It is in Cibber's Mercutio's only other scene, 2.3 (based on
Shakespeare's 1.4, 2.1, and 2.4), that most of the cuts, splices, and
other alterations appear.

The scene begins with the entrance of Benvolio and Mercutio,
and a version of the opening interchange of Shakespeare's 2.4. It
might seem that Cibber's altered opening line, "*Merc.* Where the
Devil shou'd our Friend *Romeo* be?" (cf. Shakespeare, "Where the
devil should this Romeo be?") is designed to augment the Shakespearean bond of friendship between the two men. In fact it seems
rather designed simply to identify Mercutio, who has not appeared
or been mentioned before, to the audience: this new fellow is another of Romeo's friends. Several other factors militate against taking this "friend" as an intensification of amicability between Mercutio and Romeo. Mercutio's "our" explicitly shares Romeo's friendship with Benvolio, thereby diluting the Mercutio-Romeo bond.
Then, Cibber deletes not only all Mercutio's bawdy but also much
of his other wit-play with Romeo, so that some of the camaraderie
is drained from their association. Finally, Cibber's alteration of Romeo's tribute to Mercutio, "my very friend" (3.2.112), to "my worthy friend" (sig. C8) diminishes intimacy.

The comparative lack of intimacy appears throughout Cibber's
entire cobbled-up 2.3. When Romeo enters there is barely time for
Mercutio's "Without his Roe" speech (sig. C3v) and Romeo's wish
"Good-morrow to you both!" before the Nurse and Peter enter, fore-
stalling fifty-three lines of wild-goose chase mainly between Mercutio and Romeo. Earlier in the scene, when Mercutio delivers the
Queen Mab speech, it is to Benvolio alone. Cibber has Benvolio
break up the long speech like a television anchorperson:

Benv. A pretty Equipage! But, to what End?

.   .   .   .

Benv. Queen *Mab* has certainly paid thee a Visit,
Thou art so full of dreaming Phantasies.

(sig. C3)

So managed and parcelled, and without Romeo's presence, the speech lacks some of the uncanniness it has in Shakespeare, at least until by some authorial, scribal, or compositorial error, it is broken off by the absent friend:

Rom [*sic*]. Peace *Mercutio*, peace:
Thou talk'st of nothing.

(sig. C3)

David Garrick saw Cibber's adaptation produced by Cibber in 1744 and found the play "tolerable," if the performance "vile and scandalous," (Garrick, *Plays*, 3:407). Four years later Garrick saw his own adaptation of *Romeo and Juliet* performed and published.[8] According to Garrick's editors, Pedicord and Bergmann,

> The alteration of *Romeo and Juliet* was made some years before Garrick established himself in the public mind as "restorer of Shakespeare." Despite a typically cautious approach, in this tragedy he cuts and adds at will. . . . he sought fast stage movement, while trying to keep as much of Shakespeare as possible. Two of the older women suffer most: Lady Montague no longer appears at all [as in Cibber], and Lady Capulet's lines are curtailed or given to her husband. Quibble and bawdry are eliminated for the most part. (Garrick, *Plays*, 3:410)

In his first edition Garrick restored the Rosaline complication, but withdrew it in his second and third editions. His greatest alterations are in Act 5, where he expands on the Otway-Cibber final conversation between the lovers and adds a funeral procession for Juliet before her entombment.

While Garrick's adaptation as a whole approximates Shakespeare considerably better than does Cibber's, the same cannot be said for Garrick's Mercutio. Garrick like Cibber makes fewest changes in 3.1, Mercutio's death scene. Where Cibber mainly abridges Mercutio's last speech, Garrick adopts all of the speech from Shakespeare and makes minor additions,[9] but otherwise the scene is largely intact. And Garrick, unlike Cibber, does provide versions of each of Mercutio's three earlier scenes. In the first of these Garrick invents some lines for Mercutio to say to Benvolio as they watch Romeo approach at the opening of the scene, and he transfers to Mercutio in this scene some of Benvolio's heartening remarks to Romeo from Shakespeare's 1.1 and 1.2, so that in this respect the role is slightly expanded over Shakespeare and made more immediately fraternal. But much is lost—not only the quibbling, and with it all the bawdy, but also the demonic and threatening. Garrick, like Cibber, omits the uncanny last lines of the Queen Mab speech, those about the angry wind and the frozen bosom of the north. Indeed Garrick proceeds farther in this direction than Cibber, cutting also the lines about the angry Mab's blistering ladies' lips.

In Mercutio's next scene, 2.1, Garrick reduces the length from forty-two to thirty-two lines, all but one of the cut lines coming from Mercutio. Here primarily what is cut is the extreme of Mercutio's bawdy, but interestingly some of it is restored, including the full catalog of Rosaline's parts (which, as we shall see, disappears again in later Mercutios) and a restrained version of the lines about raising a spirit in his mistress's circle. Finally, Garrick's greatest cut in the part is in 2.4, reduced from 212 to 120 lines, the largest single passage cut being the wild-goose chase (2.4.56–100), including Mercutio's celebratory and welcoming, "Now art thou sociable, now art thou Romeo."

ALONGSIDE these adaptations in the seventeenth and eighteenth centuries Mercutio has a somewhat separate line of evolution and transmission in the editions of Shakespeare from F3, 1664, through Warburton, 1747. In this line he is of course far more stable, though here too some bowdlerization is at work, in the regular deletion of Mercutio's wish that Rosaline were an open et cetera and Romeo a poperin pear (2.1.37–38). But this comparative stability appears only in the dimension of brute text. That text's legibility, comprehensibility, and significance vary continuously as functions of innumerable other variables in the historical continuum, so that the read Mercutio too, like any other read character, is protean. While nothing like a complete tracing of his evolutions in the minds of readers is possible, it does seem certain that one major determinant on the securely textual and entirely "Shakespearean" Mercutio as read would be the adaptations considered here, which separately and to-

gether work to deny Mercutio much of the significance considered
in preceding chapters, and which in particular deny him his fraternality, his demonic uncanniness, his phallicism, and much of his
eloquent wit.

As Odell (*Shakespeare*, 2:15–16) points out, the adaptations
evolve more or less directly into the standardized acting versions of
Shakespeare that begin to appear with Bell's Shakespeare (1774).
Bell's *Romeo and Juliet* is "almost precisely" the version used by
Garrick (Odell, 2:30), but it includes copious commentary in notes
by its editor, Francis Gentleman, author of *The Dramatic Censor*
(1770). It seems suitable, then, to conclude this survey of Mercutio
in adaptations with a few of Gentleman's "fresh and charming, . . .
naively humorous" (Odell, 2:18) remarks about the character as a
terminus ad quem for the line of development.

Gentleman would censor the role slightly differently than Garrick. He would restore the second half of Mercutio's speech about
the wind: "we see no reason against retaining these lines, which are
poetical and applicable" (sig. K1), but Garrick's restored "And the
demesnes that there adjacent lie" makes him uncomfortable: "A
very indecent line of ludicrous conjuration this: indeed most of
what *Mercutio* says, in this scene, is rather in the same stile" (sig.
K4v). In *The Dramatic Censor; or, Critical Companion* his disapproval of this bawdy is more categorical: "two passages more unpar-
donably gross than those . . . are scarce to be met; they call loudly
for obliteration; it is not what such a man as Mercutio might probably speak we are to consider, but what is fit for readers to peruse, or
spectators to hear" (sig. Aa12). Gentleman's favored term of approbation for Mercutio is "whimsical." The first act "has as much
spirit as a First Act should have . . . and *Mercutio's* whimsical dissertation upon dreams, enriches it vastly" (sig. K4).

In 2.4, where Garrick's surgery is most extensive, while Gentleman finds that "Throughout this whole scene, *Mercutio* is peculiarly and most entertainingly whimsical," still more radical surgery might be appropriate: "but we could have much better dis-
pensed with him, the nurse and her man, as attendants of the
Comic, than the Tragic Muse" (sig. L2v). Gentleman writes of 3.1
that Mercutio "taking Romeo's quarrel upon himself shows something of generosity" and that "after receiving his death wound he
utters a strange incoherent rhapsody, and so much preserves uniformity that his death commonly proves a very laughable incident"

(sig. Aa3). This last manifests again the instability of genre we have seen accompanying the character and, if it is not merely an incoherence of Gentleman's own, it also reveals some of the effectiveness of the reduction and containment documented here. Gentleman's summary judgment (sig. Aa3) is that, while Mercutio is "a fine effort of genius," on balance the play would have been better if he had been left out altogether.

Promptbooks, ca. 1780–1904

PERHAPS the most Mercurial of the texts through which Mercutio evolves are the promptbooks, "tricky, secretive, stubborn informants" that "tell lies" (Shattuck, *Promptbooks*, p. 3) and that by their very existence determine a thoroughly liminal region between the printed page's handwritten marginalia and the stage enactment they determine and record. Shattuck (p. 4) warns against dealing with any given promptbook in isolation, and advises that "The working of 'traditon' is more likely to be detected in books of, say, pre-1920 vintage, before the modern director, whose price is gauged by the originality of his inventions." Both cautions have been heeded in the present consideration of Mercutio in the *Romeo and Juliet* promptbooks in the Folger Library's collection as of 1985.[10] While a substantial number of them show little or no alteration of the role as printed, significant alterations do appear in the large majority.[11] The alterations are of two sorts, with any given Mercutio affected mainly by one or the other. On the one hand some promptbooks seem products of a revisionary momentum that forces Mercutio still farther along lines initiated in the adaptations just discussed. On the other hand, in some of the promptbooks Mercutio sets out in surprising new directions, which in turn comprise two main kinds of path—one leading to a Mercutio with characteristics not previously encountered and another leading in a roundabout way back toward the Mercutio who came to life in Shakespeare's mind.

The curtailed bawdy that Garrick permits Mercutio survives in the earliest Folger promptbook (*Rom.* 39), an eighteenth-century rehearsal copy with cuts elsewhere in Garrick's text,[12] but in most nineteenth-century promptbooks the bowdlerization proceeds further, as in Folger *Rom.* 15, a rehearsal copy used from 1838 to 1886,

mostly by an actor playing Mercutio.[13] Here in 2.1 Mercutio conjures Romeo only by his lady love's eyes, forehead, and lip, and the
lines "By her fine foot, straight leg, and quivering thigh / And the
demesnes that there adjacent lie" (2.1.19–20) are cut, as is the talk
of raising a spirit in his mistress's circle. Mercutio's bawdy is eliminated more ingeniously in Folger *Rom.* 29 (1906),[14] where cutting
in 2.1 gives, "I conjure thee by Rosalind's [sic] bright eyes / And the
demesnes that there adjacent lie," which may have conjured disconcerting images in the minds of auditors familiar with the original Shakespeare.

Other promptbook cuts, in addition to the bowdlerizing, also
work in a direction tending toward Gentleman's desideratum of the
complete removal of Mercutio from the play. In Folger *Rom.* 16, a
rehearsal copy using the nineteenth-century Samuel French acting
edition,[15] Mercutio's request for a mask (1.4.29–32) is cut, so that
he loses some characterizing scornfulness as well as the poetic link
to the Apothecary discussed above. Folger *Rom.* 21, based on the
1855 Lacy acting edition,[16] cuts not only the restored lines about
the angry Mab's blistering ladies' lips (1.4.74–76) but also the two-
speech interchange between Mercutio and Benvolio beginning with
Mercutio's "Any man that can write may answer a letter" (2.4.10),
thus depriving Mercutio of some of his pragmatic wit.

If such reductionist whittling away were the only trend in the
promptbooks, Gentleman's wish might eventually have been fulfilled, at least for the play as performed. But other trends are in
evidence, constituting two different sorts of augmentative pressure
on the character. The first attempts to contain Mercutio's subversiveness not, as with the whittling, by reduction, but rather by
co-optative transformation. The transformation, effectively a sentimentalizing, comes about mainly through extensive added stage
business for Mercutio in the ball scene, 2.5, and added business and
dialogue in his death scene, 3.1.

In the ball scene, where Shakespeare has no mention of Mercutio, the promptbooks begin by having Mercutio prevent the Nurse
from interrupting Romeo's attentions to Juliet. Folger *Rom.* 27
(1847)[17] at "*Nurse.* Madam, your mother craves a word with you"
(1.5.110) adds "Mercutio wishing to aid Romeo runs to L of Nurse
and drags her away by the dress from the lovers than gets between
her and them." While this obstructing of the Nurse may grow out
of the light sparring between the two characters in Shakespeare's

2.4 (as does the nineteenth-century stage tradition of Mercutio's imitating the Nurse's gait and posture, as in many of the Folger promptbooks and in the 1908 film discussed below), at the same time the business gives Mercutio the surprising role of accomplice in his friend's flirtation. This undecidedly un-Mercurial role of fostering, rather than opposing, a romantic entanglement develops further in some later promptbooks. In Folger *Rom.* 3 (ca. 1868), after Tybalt's angry exit (1.5.91), Juliet and Paris enter together, whereupon "Mercutio engages Paris' attention and talks with [him]," so that Juliet will be free to talk with Romeo. In Folger *Rom.* 22 (1876)[18] Mercutio becomes an all-out matchmaker. As Capulet and Tybalt talk (ll. 53–63), Mercutio leads Romeo to Juliet and introduces him to her, and then leads Paris away to conversation with Benvolio. In these and certain other promptbooks[19] not only has Mercutio given up his opposition to love but he has also become its promoter, so busy a servant of Cupid as to add dramatic irony to his later calling the Nurse a bawd.

In some of these same promptbooks, and in others, Mercutio at his death undergoes an analogous, if less extreme, transformation visible in three early Victorian promptbooks, three from later in the reign, and one undated.[20] Folger *Rom.* 18, at Mercutio's "Ask for me tomorrow and you shall find me a grave man" (3.1.98–99), adds the stage direction, "Smiling faintly." This bit of sentimentalizing, which replaces Mercutio's dying rancor with acquiescence, clearly means to wring added pathos from the death. The same intention appears in other alterations of the moment. In two of the Folger promptbooks a line is added before the grave-man sentence: "You were wont to call me a merry fellow" (*Rom.* 17) and "You were wont to call me merryman yesterday" (*Rom.* 41, owned by John Doud who played Mercutio). These additions provide a certain retrospective sentimentalization of Mercutio, and also prepare for sentimentalization of the grave-man sentence.[21] Folger *Rom.* 19, used in 1845–77 in England and the United States, provides an especially full version of this sentimentalizing, at "or I shall faint" (l. 108) adding the stage direction "emphasizing *faint* and smiling," and at the grave-man sentence adding, "laughs slightly—then appears to have a sudden pang."

In this group of promptbooks Mercutio's death is further sentimentalized, and his character further revamped, by the creation of a reconciliation with Romeo, effected by a gesture added at Romeo's

"I thought all for the best" (l. 106). Here the added stage directions range from "Mercutio squeezes Romeo's hand and looks kindly at him" (*Rom.* 19), through "Mer extends his hand. Rom grasps it affectionately" (*Rom.* 14), to the fulsome "Mer stretches his right hand to Romeo (who takes it) as if to say 'I am sure you did all for the best.' When a sudden pang seized him, and [he] exclaims 'Help me.' " (*Rom.* 27), to the businesslike "shakes hands" (*Rom.* 17). This reconciliation would of course tend to exempt Romeo from Mercutio's dying malediction, which could then become a mere protest against the fact of the feud, a protest of a sort Romeo (though never Mercutio) has earlier given utterance to, or it could become a kind of stiff-upper-lip affectionate mock insult. But the malediction, like the bawdy, is a potential impediment to the sentimentalization of Mercutio, and in one of the promptbooks (Folger *Rom.* 37) it like the bawdy is cut.

Mercutio's third path in the trivium of the promptbooks is augmentative like the second, but here the augmentation serves not for sentimentalizing but rather for the restoration and accentuation of some of the characteristics and significances considered above in chapters 4–6, even when the alterations do not themselves constitute restoration of Shakespeare's text.

In a few of the alterations atavistic traces of Mercutio's predecessor Mercury may be visible. Folger *Rom.* 22, in the ball scene at Capulet's "This room is grown too hot" (1.5.28), adds the stage direction "Merc. chats with Cap," and a blocking diagram placing these two upstage center, with the other characters fanning out down from them on either side, a design homologous with the Reusner synod of gods (fig. 14). A similar association of Mercutio with the patriarchal or ranking male occurs in Folger *Rom.* 44,[22] which brings the Prince to the ball in 1.5, and has Mercutio, Tybalt, and him "converse with the maskers." And some of Mercutio's accoutrements have a Mercurial resonance. In Folger *Rom.* F02,[23] as the three friends enter at the opening of 1.4, Mercutio appears like the scribal Mercury "carrying a scroll," which he "opens . . . and is about to read," when Romeo and Benvolio decide against the prologue. There may also be a distant echo of the petasos in the feathered cap Mercutio doffs mockingly and then "*Puts on . . . and almost brushes Tybalt's face with his feather*" at 3.1.43 in Folger *Rom.* 19.

A different sort of augmentation, making explicit in performance the Shakespearean Mercutio's liminal bondedness, happens in those promptbooks (*Rom.* 14, 3, 29) in which at Mercutio's French saluta-tion to Romeo (2.4.45) they embrace and Mercutio kisses Romeo on both cheeks, and in those books in which the mortally wounded Mercutio falls into Benvolio's arms (*Rom.* 22, F02) or into Benvo-lio's and Romeo's (*Rom.* 29).

Some of Mercutio's most interesting augmentation is at the ex-pense of Benvolio. Shakespeare's stage direction opening 2.4, "*En-ter* Benvolio *and* Mercutio," is altered in *Rom.* 21 and 22 so that Mercutio precedes Benvolio, the order reflecting their respective importance in the scene. Mercutio also appropriates some of Benvo-lio's lines (Folger *Rom.* 41).[24] There, in 1.1, Mercutio enters after Benvolio's speech to Montague about the brawl (ll. 104–13) and he, not Benvolio, answers Lady Montague's question about Romeo's whereabouts with the tale of the predawn sighting outside the city wall (ll. 116–28), a fairly Mercurial episode. Another potentially Mercurial moment of Benvolio's is altered somewhat and trans-ferred to Mercutio in Folger *Rom.* 45.[25] Here, near the end of 1.5 where, after Romeo discovers that Juliet is a Capulet, Shakespeare has "*Ben.* Away, be gone, the sport is at the best" (l. 118), the promptbook gives Mercutio Romeo's "Is she a Capulet?" followed by the stage direction "Runs ax [across] to L. Seizes Romeo's L. Arm," and the line "Come, Romeo, let's begone."

In several of the promptbooks of this third line of development for Mercutio, some of the wit suppressed with the bawdy returns as mockery of Romeo's lovesickness in the form of stage-direction laughter (*Rom.* 14, 22, 29) and as added mockery of the Nurse in the form of imitating her gait and stance, and persuading Benvolio to join in the fun, as with the stage direction in *Rom.* 29 at 2.4.140, "Mer whispers to Ben." in preparation for their exit "imitating Nurse & Peter."

Finally, we may notice three additional specific promptbook al-terations of the sort that serve to restore Mercutio to himself, alter-ations here cited in order of decreasing intrusiveness. First, Folger *Rom.* 29 adds an emblematic dumb show before Mercutio's first scene, 1.4. As the maskers enter, Cupid aims his bow at them and they run off to the sides, showing some effects of Cupid's such as "bus. of kiss & slap," until "Enter Mer R. . . . wearing domino & to Cupid. lifts him down from bench—Cupid aims at him [and] he breaks bow. Cupid pretends to cry—runs of [sic] C. to L. laughing."

Mercutio's invulnerability to love and his active obstruction of it are authentic, as is also the fact that Cupid has the last laugh. Then, in Folger *Rom.* 21, at Benvolio's "That gallant spirit hath aspir'd the clouds / Which too untimely here did scorn the earth," the added stage direction "slowly" acknowledges the gravity of Mercutio's death. Finally in Folger *Rom.* 43[26] the party responsible for cutting much of Mercutio's wit throughout, and most of his bawdy, is nevertheless to be commended for allowing him to retain his welcome to the friend he thinks has come back to the fraternal band, "Why, is not this better now than groaning for love? Now art thou sociable, now art thou Romeo" (2.4.88–89).[27]

Stage Performances, 1845–1976

IN live performances before a live audience Mercutio's aspiring spirit rises most tangibly. Goldman, *Shakespeare and the Energies of Drama*, 1972, has explored perhaps most extensively in recent years the significances of the corporeality of theater, that distinctive feature David (*Theatre*, p. 6) addresses:

> The factor that most surely demarcates film and television from theatre is . . . that the art of the theatre is 'live.' . . . I mean to call attention to the very founding of that art upon the human, living, physically present actor. . . . The reaction of one human animal to another human animal is more immediate, more visceral, as well as more complicated than his reaction to an inanimate object, to a representation of a human being, or even an actual beast of another species. The presentation . . . by a great actor on a stage is a more direct, more comprehensive, and a more stirring communication than is to be received from the most sensitive reading of the text in the study or, indeed, from the same actor in a film.

Of course, as David and Goldman maintain, performance may give such directness and immediacy to any dramatic character, but Mercutio seems to acquire an exceptional share of it. He does so in part because he is both theatrical and dramatic to an exceptional degree, in ways suggested by the preceding chapters and in ways that make the role "irresistible in almost any hands" (Webster, *Tears*, p. 154). To an exceptional degree, that is, Mercutio seems readily, naturally, and fully realizable in performance. And in particular his urgent and largely attractive physicality, the bodiliness that survives even the bowdlerization of the bawdiness, contributes to the exceptionally dangerous and vulnerable physicality realized in his performance.

All this is by way of preface to acknowledge the irony in the fact that, because of another of David's defining characteristics of the art of the theater, its ephemerality, the stage Mercutios treated here are the least immediate of all those considered in this study inasmuch as none of the evidence is better than secondhand.

AFTER the nearly two centuries of adaptations following D'Avenant's 1662 revival, in 1845 Charlotte and Susan Cushman "returned to Shakespeare's text" (Halliday, *Companion*, p. 420). The return is far from complete, however, as is apparent in their bowdlerized text printed by Lacy in 1855. Not only is Mercutio bowdlerized but he is also otherwise reduced and suppressed, and the role was given to minor actors. Thus even in the midst of this "return," the momentum we have been considering continues to carry Mercutio away from Shakespeare and toward the complete elimination envisioned by Gentleman. The reasons have everything to do with the time and with the particular production.

Mercutio's exceptional suppression at the moment of the play's relative restoration to Shakespeare results from the fact that in this production Romeo was played not by a man but by Charlotte Cushman. Actresses before and after Cushman's 1845 London Haymarket Romeo took "breeches parts," particularly Hamlet, among Shakespearean roles. Cushman herself had played Romeo earlier, presumably in Garrick's adaptation, in 1837 at the Pearl in Albany where, one biographer assures us, her impassioned words and athletic gestures "carried such conviction that few in the audience remembered that a woman's skill lay behind them" (Leach, *Star*, p. 65). But the 1845 *Romeo and Juliet* was at the center of the empire, to which the "American Indians," as the Cushmans were called, had come from the upstart periphery with the restored Shakespeare. Furthermore, Juliet was played by Susan Cushman, Charlotte's sister.[28]

At least some of the rationale of Charlotte Cushman's suppression of Mercutio is clear. She thereby reduced the very gender-specific Mercurial attractiveness that always threatens to undermine

Romeo even when he is played by a man, and thus she made her Romeo's domination of the play more secure. Furthermore in 1845 Mercutio more or less as written was more or less familiar to a large portion of the audience, three editions having appeared in the previous twenty years,[29] so that his subversive fraternal genitality would persist even in a bowdlerized script, and more or less threaten a female casting of Romeo. Benvolio, in contrast, could be left alone.

The Cushman *Romeo and Juliet* was a theatrical success and was revived ten years later. Some of its success derived from the scandal that dogged it from the beginning, a scandal in which it is tempting to see the merry trickster-god's revenge for the suppression of his avatar. The scandal began in Edinburgh where, during the trial run of the play, the neighbors of the Cushman sisters' host "objected strongly to Charlotte's 'masculine' demeanor as Romeo, her straight limbs as 'strident as those of a youth,' her amorous advances toward her sister so erotic 'that no man would have dared to indulge in them' publicly. In due course . . . [their host] was writing . . . for details about Charlotte's family, reputation, and 'private virtue' " (Leach, *Star*, p. 169). But the suggestion of incestuous lesbianism seems if anything to have helped fill the London theater, where one viewer found "Romeo so 'ardently masculine' and Juliet so 'tenderly feminine,' that . . . the least Miss Cushman could do, once the engagement was over, was marry her sister" (Leach, p. 175). The production ran more than eighty performances and received the tribute four years later of a production at the Theatre Royal, Marleybone, that "out-Cushmaned the great Charlotte . . . in an epicene version" (Odell, *Shakespeare*, 2:254) in which Romeo was played by another woman, Fanny Vining. While she was unrelated to the actress playing Juliet, she was married to the actor playing Mercutio, so that here too the performance generated a suggestion of homosexuality, though here male as in the fiction, and thus more authentically Shakespearean than the Cushman scandal.

Cushman's lead in the reestablishment of the Shakespeare text in performance was followed by Samuel Phelps, whose Sadler Wells "probably did more to popularize Shakespeare in the course of eighteen years (1844–62) than did any other theatre in the whole domain of English Theatrical history" (Odell, 2:247). And in his democratic and marginal theater, "far from the theatrical and fashionable centre of London" (Odell, 2:248), Phelps, himself playing

Mercutio in the 1846–47 season, led the way in the reestablishment of the character in the performance of the Shakespearean play.

Thenceforth Mercutio maintains his place. In Booth's 1869 New York production, "Mr. Edwin Adams played Mercutio in a properly dashing and altogether delightful way. There is a winning quality of good-fellowship, of honest manliness and heart, in this actor . . . which make his identification with the gay Mercutio an easy matter" (*New York Tribune* 4 February 1869). Six years later in the Mary Anderson production J. B. Studley lacked Mercutio's "spontaneity, lightness, gaiety, and effervescence" (*Chicago Herald* 20 November 1877). In the "sickeningly obscene play," this actor's "deep, guttural voice, and powerfully set figure [Not to mention his name.] are at variance with the general notion of the Mercurial Mercutio" (*New York Dramatic News* 24 November 1877). That general notion was better represented by Milnes Levick at McVicker's in 1882, whose enthusiasm "he threw into the reckless gayety of that reckless and fearless wit . . . full of airy life and daring spirit" (*Chicago Herald* 29 August 1882).

Something of the later nineteenth-century opposition between depth and power on the one hand and airy lightness on the other recurs in John Gielgud's 1935 production at the New Theatre with himself and Laurence Olivier alternating in the roles of Mercutio and Romeo. While the promptbook for this production is not extant, clear evidence recently surveyed in Levenson, *Performance*, indicates that nearly all Mercutio's bawdy was restored, and the alternation of roles raised Mercutio to a prominence commensurate with Romeo. Gielgud furthered the suggestion of parity between Mercutio and the titular characters by his use of a rapid, fluid, quasi-Elizabethan staging that permitted the play to run with only a single intermission, so that of the production's two curtains, one followed Mercutio's death and the other Romeo's and Juliet's. These symmetries naturally encouraged comparison of the acting styles of Gielgud and Olivier—the one lyric, sustained, and elegant, the other realistic, staccato, and passionate.

Olivier compares the two styles as follows: "I've seen, as if you had a coin, the top half John, all spiritual, all spirituality, all beauty, all abstract things; and myself as all earth, blood, humanity; if you like, the baser part of humanity without that beauty" (Burton, *Acting*, p. 17). Given Gielgud's expressed intention to "set Romeo and Juliet in contrast to the other characters . . . to set them almost on an operatic plane, so that they shall *sing* those marvellous duets while the other characters *speak* their lines (*Evening Standard* 10 October 1935), the more obvious casting for Mercutio would have been of Olivier, speaking the words of Mercury against the songs of Apollo.[30] But the style Olivier attributes to Gielgud also has its appropriateness with the gallant spirit that aspired to the clouds.

Peter Brook in his 1947 production at Stratford-upon-Avon cast unusually young actors in the lead roles, and cut widely and deeply, to avoid both sentimentality and what he took to be structurally extraneous or awkward material. Under these circumstances his Mercutio, played by Paul Scofield, was perhaps most notable for the integrity of the part, only thirty-two of his lines being cut or given to another character.[31] Brook seems to have encouraged the "sullen whimsicality" (*The Times* 7 April 1947) with which Scofield made Mercutio more vivid and memorable than either Romeo or Juliet.[32]

In Franco Zeffirelli's 1960 production at the Old Vic Alec Mc-Cowen played Mercutio as a youthful, disdainful, exhibitionistic, spirited, and loving member of a gang of "medieval teddyboys" (*The Observer* 9 October 1960) in a production analyzed extensively in Brown (*Performance*, pp. 167–79). Brown finds the production, variously hailed as revelatory and revolutionary (p. 167), especially notable for "Zeffirelli's unity of speech and action, his enfranchisement of the elaborate dialogue as the natural idiom of the characters of the play" (p. 179). As an example Brown cites the "mixture of daring and mockery" (p. 170) in the fight between Mercutio and Tybalt that "reflected the exaggeration of the text" (p. 170) at 3.1.45–48, "Consort! what, dost thou make us minstrels? . . . Zounds, consort!"

On the same page Brown continues:

> Zeffirelli made the fight high-spirited, like the words: Mercutio, gaining possession of both swords, used one as a whetstone for the other before handing Tybalt's back—stopping to wipe its handle with mocking ostentation. With such preparation, Romeo could respond to Mercutio's sour jests after he is wounded as casually as the text demands—"Courage, man; the hurt cannot be much"—without appearing callow; the dying man's protestations could be taken as the holding up of an elaborate jest.

Zeffirelli cut a third again as many of Mercutio's lines as Brook, but he too seems to have taken particular care with the part, and

McCowen's presentation, according to Levenson, "best represents Zeffirelli's intentions, method, and results in staging *Romeo and Juliet*" (Levenson, *Performance*, p. 97).[33] The claim of John Stride, who played Romeo, that Zeffirelli's Mercutio "no longer competed with Romeo as a romantic figure" (Levenson, *Performance*, p. 98) seems to contain an element of wishful thinking, for reviewers seem generally to have found Stride's Romeo less adequate than McCowen's Mercutio, and Zeffirelli's pacing, allowing an hour and forty minutes for the play through Mercutio's death scene and only an hour and ten minutes for the remainder of the play—apparently an attempt to quicken the problematic second half of the play—in fact seems to have done more harm than good. According to Brown, in Zeffirelli's as in many other productions, with Mercutio's death the "tragedy . . . seemed to have lost its momentum and lifelike qualities" (p. 179).

Finally, two more recent productions by the Royal Shakespeare Company at Stratford may be mentioned. Terry Hands in 1973 chose as a motto for his direction Friar Lawrence's warning, "These violent delights have violent ends" (2.6.9), and staged the action on several levels, with the Apothecary alone appearing at the highest level, not only for Romeo's purchase of the poison, "but also at the very beginning of the play as the apex of the assembled company, and once more in a sudden unscripted entry to mark and as it were to consecrate the final return of Tybalt to be killed by Romeo and so precipitate the final disaster" (David, *Theatre*, p. 109). The Mercutio in this production, played by Bernard Lloyd, elicited notably divergent readings from viewers. David finds a "devil-may-care cynicism [that] did not too much overlay that natural attractiveness and easy primacy that must be found in the leader of any such group" (p. 112) as the gang of young men "for whom woman meant simply sex and gangs were for bangs" (p. 111); and David finds the Hands Mercutio's tearing to pieces of a life-size rag doll in his ridicule of love "an effective if perhaps excessive device to bring out the distance between a kind of Hell's Angels . . . and the convert for whom woman had become Juliet and sex a sacrament" (p. 111). Evans, on the other hand, in his Introduction to *Romeo and Juliet* (p. 45), holds that this same Mercutio was "an aggressive homosexual" and (illogically, if unsurprisingly) cites his dismemberment of the female doll as evidence. Evans laments that "only if the friendship of Romeo, Benvolio and Mercutio can be given an exciting nuance of homosexuality does the play become relevant for a modern audience—so runs the directors' justification" (pp. 45–47). However much present in the production in question, precisely that nuance is, as we have seen, so deeply embedded in Mercutio as to be partly constitutive (see also Thomson, "Straight," pp. 150–51).

Obviously the mid-late twentieth-century restoration of Mercutio to a place of importance and at least marginal centrality is a direction that may be followed past points of diminishing returns, as happened, according to David, in the 1976 Royal Shakespeare production directed by John Barton and Barry Kyle, with Michael Pennington as Mercutio. This Mercutio, according to David, was overly and mistakenly developed into "the adored funny-man in a group of . . . casual companions," and one of the disappointments of the production was its "failure to give the young gallants the edge and concerted impact that had been such features of Hands' version" (David, *Theatre*, p. 115). In fact this Mercutio, while certainly more present than many of his nineteenth-century predecessors, sounds as if he was the victim of the sentimentalizing by which we have seen Mercutio repeatedly contained and reduced through his history.[34]

Film Versions, 1908–1978

MERCUTIO makes an auspicious cinematic debut in the first film *Romeo and Juliet*, the 1908 version directed by William V. Ranous. Early in the film's eleven minutes a handsome Mercutio appears, not only more vivacious than Benvolio but also seemingly younger. Traditional nineteenth-century stage business survives in the scene with the Nurse and Peter. Here, as Romeo sighs, his elbow on the balcony, Mercutio and Benvolio watch the approach of the Nurse with a walking stick and Peter with the fan, and then the guying imitation proceeds, with Mercutio using his sword as a walking stick to do the Nurse. She is scandalized, and Peter comically threatens the mockers with a dagger, whereupon they exit. At the fight, Mercutio's white costume sets him apart and gives him something of a sacrificial air. He and Benvolio both seem incensed at Romeo's refusal to fight, and they display identical provocative gestures toward Tybalt, with Benvolio actually drawing first. Having received the wound, Mercutio drops his sword, which Romeo then picks up and uses in his fight with Tybalt.

After a bit of an abeyance in two subsequent silent films[35] Mercutio makes a splashy cinematic reappearance acted by John Barrymore in 1936, directed by George Cukor in one of the character's two most important film versions. With Leslie Howard as Romeo, Norma Shearer as Juliet, and Basil Rathbone as Tybalt, the version preserves most of the text intact and is, as Evans says, "conventionally staid and rather stolid," apart from Barrymore's "somewhat outrageous" Mercutio (Introduction to *Romeo and Juliet*, p. 47n3). While both Barrymore's effeminacy and his phallic zaniness are flamboyant, neither seems necessarily intended to connote homosexuality.

Mercutio first appears on his way to the Capulet ball, and in an introductory establishing bit of business he leans in a window on an impulse to kiss a Veronan beauty, and has to be pulled away by Benvolio. In this scene he wears a pendant pearl earring (as in his next a hoop) and here, even as Benvolio pulls him away from the heterosexual flirtation, his gestures and wide-eyed manners are exaggeratedly effeminate.

His phallicity appears in this scene in the long-nosed domino he dons for the ball, and also, far more outrageously, in the business that follows a mimed jousting. Here Barrymore has unmasked and is walking away, bowing, when one of the performers thrusts the round-tipped lance between his legs from behind, providing a hint of sodomy as it surprises him, before it continues through for him to ride, the lance now resembling a giant phallus. So with Romeo and Benvolio beside him he mounts a stair like an accompanied Priapus.

Nothing quite so phallic follows, but the effeminate zaniness continues in the following scenes, as when in 2.1 Mercutio ends a speech with a mock faint, falling into the arms of a bystander. The initial kiss of the woman in the window proves a kind of leitmotiv as in 2.4 Mercutio sends up a carafe of wine to a group of décolleté women on a balcony, and then plays to them in his mischief with the Nurse. These same women are affrighted in 3.1 when the swordplay begins, and then the mortally wounded Mercutio, in his final significant action, blows a kiss up to them. All this business is clearly considered, and it may be intended to give Mercutio a lighter, more playful parallel to Romeo's balcony scene. It has no textual basis though, and it tends to contain, normalize, and senti-mentalize Shakespeare's creation. At the same time, Barrymore's Mercutio's persistent eye for the ladies is itself subverted by the conspicuous effeminacy of all his flirtatiousness.

In 3.1, in his near-disbelief in Romeo's behavior with Tybalt, Barrymore for the first time looks more virile than effeminately zany, and some of the virility persists in his sword fight through the moment when, mortally wounded, he starts to join Romeo and give chase to the departing Tybalt. But then he falters and is supported by Benvolio, in a reprise of his earlier mock faint. Romeo returns and stands on the other side of him, their positions echoing the earlier priapic ascent, and Mercutio returns to his earlier tipsy sen-timentality. With his left arm around Benvolio's neck he pats Ro-meo on both cheeks, after Romeo's "I thought all for the best," in a debonair version of the sentimental pardon we have already seen examples of.

Thus Barrymore's performance, the most remarkable thing in Cukor's film, is perhaps also the most unsatisfactory, and unques-tionably it has had some important influence on general percep-tions of the character. Our vantage makes it possible to see the roots of Barrymore's sentimentalization in eighteenth- and espe-cially nineteenth-century ways of processing the character. And we can also see roots for what is most "outrageous" in the performance —the effeminacy, the mock-sodomy, and the mock-priapism—in Shakespeare's Mercutio and in his Mercury. Furthermore the very aberrations of Cukor's and Barrymore's Mercutio may well have contributed to the second major film version, which in many ways reads like a reaction.[36]

This is of course the 1968 Zeffirelli *Romeo and Juliet*, with John McEnery playing Mercutio, and Leonard Whiting and Olivia Hus-sey as the leads.[37] It is easily the most popular and influential film version to date, and indeed according to Jorgens (*Film*, 1977, p. 80), it is "the most popular and financially successful Shakespeare film yet made." Zeffirelli's experience with the 1960 stage production naturally figures in his direction of the film, which nevertheless is based only loosely on the stage version (Jorgens, p. 80). With this as with the stage version, Mercutio stands as something of a key, and indeed the most significant evolution in Zeffirelli's thinking about the play seems to have been about Mercutio. A major change ap-pears at the first sight of John McEnery: where the stage Mercutio was of an age with Romeo and Benvolio, McEnery may seem, in Colman's (*Bawdy*, p. 70) memorable phrase, "an aging manic-depressive, idling his time away in the company of men half his own age."

The film has been discussed extensively by Jorgens and others and, especially given the consensus about the principals' lackluster performances, a fair amount of that discussion has naturally focused on Mercutio. Jorgens notes the visual thematic element of the white shroud, recurring from the morning fog in the opening panorama to the winding sheets in the Capulet tomb, and appearing importantly as Mercutio's white handkerchief, which becomes his apron and then his needlework as he mimes in the Queen Mab speech, his contraceptive as he jests with the Nurse, his deathlike mask and facecloth in the hot square, and finally his bandage with which he hides his wound, and which Romeo then rubs in Tybalt's face (pp. 81–82). Though the motif has passing associations with other characters, the primary association is with Mercutio, and thus the initial manifestation of the motif as fog over Verona prepares for his talk of air and wind in his first scene and for Benvolio's talk of his spirit's aspiring the clouds, activating some of the character's latent Mercuriality and giving him a visual immanence after his death that corresponds to the immanence created in Shakespeare by such verbal associations noted above as make the Apothecary echo Mercutio.[38]

The Cukor-Barrymore sentimentality is largely removed, and indeed this Mercutio restores and embodies much of the semiotic complexity discussed in preceding chapters. McEnery does no flirting with Veronan damsels, and in the liminal band of males he leads, his attachment to Romeo goes deeper than Cukor dreamed of, as Jorgens (*Film*, p. 84) notes: "There is deep friendship, even love, between Romeo and Mercutio. Mercutio's mercurial showmanship seems aimed at Romeo, and his anger, when Romeo is off sighing for love or making a milksop of himself before Tybalt, is tinged with jealousy. How could a friend abandon his male comradery for 'a smock'?" Since McEnery displays none of the Barrymore effeminancy, a more coherent phallicity appears when his sword rises at a phallic angle out of the waist-deep water of the watering trough, or when, at "hide his bauble in a hole" (2.4.92–93) he makes the obscene gesture of the fist.[39] Zeffirelli restores a decided trace of the demonic or possessed to the Queen Mab speech, making Mercutio deliver it "in the empty square bathed in eerie blue light" (Jorgens, p. 89) and seem "to unnerve ... himself no less than the others" (p. 70). Perhaps most important, Zeffirelli admits the resonance with Mercury as psychopomp, which has been suppressed through most of Mercutio's history. That resonance appears in the train of visual association connecting the fog, the handkerchief, and the winding sheet; in the eeriness of the visual style of the Queen Mab speech, which itself foreshadows the change in visual style that follows Mercutio's death, when the film is "drained of its busy look and festive colors" (Jorgens, p. 89); in the fact that he himself breaks off the Queen Mab speech at the soldier's frightening dream; and perhaps most strikingly in his visor, an owlish death's head that, when he pushes it up onto his head for the Queen Mab speech, becomes a petasos.[40]

Mercutio's death, deriving partly from the Zeffirelli stage version—Mercutio's sword-sharpening business reappears—seems one of the least sentimentalized under review here. Michael York's Tybalt makes Mercutio sweat, holding a blade to his throat, but at the same time Mercutio maintains his wit and bravado, whistling nonchalantly (a touch made for film) when cornered. Even if we don't know the play, we in the audience know Tybalt's mortal thrust is serious as we see him surprised at the blood on his sword; but Mercutio's cohorts suppose he is playing, and the page, thinking the request a joke, doesn't leave to fetch a surgeon. Mercutio hides the wound with his handkerchief and lets his extremity be taken as play through his final living moment when, forehead to forehead with Romeo (a posture forecast in the Queen Mab speech), he speaks his final words. Here finally some sentimentalization does occur even in the Zeffirelli film, in the denaturing of the curse taken (and intended to be so taken) as play.[41] Nevertheless, the Zeffirelli-McEnery Mercutio is a major achievement of the film. As noted above, Colman suggests that this Mercutio necessitates "a good deal of critical reorientation" (*Bawdy*, p. 171) toward the play. A part of such a reorientation would be a recognition of a possibility entertained in the present study, the possibility that for our time Mercutio, with his history, is in fact the hero of the play, and keeps it alive.

The 1977 film version directed by Paul Bosner, with Mercutio played by David Collings, in various ways ratifies Zeffirelli's recognition of Mercutio's significance. This version includes the reading of the guest list for the Capulet banquet, and when Romeo reads "Mercutio and his brother Valentine" he slows a bit to show his knowledge of Mercutio. In the fight scene Bosner uses a less striking version of Zeffirelli's Romeo's temporarily delayed comprehension of the gravity of Mercutio's wound. At the moment of the wounding Bosner employs an ironic turn on Mercutio's affection for Romeo when, having come between Mercutio and Tybalt, Romeo is effectively embracing Mercutio to stop the fight as Tybalt thrusts under his arm.

CHAPTER EIGHT.

MERCUTIO'S SHAKESPEARE

CLIFFORD LEECH, "The Moral Tragedy of *Romeo and Juliet*," p. 73, holds that "moral tragedy" is a contradiction in terms since "tragedy is necessarily at odds with the moral: it is concerned with a permanent anguishing situation, not with one that can either be put right or be instrumental in teaching the survivors to do better." He finds a certain sanguineness about the conclusion of the play that prevents the deaths of the lovers from achieving genuine tragic status. The sanguineness, according to Leech, inheres in the "long-drawn-out ending, after the lovers are dead, with the pressing home of the moral that their deaths will bring peace" (p. 73), which features themselves derive from the tradition of sixteenth-century moral drama, a tradition Shakespeare in *Romeo and Juliet* has not yet "worked as free from . . . as Marlowe had done in *Tamburlaine*, *Faustus*, and *Edward II*" (p. 73).

It might seem to some that Leech's finding of a however restrained sanguineness grants insufficient weight to the "glooming . . . sorrow . . . sad . . . woe" of the Prince's final speech, but the question is a nice one of emphasis, and it seems likely that most playgoers and readers through most of this century would find themselves in substantial agreement with Leech that the woeful story of Juliet and her Romeo falls short of the tragic idea embodied in *Hamlet*, *Othello*, *King Lear*, and *Macbeth*.[1]

What Leech says about Mercutio, however, would seem likely to be a good deal more surprising to most of the play's audience in this century until very recently, and even now it would seem easily the most controversial of his claims about the play. I quote at some length because Leech's observations seem to me to stand as a landmark of the revision of character, play, and author. Even though the titular characters fall short of tragedy, Leech writes,

> Even so, there is a small achieved tragedy embodied within this play. I have described Mercutio as "daemonic," and that is

an adjective we can appropriately apply to every tragic hero: he has fire within him . . . and the fire ultimately consumes. We can call this "hubris," but the rashness implied in that word is not a matter for moral comment. . . . Mercutio, careless of what may come . . . draws his sword and goes to his death. His last words are ironic and resentful. . . . No lesson is drawn from this destruction; there is no suggestion that good may come out of it. It has simply happened, to the world's impoverishment. . . . [The Queen Mab speech] puts Mercutio outside the general Christian framework of the play. . . . his last call is for a surgeon, not a priest. There is an angriness in him that is a link with Hamlet, Othello, Lear, Macbeth: . . . their final acts are those of men standing alone, without help from the general current of thought in their world, with a full realization too of their loneliness. Here . . . we find the true germ of Shakespeare's later development. One may suspect that Mercutio haunted this playwright, that the character and his death provided a foundation on which the later tragedies could be securely built. ("Moral Tragedy," pp. 74–75)

In the context of the previous chapter these remarkable observations, with which the present study is very much in accord, exemplify a further stage in Mercutio's evolution, and reveal some of the ways his transformation, still in progress, figures in the transformations of his play, his author, and his audience. This concluding chapter considers these matters in three somewhat artificially separated ways. First I treat Mercutio as an index of larger cultural and critical changes he participates in, with particular attention to the issue of postfeminist criticism. Then from a different vantage I treat him as a particular kind of poststructuralist and postmodernist entity, the diachronic dramatic character. Finally I treat Mercutio as constitutive or catalytic, as I consider changes currently under way in our understanding of Shakespeare—which is to say, in our understanding.

ALTHOUGH Leech includes Zeffirelli by extension among recent directors whose handling of the Queen Mab speech he disapproves of,[2] in fact Leech's Mercutio continues in the same general direction as Zeffirelli's, a direction of recovery from the various kinds of reduction, suppression, containment, and marginalization that intervene between 1595 and the recent past, reaching their peak with the peak of Victorianism. But Leech's Mercutio proceeds along that road, or at least one branch of it, well past Zeffirelli's. Indeed in Leech Mercutio goes well beyond restoration of his Shakespearean prominence, and he pulls after him the entire play. In Leech Mercutio stands forth as the rightful, if not the actual, titular character of *The Tragedy of . . . .*[3]

It is an extraordinary itinerary that runs from the simultaneously subordinated and foregrounded god of boundary and agora, calculation and dream, through Shakespeare's gallant spirit and saucy merchant, and through his decline and marginalization during the seventeenth and eighteenth centuries to his nineteen-century nadir, followed by his twentieth-century recovery and increasing centrality. As Brown and Burkert show with the earliest portions of that itinerary, so with every succeeding step of the way: it reflects prevailing cultural and political constructs of many sorts. The present study, primarily in chapters 4–6, has paid most attention to a single stage of that journey, the moment in 1595 when Brooke's trace Mercutio flowers in Shakespeare's mind. Any other stage of the journey might repay equivalent attention, and one other stage, the present, is inevitably of particular interest. Inevitably too, that stage, whether invoked or not, is more or less legible in everything said above. It seems well, then, here to invoke that stage once more in a consideration of a contradiction apparent in the present critical assessment of Mercutio. For, as will be remembered, current feminist and psychoanalytic assessments run decidedly counter to Leech's. But this current contradiction reveals itself most fruitfully, I believe, when it is set in relief against a particular stage of Mercutio's itinerary.

The Victorian documentation of the previous chapter may have seemed almost superfluous inasmuch as even the most nodding acquaintance with the period and with Mercutio would lead to the conclusion that this must be the nadir of his journey. Of course his bawdiness grows most indecorous then, and much else about him does also. In an age celebrating domesticity and middle-class marriage, Mercutio's ranging liminality and his scorn of love and houses grow exceptionally indecorous. So too does his frank corporeality even when it is not bawdy, and so too his traces of misogyny. The story of male attitudes toward women during Victoria's reign is a long one still being told, but there seems at the moment to be at least something of a consensus suggesting that the obverse of the familiar sentimentalization is a rapacious degradation. By contrast, Mercutio's light intermittent misogyny comes across as a reflex of a fundamental lack of interest in women. While this stance of his, with antecedents in Mercury and in Marlowe, is restrained by the fact that it first takes shape under a female monarch, at the same time the stance is authorized by her own mercurial holding off from marriage—whereas Victoria by her own example stood firmly for marriage and married procreation. Other rationales for the suppression of Mercutio may also be found in Victorian England. An empire the sun never sets on, for instance, might be expected to have peculiarly little use for a liminal figure descended from the god of borders.[4]

Mercutio's recovery from the extremes of Victorian censorship, then, may be read as an index of the supercession of these Victorian verities. Analogously his present status indicates verities of ours. In particular, his present status is a function of changes and hindrances to change in the realm of gender relations. Specifically, Mercutio's current contradictory assessments seem to mark a crisis in the evolution of feminist critical thought.

It can hardly be accidental that, as discussed above in chapter 6, Mercutio's post-Victorian advance in status meets roadblocks in feminist accounts. His advance, especially in its acceleration over the past two or three decades, is most obviously an index of a nearly unprecedented lessening of moralistic censorship combined with a widespread interest in sexual matters, an interest so vigorous as to have been at times obsessive. Mercutio, with his easy bawdy and, perhaps more important, his quick contempt for what may be called the antibawdy, thus finds a more receptive audience in the present than he has found since Shakespeare's time. Similarly, a sophisticated and variously materialist (and anti-idealist) time such as ours naturally finds Mercutio to its taste. But these reasons for Mercutio's advance in status seem not to lie behind the feminist resistance to that advance. True, some of our time's kinds of materialism and interest in sexuality are unquestionably antifeminist and antihumanist, but here, despite feminist sniping at him, I find Mercutio largely innocent. The causes of the sniping seem to lie elsewhere.

The continuing recognition of Mercutio's importance, not only in his play but also in his author's development—Shakespearean tragedy itself, at least in Leech's view, stems from Mercutio—that recognition depends on numerous features of the present moment, including our increasing enfranchisement of the previously marginal, our increasing reluctance to be bound by received interpretations and constructions of "reality," and our increased familiarity with the entirely realistic and unsentimentalized possibility of entire absolute loss. But if this much seems clear, the question remains, why the new reactionary feminist attempts to contain and suppress Mercutio?

A documented answer to the question is obviously beyond the scope of this study, but the preceding consideration of Mercutio may provide the basis for an educated hypothesis. In brief, Mercutio by his phallocentrism, his scorn of heterosexual love, and his own invulnerability to the wounds of heterosexual love, seems subversive to the project of feminist (and psychoanalytic) criticism of a certain sort, that project being the continuing politicization and prescriptivization of gender and affectional orientation, in ways that exclude Mercutio. The contemporary impulse toward a re-reduction of Mercutio then, is an index of an important, and probably inherent, inadequacy in the feminist critical stance. For that stance itself is paradoxical: feminism as a reaction to antifeminism tends to render itself superfluous by its successes, and yet no beachhead as hard won as the feminist is likely to be abandoned easily.[5] It is for some such reason, I believe, that feminist criticism, which is effecting revolutionary change in our understanding of much of Shakespeare, stalls and turns regressive when it comes to Mercutio.

But such need not be the case. Mercutio's light intermittent misogyny does not in the least entail antifeminism. It may well be that Romeo's and even Juliet's stances may come to seem antihumanist and so antifeminist—there is reason to suppose that some such evolution is under way—but as for Mercutio, his stance seems postfeminist rather than antifeminist. What he bodes fair to indicate for criticism at the present moment is whether the gains made by feminism will seem sufficient, and we stall in an equally tyrannical negation of the old sexist tyranny, or whether we will be able to make our way into a genuine postfeminism that subsumes the gains of feminism.

I N the preceding pages I have intentionally refrained from any careful acknowledgment at every turn that Mercutio is fictional, and indeed I have at times let myself speak of him as if he were not fictional. In part the procedure grew out of simple curiosity about a fashion so old as no longer even to be démodé. So much time has passed since we concerned ourselves with Lady Macbeth's children, and we are so irreversibly insulated from that sort of naiveté, that we may permit ourselves to slip into the old garment, if only for the sake of gratifying some nostalgic curiosity about how wearing it might have felt, even though we know that that curiosity can only be gratified with a sense of knowledge, and never with knowledge itself.

Then too we have progressed so far in our understanding of the constructedness—indeed the fictionality—of the "true" and the "real" that, even though in a general way we routinely distinguish between personages like Mercutio and persons like Shakespeare, like ourselves, still any careful policing of the border would seem at present to be a waste of troop strength at best.

But the main reason for my letting myself sometimes talk about Mercutio much in the way I talk about Shakespeare has to do with the postmodernist disintegrationist denial of the usefulness, and even the very viability, of the notion of fictional character or personhood, a matter addressed briefly above in "Part Two: Shakespeare's Mercutio" and to which I return for a moment here, to say once more that I find the position untenable. The commonplace about Shakespeare's characters' seeming more real than real people may have worn threadbare as praise, but its psychological basis seems as sound as ever, for surely we all automatically think of all fictional personages as if they were real persons. We make the initial assumption that personages are persons not only because they are so meant—so conceived by their authors—but also because it is otherwise nearly impossible for us to find any mental purchase on a fiction. The "we" here is meant to include all of us who concern ourselves in any way with fictional personages—the student taking care to spell Nausicaa correctly, the machinist amused by Dagwood's morning adventure, the critical polemicist staking a new claim. We think of fictional people as real in part for the same reason we think of real people as real: it is the only way to arrive at any coherence.

Of course at the same time, as noted, we routinely distinguish between fictional and nonfictional people. Among the numerous grounds we employ for the distinction, one seems especially noteworthy here. With luck, Dagwood will continue to solve a new problem every morning of the future, but leaving him aside for the present we may say that a basic difference between Mercutio and Shakespeare is that with Mercutio we suppose we have the full dossier, at least at one level—an unsurpassably complete record of what he says and hears, all that he does and all that is done to him—whereas with Shakespeare we feel sure that more evidence may always come to light and that, furthermore, however much is included, with him as with us the dossier can never approach completeness.

With real persons the availability of information varies considerably in degree and kind, as is made clear by a moment's reflection about the vastly different ways we develop a sense of the characters of acquaintances, public figures, and historical figures such as Shakespeare and Elizabeth I. The similar and perhaps commensurate variety of accessibility that obtains with fictional personages is exemplified by the two with which the present study has been concerned. Mercury like all gods has a long and only partly recoverable history of communal production and modification, a history that includes denials of his fictionality. To Shakespeare, as to us, Mercury is accessible in the manifold treated above, a manifold that is distinctive to Mercury among gods in innumerable ways, including in particular the fairly distinctive combination of his great popularity, the nearly complete absence of ecclesiastical bodies instituted for the canonization and promulgation of his story, and the exceptional complexity of his own array of characterizing traits. The avenues of Mercury's accessibility to us, as perhaps also to Shakespeare, include the other fictional character with which this study is concerned, the modes and degrees of whose accessibility to us differ in turn in countless ways from the god's.

The foregoing study seems to bear especially on two determinants on Mercutio's accessibility to us. I wish briefly to postpone review of one of these determinants, Mercutio's authorship, as we look back for a moment at the other, his dramaticality.[6] And here, among the (again) innumerable ways in which the exigencies of genre make dramatic personages distinctive, two are of particular note, and both are functions of the performability of drama.

First, there is the foregroundedness that dramatic characters seem not to share with fictional personages of any other sort. It derives from the fact that we have direct access to nothing more of an entirely fictional dramatic character than the things said and done in the character's play(s), of which the most significant are obviously the speeches assigned to the character himself by his name in the speech headings. In narrative, the other mega-genre with significant room for character (character in lyric being generally variously diffused, displaced, or otherwise absent), the narrator may provide many sorts of additional information about a fictional personage, and may provide the information with various colorings and degrees of specificity or summary, so that of necessity a fictional personage in narrative has at least a potential—and therefore actual, in the paradoxical logic operative here—kind of depth or penumbra denied dramatic characters. A dramatic character by contrast is quite determinate. Since no narrator stands between Mercutio and us, we may witness his story immediately.

But on the other hand Mercutio varies from performer to performer, indeed from performance to performance, and he is meant for performance. Herein a dramatic character is more endlessly mutable, and so more indeterminate, than any other sort of fictional personage. Received as he was meant to be received, in performance, Mercutio appears only as played in a certain way by a particular actor in a given production of *Romeo and Juliet*. Thus the actor and the production have a mediating role in the constitution and transmission of fictional character analogous to that of the narrator in narrative, but arguably still more interventionist. While in a narrative the narrator stands apart from the character presented in various ways including the fact that the narrator generally has an existence independent of the characters presented, in performed drama an absolute linkage between character and mediating performer makes the performance so interventionist as to seem constitutive. At the same time, actors in plays act as you sing prick song, speaking the already written part, enacting the written gestures and acts. The hierophantic and scribal Mercury seems to hover over the fact that the authorial strings of written characters that make up a part, a dramatic character, efface themselves in any realization of the part in performance. And yet at the same time, at least in so literary a medium as Shakespearean drama, the writtenness of the spoken words, their authoredness, calls attention to itself steadily, as is not the case, for instance (except inadvertently), with such other scripted spoken words as those we may hear in television soaps and sitcoms.

These distinctive attributes of dramatic character seem to make Mercutio more susceptible than nondramatic characters to the kind of poststructuralist consideration undertaken above. The notion of character operative here is poststructuralist inasmuch as, while availing itself of structuralist methods and insights, it does not bind itself by them. The structuralist (and modernist) component of the study treats Mercutio as a product of the contrastive relations distinguishing him from other characters in his play. This mode of conceptualization of characters derives, of course, from Saussurean synchronic linguistic analysis as well as from both modernist and new-critical assumptions about the unity and integrity of the individual work of art. It serves in some of the contrastive descriptions of Mercutio's characterizing speech acts and his characterizing bawdy, and more generally in the prevailing sense of him as mutually determinative with the rest of his play. But I have hardly been bound to the structuralist axiom that would make Mercutio inseparable from—that is, meaningless apart from—his play. The poststructuralist (and postmodernist) component of the foregoing does treat Mercutio as separable from, meaningful apart from, his play. In a sense the poststructuralism of the notion of character operative here manifests itself most conspicuously in an absence—the absence of any programmatic corresponding attention to the rest of the cast list.[7] The poststructuralism of the foregoing is, incidentally, closely analogous with its postfeminism: here too the method aims to incorporate insights and discoveries of a preceding critical moment even as it moves beyond limitations inherent in that moment.

Poststructuralist separability and isolatability of dramatic character as conceived here figures importantly in one additional feature of the foregoing consideration of Mercutio. Indeed separability would seem a precondition for the treatment of Mercutio as a diachronic entity. The linguistic model is very apt: just as a lexical or a syntactic unit of a language may be described diachronically, more or less separately from the rest of its language, as a single evolutionary history of which all parts are invoked, so with "Mercutio" as described here. The diachronic Mercutio manifests the operation of numerous, perhaps innumerable, general principles and other determinants governing his history, determinants that may similarly govern many other such histories, as with the nineteenth-century sentimentalization and bowdlerization, or that may govern relatively few, as with the mercurial deathliness shading Mercutio's on-going corporeality. The sum of those determinants, however, must surely be unique for any so substantial a character as Mercutio.

When I was beginning this study and described to a colleague the little I could then see of what it was I wanted to find out, she asked whether what I envisioned wasn't simply a source study. Even though she hastened to assure me that there was nothing wrong with source study, I resisted concurring, without then being able to justify the resistance beyond saying that the phrase didn't quite seem to mark the route I expected to be traveling. A clearer explanation seems possible now. The term "source study" seems wrong for the present inquiry for two particular reasons, each having to do with one extremity of the history I have been writing considered as a determinate line. On the one hand the Derridean deconstruction of the Western story of origination has variously discredited the old notion of the source as point of origin. On the other hand, while a source study generally takes a particular point in a history—1595, 1988—as its terminus and culmination, the end of the voyage and the vantage point for its survey, the present study's preconceptions are somewhat different. It is true that I have dwelt more on 1595 than on any other moment in the history, and that the present moment of Shakespeare study in the 1980s has also frequently been in view. But the diachronic Mercutio here in view is no more stable now than he ever was. This study is itself one part of an evolution that will continue well after it, if anything does.

FINALLY we may consider briefly wherein the Shakespeare entailed and revealed by this Mercutio seems distinctive. One need not have any particular Shakespeare study in hand to be aware that, as with Mercutio, so with "Shakespeare": the entity in question is highly variable. At present, one need only have an ear to the ground for an awareness that Shakespeare seems to be in a state of flux proceeding with unusual rapidity and depth. Furthermore, while some research projects might imaginably insulate one from awareness of the flux, the present study seems to have had rather the opposite effect on me. I wish therefore in the space remaining briefly to address the subject of Shakespeare's diachronicity, and then finally to look momentarily at some of the ways the creator of this study's Mercutio differs from other Shakespeares.

A significant part of the current general historicization of all semiological systems including, in particular, those most of us were taught to think of as literary and more or less canonical, has been the historicization of Shakespeare. Jonathan Dollimore and Alan Sinfield (*Political Shakespeare*, 1984), John Drakakis (*Alternative Shakespeares*, 1985), and Terence Hawkes (*That Shakespeherean Rag*, 1986) come to mind as but three notable works among many that have lately helped lay bare the contingent and diachronically variable constitutedness of "Shakespeare," as well as some of the forces and stakes involved in his constitution. It seems unlikely that in the foreseeable future Shakespeare will regain the semblance of immutability and immediacy that attends him through nearly all of his preceding history, and that happens to gain greatest strength and confidence just when (as now seems) his transformations are most extreme, as in the nineteenth century. It also seems unlikely that we have yet made available to consciousness or brought into question all we need about Shakespeare's diachronicity.

The Mercutio surveyed here provides a good index of Shakespeare's diachronic variation. Across the range of Shakespearean characters there is, of course, no uniformity of degree of variation through time. Alongside such comparatively stable characters as Rosalind and Macbeth, others vary appreciably. Isabella, Hal, and Shylock come immediately to mind as examples of comparatively protean beings who pull their plays, and their plays' author, after them in their transmutations. Shylock's transmutations, the best known of these, certainly outdo Mercutio's in terms of elicited or hypothesized general public attitude toward him, but the two cases resemble each other in terms of generic conventions supposed appropriate. And in fact the amplitude of Mercutio's swing between near-vanishing marginality and essential centrality as the unique exemplar of the genre named in his play's title exceeds anything comparable with Shylock or, I believe, with any other Shakespearean character. Thus while Rosalind or Macbeth or, to name cases closer to hand, Romeo and Juliet, contribute (to date at least) to the stability of "Shakespeare," Mercutio is an outstanding member of that smaller band of characters who catalyze change there.

With respect to the question of Shakespeare's own stability or his instability of whatever form, all parties are of course interested. Recent Marxists, feminists, and deconstructionists have in their various ways brought forcefully to our attention the complex of interests and interested assumptions that determine the repeated denial, from Jonson's "not of an age" down to the present, of Shakespeare's contingency and diachronic variation. In its present form that complex comprises most of the various sorts of investments made in maintaining the Shakespeare "industry" much in its present form, as well as a number of predictable philosophical and political commitments. On the other hand, those showing us the undisinterestedness of proponents of an invariant Shakespeare are themselves interested, as they more or less readily admit. They have their own various sorts of investments in decisive change in the Shakespeare industry, as well as their own more or less predictable philosophical and political commitments. Similar states of affairs obtain with other literary texts, but the battle being joined in Shakespeare studies is exceptional in at least two related respects. The stakes are higher because of the very size of the Shakespeare industry. More important, the stakes are also higher because in Anglophone culture Shakespeare's works are the most canonical of the received canon of literary texts.

One particular kind of change in Shakespeare that seems possible, and is even being forecast by some, is his displacement from the centered position he still generally holds in Anglophone culture, and even his marginalization. Some general benefit would necessarily attend such a change, but I (interested as anyone) must here record my sense that the general cost would very far outweigh any benefit. And, without arguing for the case, I do wish to suggest how part of such an argument might be mounted. It seems to me that the marginalization of Shakespeare would have one regrettable effect shared by the denial of his diachronic variation: in both cases some of the valuable history, not only of Shakespeare but also of Anglophone culture as a whole, is suppressed. A fundamental tenet of all the foregoing is the partial legibility of Shakespeare as a palimpsest, the partial recoverability of his diachronic mark. Because of the continuity and centrality of that mark, then, to see or read Shakespeare is to track who we ourselves have been for the past four hundred years, and also well before. The linguistic metaphor is helpful again. Some words in our language seem more or less key or central, and, although they may always be used as if there were no etymology, and they may always be shunted out of a vocabulary, still they seem to me to serve us best when kept in use, and used with a consciousness of their histories.

But should the marginalization of "Shakespeare" come to pass,[8] it may be that the Shakespeare of this study's Mercutio has already faced such an eventuality better than, say, Garrick's or Gentleman's or Barrymore's Mercutio's Shakespeare, and better than the Shakespeares of the corresponding Romeos and Juliets. Our Mercutio's Shakespeare of 1595 has in fact himself not yet quite found his way to the sovereignty he very soon begins to exercise, but Mercutio blooming in his mind is showing him the way there. That way lies past the gilded monuments of princes and the gold effigies of lovers, past institutional sanctions and pieties, and beyond authoritative determination. This Shakespeare's way to sovereignty is a never quite complete withdrawal, from fratricide and perhaps from friendship too, a withdrawal already far advanced in Mercutio's play, where Shakespeare's will already can give way to the conjuring, the call to the wild margins, and the welcome there.

NOTES

INTRODUCTION: MERCUTIO'S BROTHER

1. Gibbons, *Romeo and Juliet*, 1980. Unless otherwise noted, all quotations from *Romeo* are from this edition. Quotations from other Shakespeare works are from Harbage, *Works*, 1977, unless otherwise noted.

2. J. J. Munro, ed., *Brooke's "Romeus and Juliet" Being the Original of Shakespeare's "Romeo and Juliet"*; quotation is from this edition.

3. See Bullough, *Sources*, p. 272, and Gibbons, *Romeo*, p. 34. The cold hands come into the story with Bandello's source da Porto.

4. Given *Two Gentlemen*'s casting of Proteus as the less true lover, the phonetic chime Proteus-Romeus may have felt inappropriate to Shakespeare and so figured in his rejection of Brooke's form of the hero's name. The charged Mercutio passage in Brooke is intriguing for its general emphasis on the manual (ll. 259, 260–62, 264, 289–90), which in Shakespeare informs the opening interchanges of Romeo and Juliet (1.5.92–103), and for its careful specification that Mercutio takes Juliet's right, Romeo her left hand. Tilley (*Proverbs*) lists as H84 (1666) "The left hand is the hand of the heart."

5. The two St. Valentines with 14 February as their feast day are (1) a priest of Rome and (2) a bishop of Terni, both third century. According to Attwater the supposed acts of (1) seem to derive from those of two other saints, while (2) is only a doublet of (1). "There is nothing in either Valentine legend to account for the custom of choosing a partner of the opposite sex and sending 'valentines' on 14 February; it apparently arose from the old idea that birds begin to pair on that date, but it may have a more remote pagan origin" (Attwater, *Dictionary of Saints*, p. 334). The "old idea" about birds is referred to by Theseus: "Saint Valentine is past. / Begin these woodbirds but to couple now?" (*MND* 4.1.138–39). See Tilley S66 (1477), "On Saint Valentine's Day all the birds in couples do join." Dent, *Language*, p. 204, calls the idea "more folklore than proverb." Jenkins, in his note to Ophelia's song about St. Valentine's day, says that Valentine means "sweetheart according to the ancient custom which recognized as such the first person of the opposite sex seen on St. Valentine's day" (Jenkins, *Ham.* 4.5.51n). Kelly, *Chaucer*, pp. 120–27, holds that Chaucer commemorates the marriage of Richard II and Anne of Bohemia by associating St. Valentine with lovers.

6. The lost first *Valentine and Orson* (to which I return below) could have just preceded *Romeo and Juliet* since it was registered in 1595, the generally accepted date for *Romeo and Juliet*. Berger and Bradford, *Index of Characters*, list dramatic uses of the name. Intriguing but beyond the scope of this study are Shakespeare's later uses of the name, especially in *Measure for Measure* ("Valentinus") with its ghostly Juliet.

7. Noted by Leech, *TGV*, pp. xliii–xliv, Gibbons, *Rom.*, pp. 27–29, and others.

8. Leech (*TGV*, p. xxxv) concludes that the composition of *Two Gentlemen* extends through several phases from 1592 to late 1593. An additional link in the Brooke-Valentine association, as was noted by Leech (*TGV* 1.2.12n), is the name "Mercatio" mentioned in *Two Gentlemen*, effecting a chime with Mercutio (see below, chap. 5).

9. See Dickson's Introduction to *Valentine and Orson*, 1937. Probable dates for the three editions are 1503–5, 1548–58, 1565–67.

10. For Thomas Gosson and Raffe Hancock, 23 May 1595, "Entred for theire Copie an enterlude of Valentyne and Orsson, plaid by hir maiesties Players" (*Register*, 2:298). The second play of the same title, by Hathaway and Munday, is from 1598, listed by Henslowe, *Diary*, 1:90 and 2:195.

11. Peck, *Dictionary*, pp. 1630–31, surveys the brothers' history. For the Code see Pharr, *Theodosian Code*, and the bibliography for sixteenth-century anthologies of sententiae. John Fletcher's play *Valentinian* is about a different emperor, Valentinian III.

12. Romei, *Courtiers*, sig. H4 (printed by Valentine [!] Sims, 1598). The speaker Barisano is cited by Henderson, *Family*, pp. 152–67, as an analogue of Mercutio. Since the book, at least in its English version, postdates *Romeo and Juliet*, the names of its author and printer are probably coincidental. (Valentine Sims, or Simmes, printed *R2*, *1H4*, *2H4*, *Ado*, and *Ham.* 1597–1604.) Ferguson (*Simmes*) nowhere suggests that the printer would have been on Shakespeare's mind in 1595.

13. Most of this introduction, in substantially the same form, appeared in *South Atlantic Review* as "Mercutio's Brother."

PART ONE: SHAKESPEARE'S MERCURY

1. Mercury's patronage of writing and scribes seems to derive both from his status as messenger and from his identification with the Egyptian scribal god Thoth. As a god of boundaries Mercury has charge of "communication with enemies and strangers" (Burkert, *Greek Religion*, p. 158) and so of interpretation.

2. Mercutio's name is affected by the *er-ar* equivalence as it comes from da Porto (Marcuccio) into Bandello (Mercutio). The same equivalence ap-

pears in the name of the messenger Marcade (*LLL* 5.2), which may be based on the name of an historical Frenchman, Marcade or Mercade (see David, *Theatre*, p. 185n; Wilson uses the latter form in his edition). The equivalence appears also in an apparently overlooked possible source for the name, Wilson's *Coblers Prophesie* (1594), where Raph Cobler calls Mercury "God Markedy" (sig. B1, B1v), "God Markedie" (sig. B2v), and "God Merkedy" (sig. F2v). The Elizabethan *er-ar* spelling alternation is so common as to turn up elsewhere with Mercury's story too: the god's victim Argus is Ergus in Riche, *Dialogue*, sig. A1v. As Kökeritz, *Names*, p. 71, points out, the god's name was susceptible to either pronunciation. Although Kökeritz there disallows Shakespeare any but our pronunciation of Mercutio, the name's history and the principles stated in Kökeritz, *Pronunciation*, pp. 249–52, and in Cercignani, *Pronunciation*, pp. 64–66, 98–100, imply the possibility of the alternative with *ar*. As my colleague Ronald R. Butters has kindly pointed out to me in a personal communication, the trill we assume Shakespeare to have given his *r*'s would have favored the *ar* pronunciation, since "it is much easier to raise the tongue from /a/ to /ī/ than to retract the tongue from /ɛ/ to a following /ī/." In any case, even should Shakespeare and his company have confined themselves to our pronunciation, the alternative would have been present as a possibility. What seems most likely is that the two phones would have been nonphonemic variants; that is, that the pronunciations we distinguish were one for Shakespeare. This phonetic equivalence would have produced sinister overtones in the Greek version of Mercury's name.

Maxwell (*TA*, p. 78n) suggests that "Ovid may have afforded a hint for the writing of the name. . . . When Io has been transformed into a cow, she first tries to tell her father who she is, but cannot any longer speak. . . . Golding translates: 'But for because she could not speak she printed in the sand / Two letters with her foot, whereby was given to vnderstand / The sorowfull changing of hir shape.' " There would thus be an associative resonance with Jove and so some reason for crediting him with inspiring Marcus. But Mercury has his own part to play in the Io story (see below, chap. 1).

3. Honigmann (*Jn.* p. 105), in his note on the passage points out that "Fripp [1930] compared Ovid's *Metam.*, I 671 ff." The comparison is also drawn by Root, *Mythology*, pp. 84–85, who suggests further that Shakespeare's "set feathers to thy heels" (l. 174) may derive from Golding—"He made no long abod, but tyde his fethers too his feete"—rather than directly from Ovid—"alas [wings] pedibus" (1.671). Since Shakespeare makes many references to Mercury's talaria (*Jn.* 4.2.174, *H5* 2.Prol. 7, *Tro.* 2.2.44, and *Cym.* 4.2.310), and nowhere to his petasos, one may assume that the wings he has in *Richard III* (2.1.89) and the feathers in *1 Henry IV* (4.1.106) are at his heels rather than at his cap or over his ears. As for other accoutrements,

Shakespeare mentions only the pipe, once (*H5* 3.7.17), and caduceus, once
also (*Tro.* 2.3.11–12). The primacy of Mercury's talaria in Shakespeare's
imagination, incidentally, accounts in part for the precise manner of Hermes' appearance in the Dauphin's description of his horse in *Henry V*
(3.7.14–17):

> le cheval volant, the Pegasus, chez les narines de feu! When I bestride
> him, I soar, I am a hawk. He trots the air. The earth sings when he
> touches it. The basest horn of his hoof is more musical than the pipe
> of Hermes.

The Mercury-Pegasus associative bond (a natural one for two abnormally
winged creatures) had already been established by *1 Henry IV*—"I saw
young Harry . . . / Rise from the ground like feathered Mercury, / To turn
and wind a fiery Pegasus" (4.1.104–9)—so that the Dauphin's fiery Pegasus
naturally enough brings Mercury into Shakespeare's mind. But here the
movement from one term of the association to the other is more circuitous
than in *1 Henry IV*. There, if Harry mounting his horse is like Mercury, the
horse can become Pegasus. Here, the reverse movement is interestingly
blocked—though the Dauphin's horse is Pegasus, the Dauphin with surprising modesty refrains from making himself a god. But Hermes does find
his way into the passage. Ostensibly it is via the pun on "horn," and the
train of association may look a bit arbitrary. But I believe the implicit and
perhaps unconscious sequence *hoof-foot-talaria* grounds the explicit one
hoof-horn-pipe that leads from Pegasus to Mercury.

Subliminally, the word hornpipe may also have facilitated Hermes' entry
into the passage; if not, it here becomes linked with other terms in the
associative cluster. The passage continues,

> *Dauphin*: . . . than the pipe of Hermes.
> *Orleans*: He's of the color of the nutmeg.
> *Dauphin*: And of the heat of the ginger.
>   (*H5* 3.7.17–19)

The cluster reappears in *Winter's Tale*. Shortly after Autolycus's mention
of being "littered under Mercury" (4.3.24–25), the Clown says that the
Puritan "sings psalms to hornpipes" (l. 43), and then speaks of nutmeg,
ginger, and other spices (ll. 43–45). Though Pegasus is not mentioned, he,
and the *talaria-foot-hoof* terms of the associative cluster may lie beneath
the horseman-footman-footman-footman-footman-horseman-hot sequence
that follows shortly (ll. 62–65). This is Shakespeare's only use of hornpipe.
See also Lever, "Fruits," p. 87.

4. The sentence appears in larger type in Q1. Wilson (*LLL*, 1923, p. 185n),
suggests that "the words, written in a large hand at the end of Shakespeare's manuscript, may conceivably have been a comment on the play by

someone to whom he had lent it for perusal." If so, the reader was uncannily attuned to the idiom of Shakespeare's imagination. In the revised edition (1962), Wilson withdraws the suggestion, but he was surely right in the beginning that the line stands as a motto, peculiarly laconic and gnomic, for the entire play. The first folio adds a speech heading giving Armado the sentence, and follows it with another, "You, that way: we, this way," which is then followed with the stage direction "Exeunt omnes," which David (*LLL*, p. 196n) says "was perhaps made by the stage-manager to ensure a tidy *Exeunt*." Harbage, *Works*, p. 178, holds that "thus the words of the quarto are made, if they were not so already, an integral part of the play." See also Evans, *Signifying*, pp. 50–65.

5. Inasmuch as "English Mercury" is the herb *Chenopodium Bonus-Henricus*, or "good Henrie" or "Good king Harry" (Gerard, *Herball*, sig. R2), the youth of England may be following their king's pattern more closely than they know.

6. "Hic primum paribus nitens Cyllenius [Mercury] alis / constit," *Aeneid* 4.252–53; "Here Mercury first took his stand, bouying himself on equal wings." Frye, *Hamlet*, pp. 172–74, discusses Hamlet Senior's combination of Mars and Mercury, adducing Gascoigne's motto "Tam Marti, quam Mercurio," and treating Mercury as signifying "the thinker."

7. Root, *Mythology*, p. 85, observes, "That the wand was wreathed with serpents was a later Latin tradition; Steevens adduces Martial, *Epig.* 7.74; Marlowe speaks of his 'snaky rod' in *Hero and Leander* I." For Marlowe, see below, chap. 5. The serpents in fact seem to have evolved from the earlier twined twigs of the caduceus by the time of Sophocles; see Waele, *Staff*, p. 35.

8. Hermes shows in Hermia as well as in Hermione. While I have carried out no deep interrogation of *A Midsummer Night's Dream*, it seems clear that Hermia is a "she-Mercury" not only in her name but also in her marked sorority, which corresponds to Mercury's and Mercutio's fraternality.

CHAPTER ONE: TO THE RENAISSANCE

1. See figs. 9 and 21 below for the stone heaps. Brown's evolution from trickster to boundary marker has been inverted by Burkert and other more recent commentators.

2. See also Kahn, *Hermès passe*, and Hyde, "Tricks." Both commentators are valuably idiosyncratic, and in their very different ways have begun to provide phenomenological and poststructuralist understandings of the god. And for the figure of the god as received and modified by Ronsard, see Welch, *Mercury*.

3. Hermes also is mentioned or appears, briefly, in *Iliad* 2.104, 14.491, 16.185, 20.35, 72, and 21.497, and *Odyssey*, 12.390, 14.435, and 15.319.

4. Mercury's history intermittently generates the notion of a fraternal radical equality, a version of which appears in the liminal society as described by Turner. See below, chaps. 4, 5, and 6 passim, for ways in which some of Mercutio's subversiveness derives from the liminal society he calls into being. In addition to the "Hymn" discussed here, the lesser *Homerica* contain a short and comparatively minor hymn to Mercury.

5. Including the Mercury in Aesop's "Fable of the Carpenter," which Shakespeare could have come across in the English translations by Caxton (1484, 1497?), Middleton (1550?), Henryson (1570), and Bullokar (1585). In Caxton the fable is illustrated with a woodcut of Mercury enthroned, nude except for a crown, but without genitals as well as wings, petasos, talaria, or other identifying appurtenance.

6. Brown, *Hermes*, pp. 93–101, argues that, since Mercury's teaching of Amphion, told by Eumelus (seventh century B.C.) as quoted in Pausanias 9.5.8, is the god's earliest association with music in literature—while Apollo is earlier associated with music—Eumelus's story, like the Homeric Hymn, is evidence of rivalry between the cults of the two gods and of Mercury's intrusion into territory Apollo had previously monopolized. Although Shakespeare mentions Niobe (*Tro.* 5.10.19 and *Ham.* 1.2.149), it is in connection with her grief for her children, and he nowhere mentions her musical husband Amphion. See Raingeard, *Hermès*, for an extended treatment of the classical cult of Mercury, and Commager, *Odes*, p. 188, for "arguments as to whether there was . . . a cult of Mercury-Augustus at Rome." Deonna, *Mercure*, p. 39, holds that the cult enjoyed particular favor in Roman Africa. The cult of Mercury also established itself particularly firmly in Gaul (and Renaissance mythographers routinely mention the fact). Hall, *History*, p. 8, describes the further conflation, by the early Christian church, of Mercury and St. Michael, and illustrates with a remarkable sequence of pictures of Anubis (c. 1400 B.C.), Hermes (sixth century B.C.), and St. Michael (1476), each using a pan scale to weigh souls or miniature warriors. And see Armstrong, *Painters*, pp. 68–73, for " 'the Mercury cult' of the early Renaissance."

7. See Commager, *Odes*, pp. 175–94. The purpose of the periphrasis, Commager suggests, is to associate the adjective *almus*, "which might sit oddly upon Mercury himself," with the god and by extension with Octavian, in the interests of peace (p. 188). Mercury is also mentioned in Ode 1.30. In Horace's more colloquial *Satires* Mercury is mentioned as patron of merchants and god of luck and gain (2.3.25, 68; 2.6.5).

8. These eyes run away with their translators in various ways. Douglas, Surrey, and Stanyhurst all reverse Virgil's meaning: "and to the deid /

Closis their ene, and brekis the stringis twa" (Douglas, *Eneados*, sig. M3); "And mortall eies he closeth vp in deth" (Surrey, *Aenaeis*, sig. E4); "Bye death eyelyd uphasping" (Stanyhurst, *Aeneis*, sig. L2v). Ridley, *"Aeneid,"* p. 125, quotes glosses by Servius and Badius that prove the antiquity of the confusion. Phaer, omitting the eyes without quite summoning the assurance that allows Caxton to omit the entire phrase, gives the caduceus still another power—"men from death defendes" (*Eneidos*, sig. K1). For comparative assessments of the five English Virgils see Lathrop, *Translations*, pp. 26, 100–101, 112–13.

9. Nashe ("Preface," p. 315) writes that Stanyhurst "with an hexameter furie, recalled to life what euer hissed Barbarisme hath been buried this C. yeere; and reuiued by his ragged quill such carterly varietie as no hodge plowman in a country but would haue held as the extremitie of clownerie." Nashe also attacks Stanyhurst in "Strange News" (p. 299). Haar, *"Aeneis,"* pp. 8–13, discusses these and other appraisals. Root, *Mythology*, p. 7, finds evidence for Shakespeare's acquaintance with Phaer.

10. In the story in question, Ovid's sexism of course also shows in the fact that the sons inherit characteristics from their fathers alone. If anything, Golding softens the picture. Ovid has "tactu iacet illa potenti / vimque dei patitur" (11.308–9), "She lay beneath the god's magic touch and endured his violence" (Miller, *Metam.* 2.143).

11. The *Lares Compitales* worshipped at crossroads "were dangerous spirits, probably spirits of the dead, who had to be propitiated," and distinct from the *Lares Familiares*. Both were sets of male twins, and in later times were identified with Castor and Pollux (Harvey, *Companion*, pp. 235–36). Thus fraternality as well as filiation associates them with Mercury and through him Mercutio. Among Mercury's other offspring the most famous is Pan. In addition he fathered the sons Cephalus, Ceryx, Eleusis, and Daphnis (Grimal, *Mythology*, p. 128; Zimmerman, *Dictionary*, p. 81). Although Shakespeare mentions none of these scions of the god, he would certainly have known at least of Pan.

12. Perseus (*Metam.* 4.753–54) sacrifices a bullock, a bull, and a cow to Mercury, Jupiter, and Minerva respectively; in 5.331 Mercury in Egypt disguises himself as an ibis to escape the giants; in 12.146 Ulysses boasts of his descent from Mercury; and in 14.291–92 Mercury's bringing the moly to Ulysses is mentioned.

13. Argus is mentioned in *LLL* 3.1.188, *MV* 5.1.230, and *Tro.* 1.2.29, Io in *Shr.* Introd. 2.52–53. The three pictures the servant proposes to show Christopher Sly are all from Ovid. After Venus and Adonis from *Metam.* 10, he proposes the two adjacent stories from *Metam.* 1 of Io and of Daphne and Apollo. Assuming that the three pictures came to Shakespeare in the order given, the associative chain is of interest. The second link can be

explained by the contiguity of the stories in Ovid, together with the popularity of the story of Daphne and Apollo. The jump from Venus and Adonis
to Io is a bit less direct, but it seems certain that the first proposed picture,

> Adonis painted by a running brook
> And Cytherea all in sedges hid,
> Which seem to move and wanton with her breath
> Even as the waving sedges play with wind
> *(Shr.* Ind. 2.48–51),

calls up the second, "Io as she was a maid / And how she was beguilèd and
surprised" (ll. 52–53), via the story of Pan and Syrinx, which is set into the
Io story, and whose conclusion Golding, incidentally, makes memorable:

> And how when Pan betweene his armes, to catch the Nymph
>   had thought,
> In steade of hir he caught the Reedes newe growne upon the brooke,
> And as he sighed, with his breath the Reedes he softly shooke
> Which made a still and mourning noyse, with straungnesse of
>   the which
> And sweetenesse of the feeble sounde the God delighted mich.
>   (ll. 879–83)

Compare *Metam.* 1.705–9. The first of the servant's proposed pictures is
itself a composite since "this is a picture not of any scene in Ovid's story of
Venus and Adonis, but of a scene in his story of Salmacis and Hermaphroditus," *Metam.* 4.285ff. (Thomson, *Shakespeare,* p. 60).

   14. Adlington (1566, 1571, 1582) "avoided the extravagance of Apuleius's
style, retaining nearly always the agitating substance, usually securing an
appropriate, or even a powerfully sympathetic tone, but expressing himself
more simply and normally than his original" (Lathrop, *Translations,* p.
159). As Whibley, "Introduction," p. xxvi, demonstrates, Adlington "attempted to amend his ignorance of Latin by the aid of a French version,"
Lucius Apuleius de Lasne dore (Paris, 1522). *The Golden Ass* appeared in a
second French translation, and in Spanish and Italian translations, before
Adlington's English (Whibley, "Introduction," p. xxvi). In addition to the
widely acknowledged echo of Apuleius in Bottom's metamorphosis, Tobin, *Favorite Novel,* pp. 40–42, finds Apuleian traces in some thirty other
works of Shakespeare, including *Romeo.*

   15. Here, as generally, Adlington tones down the eroticism of his source:

> et in modum Paridis Phrygii pastoris barbaricis amiculis humeris de-
> fluentibus pulchre indusiatus adolescens, aurea tiara contecto capite,
> pecuarium simulabat magisterium. Adest luculentus puer nudus, nisi
> quod ephebica chlamida sinistrum tegebat humerum, flavis crinibus

usquequaque conspicuus, et inter comas eius aureae pinnulae cognatione simili sociatae prominebant, quem caduceum et virgula Mercurium indicabant. Is saltatorie procurrens malumque bracteis inauratum dextra gerens. (10.30)

a young man, a shepherd representing Paris, richly arrayed with vestments of barbary, having a mitre of gold upon his head, and seeming as though he kept the goats. After him ensued another fair youth all naked, saving that his left shoulder was covered with a rich cloak such as young men do wear, and his head shining with golden hair, and as it hung down you might perceive through it two little wings of gold; and him the rod called Caduceus and the wand did shew to be Mercury. He bare in his right hand an apple of gold, and with a seemly and dancing gait went towards him that represented Paris, and ... delivered him the apple. (Gaselee, *Golden Ass*, p. 527)

But this Mercury is more of a cynosure than even Gaselee will quite allow. Butler, *Metam.*, renders "usquequaque conspicuus" (Gaselee, "shining") more faithfully as "a mark for all men's eyes."

16. In the original, Anubis is not identified as Mercury explicitly as in Adlington, though the repeated appurtenances and the mention of Anubis's office of envoy to the dead make the identity apparent enough. For the identifications of Mercury with Anubis and Thoth, see, among others, Harvey, *Companion*, p. 33; Zimmerman, *Dictionary*, pp. 25, 270–71. These identifications are of course the outcome of a complex network of factors, including, for instance, the congruence between Thoth's offices—scribe, god of wisdom and magic—and Mercury's. In later classical times the identifications are rationalized in myths of Mercury's flight into Egypt with other members of the pantheon where, to escape a dragon, Mercury disguises himself with a dog's head or, to escape the giants, he disguises himself as an ibis (Butler, *Metam.*, 5.331). Schrickx, *Contemporaries*, pp. 229–30, notes that the Greeks identified Thoth with Mercury (Hermes) from the time of Herodotus, though the identification is not made universally. Thoth "fulfilled the function of scribe of the gods with the result that he was soon converted into an inventor of speech and letters; from this invention many other sciences dependent on speech and writing arose and it was but natural to ascribe these to him as well" (Schrickx, p. 230).

17. According to most authorities Pan's parents are Mercury and the nymph Dryope, though there are other versions with different fathers and mothers, including one that makes Mercury father Pan by his granddaughter-in-law Penelope. See Harvey, *Companion*, p. 304; Zimmerman, *Dictionary*, p. 190; Jacobson, *Heroides*, p. 246.

18. Mercury's patronage of gymnastics

seems to be of late origin, for in the Homeric poems no trace of it is found; and the appearance of the god . . . is very different from that which we might expect in the god of the gymnastic art. But as the images were erected . . . at the entrance of the gymnasia, the natural result was, that he . . . was regarded as the protector of youths and gymnastic exercises and contests . . . and that at a later time the Greek artists . . . represented him as a youth whose limbs were beautifully and harmoniously developed by gymnastic exercises. (Smith, *Dictionary*, 2:413)

19. Although the entire work appears before *Romeo and Juliet* in six continental editions and one Italian translation (1499–1592), and Books 1 and 2 appear in a separate edition in 1516 (Stahl et al., 1:75–77), still "Martianus has never been a popular author in the British Isles" (1:60).

20. For the critical history of Martianus see Stahl et al., *Martianus*, 1:55–79, 2:231–43, and LeMoine, *Martianus*, pp. 1–4, 229. The best-known modern assessment may still be Lewis, "this universe, which has produced the bee-orchid and the giraffe, has produced nothing stranger than Martianus Capella" (*Allegory*, p. 78). See also Allen, *Mysteriously Meant*, pp. 208ff.

21. The brotherhood of Mercury and Apollo retains some of its classical richness and ambivalence. Identification with astronomical bodies emphasized their closeness (Martianus, *Marriage*, p. 8), as does the fact that Gemini is "a sign kindred to them" (p. 17). And it is to Apollo that Mercury applies for the nomination of a bride (pp. 8–14). On the other hand Prophecy, whose "splendid beauty inflamed his [Mercury's] desires, and whom Mercury by his own lights elects to marry, "went . . . to young Apollo and . . . became his lover" (p. 6).

22. Seznec's is the best account of the medieval transformations and Renaissance reintegrations of the classical gods, and he treats Mercury in particular, discussing his astrological appearance and reproducing a number of pictorial illustrations of the god from Arab and continental texts. There is of course a vast commentary on the subject of medieval astrology and its influence. See especially Parr, *Malady*, pp. 112–50.

23. "Every alchemist . . . knew perfectly well that ordinary sulphur and mercury could not be the constituents of metals because when combined they form cinnabar (mercuric sulphide). This might have led alchemists to abandon the original theory, but instead they simply described *their* sulphur and mercury as 'sophic,' 'philosophic,' 'ideal,' or just 'not vulgar'" (Coudert, *Alchemy*, p. 21).

24. The recapitulation in a happier key by Hermione's "statue" of the effigies of Romeo and Juliet is another of the numerous links between the two plays; another is the echo, in "Paulina," of the "Christian Mercury" (Acts 14.12), Paul. See Davies, *Feminine*, pp. 168–69. For a more inten-

sively and exclusively alchemical reading of Shakespeare than I undertake here, see Nicholl, *Theatre*, pp. 136–239. Nicholl sees the alchemical process of transmutation as informing *Lear*, with the Fool playing the role of mercury or the alchemical "Our Mercury," and he draws connections between the alchemy he finds in *Lear* and that in *Eastward Ho* and *The Alchemist*. For a more general treatment of what Artaud (*Theatre*, p. 48) calls a "mysterious identity of essence between the principle of theatre and that of alchemy," see Knapp, *Theatre*. Jung has of course written extensively on psychology and alchemy, and commentary on the subject as a whole is by now vast (see Pritchard, *Alchemy*). Shakespeare's general familiarity with the subject is unquestioned. For the particular influence of John Dee on Shakespeare's later works see Yates, *Last Plays*, pp. 129–34. Dee had been back in England for some five years at the time of the composition of *Romeo*. The governing emblem of Dee's cabalistic and alchemical *Monas Hieroglyphica* (1564) is based on the alchemical sign for mercury (see Brooks-Davies, *Monarch*, pp. 3–4). Finally, it seems possible that the presence of the alchemical mercury as a constituent of Mercutio provided an additional trigger for the name of Mercutio's brother in the name of the alchemist Basil Valentine. See also Casaubon, *Relation*.

25. For reproductions and discussions of frescoes of Mercury and his medieval "children"—scribes, scholars, and other users of the written word—see Seznec, *Survival*, pp. 71–75.

26. In the heightened and dense phonetic texture of these lines of Mercutio and their immediate context—

> Give me a case to put my visage in:
> A visor for a visor. What care I,
> What curious eye doth quote deformities?
> Here are the beetle brows shall blush for me.
>
> (1.4.29–32)

—there may be a subliminal chime with the god's name in "*curious*," foreshadowed and then echoed in "*care I*," "*eye*," and "*quote*." The likelihood is increased by the appearance of "beetle," which in Shakespeare carries with it, as Armstrong, *Imagination*, pp. 18–24, demonstrates, an association with the idea of death. That term, usually explicit in what Armstrong calls "the beetle image cluster," here grounds the associative train Mercutio-Mercury-psychopomp-death, and appears explicitly later in the scene in Mercutio's Queen Mab speech (l. 83) and in Romeo's misgivings (l. 111). See below, chap. 4.

27. "Alchemists laboured to 'fix' this mercury in stone, and they often illustrated this procedure in gruesome pictures of the god Mercury with his hands and winged feet hacked off" (Coudert, *Alchemy*, p. 5). The second

derivation for "Cyllenian" cited by Cartari (*Le Imagini*, 1571) must also have played a part in fixing the image of Mercury the amputee:

> E benche molti scriuano che Mercurio fu chiamato Cillenio do un monte dell' Arcadia de questo nome, oue ei nacque, nondimeno ui sono stati anco di quelli che hanno uoluto ch' ei fosse cosi cognominato da queste imagini quadre, le quali si poteuano dire tronche, e mozze non hauendo altro membro che il capo, perche i Greci chiamano Cilli quelli, alli quali sia mozzo alcun membro, e mostrauano la forza del parlare, il quale non ha bisogno dell' aiuto delle mani, come scriue Festo. (sig. Rr4v)

> [Although many write that Mercury was called "the Cyllene" from a hill in Arcadia so named, nevertheless some have wanted to give him that name because of the square statues [the herms] which might be called truncated, having no extremity other than the head. Because, as Festus writes, the Greeks called "Cilli" those who had a limb amputated and who demonstrated a powerful speaking ability because when they spoke they did not need the help of their hands.]

28. Unless otherwise noted, all translations of foreign extracts are my own.

CHAPTER TWO: RENAISSANCE PICTURES WITH TEXT

1. Mitchell, "Archaeology," p. 473, holding that "From his wintry medieval disguise Hermes sprang forth in his true Greek character" in Cyriac's drawing, fails to address Seznec's account of the figure as "ancient but not classical in the strict sense of the word . . . in its picturesque oddity . . . an antique figure . . . grafted onto the medieval stem" (Seznec, *Survival*, p. 201). Mitchell provides a brief account of Cyriac's career and quotes one of his prayers to Mercury (p. 473). See also Starnes and Talbert, *Study*.

2. Waage, "Stone," pp. 65–73 passim, treats some of the "voluminous" (p. 65) discussion of Shakespeare's reference to Giulio. While Waage provides a number of textual avenues by which Shakespeare could have known something of Giulio's work and of its environment of aesthetic theory, he does not concern himself much with particular works of Giulio; nor does Fairchild, *Design*, pp. 71–76, in what Waage (p. 83n47) terms the definitive discussion.

3. Mercurys attributed all or in part to Giulio by Hartt, *Giulio Romano*, include that mentioned in 1:125 (not visible in the plates) and those mentioned there passim and visible in vol. 2, plates 192, 245, 305, 306, 347, 401, 493, and 501. In all likelihood Giulio would also have been associated

in some minds with the fresco of Mercury with Psyche in the Farnesina (which Hartt, p. 32, gives to Penni), inasmuch as six of the work's companion frescoes seem certainly by Giulio.

4. The Venetian Cartaris discussed here are from the presses of Valgrisi (1571) and Ziletti (1571, 1580, 1581), and the Lyonnais from the press of Guichard Jullieron (1581). Other printings of the popular work survive from the period.

5. "At all events, it is to the *Imagini* that one must turn for help in solving the enigma posed by a Shakespearean heraldic emblem devised by Bacon" (Seznec, *Survival*, p. 315). Seznec cites "William Goldsworthy Lansdown," actually William Lansdown Goldsworthy (*Heraldic Emblems*, 1928), to the effect that the figures of Castor and Pollux in "the emblem" derive from Cartari.

6. By my rough count, omitting a shipload synod where the gods are too small to be very impressive individually, and setting aside for a moment the case of Bacchus-cum-satyr, in descending order Cartari's gods with their frequency of appearance are:

Mercury	12	Cupid	7	Neptune	2
Appollo	8	Minerva	5	Pan	1
Venus	8	Saturn	5	Pluto	1
Juno	8	Janus	3		
Jove	7	Diana	3		

Bacchus is problematical because he often is indistinguishable from the satyrs who accompany him. If we chose to let all such figures count as Bacchi, he would have seventeen appearances.

7. "Horapollo and Valeriano are continually cited. . . . But the real sources are Macrobius's *Saturnalia* and Martianus Capella and the early neo-Platonists" (Purdon, *Mercury*, p. 59). Compare "Mercurivs" in Batman, *Golden Booke*, 1583 (sig. A4):

MErcurie was portraicted with wings at head and feete, wearing an Hat of white & blacke colloures: A Fawlchon by his side, in one hande a scepter, & in the other a Pype, on the one side stode a Cocke and a Ramme, and close by his side a Fylcher or Cutpurse, and a headlesse Argus.

The "Fawlchon" is of course the scimitar with which Mercury beheads Argus (cf. fig. 9). While there are rams in Mercury's story, he usually carries them as in fig. 9, and the quadruped pictured standing beside him is more often said to be a goat, as in Cartari (fig. 4), or in the antique medal described and illustrated in Du Choul, *Discours*, 1556, where two additional commonly associated animals appear:

En l'autre est vn Mercure graué de telle maniere, ieune, sans barbe, qui ha des aesles sur son chapeau, tout nud, hors mis son manteau, qu'il porte sur le bras droit, tenant de la main gauche vne bourse, & vn Gal sur son poing, & de la droitte son caducée: & à ses pieds accoustrez de ses talaires, se voit vn Bouc: & de l'autre costé vn Escorpion, & vne Mousche, choses toutes appartena[n]tes à Mercure. (sig. v2)

[The other side is engraved with a young beardless Mercury with a winged cap, completely nude except for his cloak, which he carries on his right arm, holding a purse in his left hand, with a cock on his fist, and holding his caduceus in his right hand, and at his talaria-shod feet is a goat, and on the other side a scorpion and a fly, all appurtenances of Mercury.]

8. "Pausonia . . . lo descriue fatto in guisa, che pareua uestirsi un manto, ne haueua poi di sotto gambe, ne piedi, ma era come una piccola colonnetta quadrata. Galeno quando esorta gli gioueni nelle buone arti dice che elle furono tutte ritrouate da Mercurio, e lo disegna giouine bello, non fatto con arte, ma naturalmente tale, allegro in uista, con occhi lucidi, e risplendenti, e che stia sopra una quadrata base, perche chi seguita la virtù si leua de mano alla Fortuna, e stando fermo, e saldo non teme di alcuna sua ingiuria. E Suida scriue, che la figura quadra è data à Mercurio per rispetto del parlare veriteuole, ilquale sta fermo sempre."

9. "Palestra . . . fu figliuola di Mercurio, & era tale, che malageuolmente si poteua conoscere se fosse maschio, o femina . . . e uago pareua essere non meno fanciullo, che fanciulla. . . . ne piu rileuauano le belle poppe in lei, che rileuino in un delicato giouine" (sig. Rr2–Rr3). If we could be sure of Shakespeare's having glanced at either version of precisely this illustration of Cartari, it would be tempting to see it as the perhaps unconscious catalyst for the growth of Mercutio out of Brooke's brief description of Juliet seated between Romeo and Mercutio.

10. "I Greci faceuano spesso la statoa di Mercurio in forma quadra col capo solo senza alcun' altro membro. . . . lequali erano dette Hermi. . . . Cicerone . . . chiama Herme ornamento commune à tutte le Academie. . . . gli Atheniese furono i primi, che facessero simili statoe. . . . le quali si poteuano dire tronche, e mozze non hauendo altro membro che il capo" (sig. Rr4–Rr4v).

11. In the English *Strife*, sig. Z4, the (unillustrated) description of the more recognizable Mercury is "an other sent from *Iupiter* . . . a yonge man, with winged buskyns, and a staffe, with two serpents winding about it." Elsewhere, alongside description of a youth with winged ankles and a "vypered caduce," sig. F4 ("vn sceptre entortillé de deux serpe[n]s" in the French translation of Martin, *Songe*, sig. Ciii), the English version risks the gloss "Mercurie." Colonna names Jupiter, Venus, and Cupid (though not

Bacchus) in contrast to the unnamed Mercury. As with Mercury's absent name in the text, so with the pictured herm's phallus in the Folger *Songe*, which has vanished under white paint. My illustration is from the 1904 facsimile of the first Italian edition, sig. X8v. In the copy of this edition in Duke University's Perkins Library we have a good example not only of censorious denial but also of a Mercurial subversion of that denial. As bound, the book illustrates "nel medio dil quadrata ... appareua lo ithyphallio signo," with a three-headed figure atop a pedestal that is quite innocently bare. A separate second leaf was printed for insert, identical in all respects except that the illustration appears as here, true to its original, and evidently distributed to selected purchasers of the facsimile. This Colonnan herm is accompanied by intriguing Mercurial echoes. The triumphal standard pictured below it is said to carry the lion-wolf-dog head of the Egyptian god Serapis, but as carried in the triumph on the following pages it looks more like a three-headed Anubis, all dog. And then there is the unillustrated "Hermopoane" (sig. X8v) worn by the nymph carrying it ("mercuriale" in the French, not translated in the English *Strife*).

12. "Et una altra ne era appresso de Tanagrei gente della Boetia, che portaua un montone in collo, perche dicesi che Mercurio andando già in quel modo intorno alle mura della città fece cessare una grauissima pestilenza. Onde fu osseruato poi, che quando si celebraua quiui la sua festa andaua un bellissimo giouane intorno alla città con un' agnello in collo" (sig. Tt1). "The motif of a herdsman carrying a calf or sheep existed in Archaic Greek art; and later it was used to represent Mercury as the protector of herds and flocks. It could be readily adapted to illustrate the Good Shepherd of the Bible and was used with this meaning in the Roman catacombs and on early Christian sarcophagi" (Hall, *History*, p. 5).

13. Commentary in English on emblem books begins with a study of Shakespeare (Green, *Emblem Writers*, 1870). Green's definition of the emblem is exceptionally elastic and his "whole book is an attempt to prove Shakespeare's debt to the emblem books, and he drew countless parallels of wording and imagery with small regard for context or method" (Freeman, *Emblem Books*, p. 63n). On this foundation Goldsworthy (*Heraldic Emblems*, 1928) builds an anti-Stratfordian case. More serious study begins with Gilbert (*Impresa*, 1933; "Crown," 1939–40; "Embleme," 1948; *Persons*, 1948), Praz (*Studies*, 1939), and especially Freeman (*Emblem Books*, 1948), and continues through Clements (*Picta Poesis*, 1960), Steadman ("Spenser's 'Errour,'" 1961), Biggins ("Problem," 1962), Scott (*Pericles*, 1969), Hoyle ("Emblems," 1971), Daly ("Note," 1977; *Emblem*, 1979), Schoeck (*Intertextuality*, 1984), and Fabiny (*Emblem*, 1984). A somewhat separate line of emblem study in German runs from Mauntz (*Heraldik*, 1903) through Henkel & Schöne (*Handbuch*, 1967), and Daly (*Emblematik*, 1976). Daly (*Emblem*, p. 134) writes, "the study of emblematic literature

has only now come of age." A useful survey of recent work is Dees, "English Emblem," 1986.

14. Clements, *Picta Poesis*, p. 28, lists the motto and plate from Giovio and Symeoni, *Sentiose Imprese* (Lyon, 1562), as one of a number of emblematists' personal emblems. In Alciati (1534, sig. B3v) the motto for the plate is "virtuti fortuna comes," and the *subscriptio* reads

> Anguibus implicitis geminis caduceus alis,
> Inter Amalthaeae cornua rectus adest.
> Pollentes sic mente viros, fandiq[ue] peritos
> Indicat, ut rerum copia multa beet.

[The caduceus with twin wings and intertwining snakes
stands up here, guiding Amalthea among the horns of plenty.
Mindful of powerful men, it shows the experienced in speaking
how abundance blesses them.]

15.   Apres sept ans lenfant co[n]duit Mercure,
> Pource qu'il est capable d'estre aprins:
> Cest à bo[n] droit, que de luy pre[n]t la cure,
> Car tous arts ont de luy fondement prins.
>   (sig. B7)

16. The motto for the dual Mercury is "Prudentia cum robore coniuncta," and the *subscriptio* is

> Viribus Cyllenius integris stat
> Iunctus con senio graui.
> Robur inuictum est, sapientia si
> Firmes: qua sine, concidet.
>   (Emblem 13, sig. B2r)

[Mercury in his full strength is
joined with heavy old age.
If wisdom is strong, strength is unconquerable:
without wisdom, strength crumbles.]

Bocchi's Mercury covering his mouth with his hand is listed in the table of contents as "Silens," his motto is "FERT TACITVS, VIVIT, VINCIT, / DIVINVS AMATOR" (sig. Tt4v) and his *subscriptio* is

> Ardenti tacitus fero, viuo victor in igne,
> Non ego diuino hoc igne mori dubitem.
> Cernis vt ad patrium sublimis fertur olympum.
> Huc nostra, vnde orta est, mens simul approperat.
> Euge beate ignis zephyri aura incense supremi,

Mortale in nobis excoque quicquid inest.
Deniq[ue] felici nos terq[ue] quaterq[ue] corona
Dignare, atq[ue] tua perfice iustitia.

(sig. Vv1)

This too then, like the next Bocchi discussed, is a figure of silence.

17. Wind, *Mysteries*, pp. 12–13nn40–41, provides much information about textual and pictorial transmission to the Renaissance of images of Harpocrates from Ovid and also of the Roman goddess of silence, Angerona, from Pliny. About Angerona, incidentally, it may be worth noting that, while one may derive the impression from Wind that Cartari gives her the Harpocratic gesture, in fact in both Cartari's text and Zaltieri's engraving she is gagged (sig. Zz3v–Zz4). Mercury appears in other of the engravings by Agostino Caracci in the second edition (Bologna, 1574) of Bocchi, e.g., as a farmer praying to Jupiter for rain (sig. Z2v), as a herm (likewise Minerva) at the corner of a building (sig. Dd4v), and as giving moly to Ulysses (with Minerva again, sig. Mm4v).

With the Harpocratic Mercury Bocchi prints the motto "SILENTIO DEVM COLE" (sig. Ss1v), and on the facing page, after a Latin version of the inscription on the pedestal, the lines

Menti, Virtuti, & Fidei delubra dicamus:
　　Esse sita in nobis cernimus illa tamen.
Cur capitolina Tritonia Pallas in arce
　　Sedem habuit? caput haec urbis, & orbis erat.
Mens decus est hominis, diuinae mentis imago,
　　Non vllis vnquàm sensibus exposito.
Noscere qui cupit hanc ipsum se noscat oportet
　　In primis, Pharium, & consulat Harpocratem.
　　　REVOCANDA MENS A SENSIBVS
　　　DIVINA CVI MENS OBTIGIT.
Revocare mentem qui protest à sensibus,
Et cogitationem ab assuetudine
Abducere, facilè ille praestat omnibus:
Nam mente viuit, atq[ue] viuit vt Deus,
Qui corpore ac sensibus, brutum vt pecus.
Hermetis hanc sententiam ter maximi
Qui cordi habebit, esse non potest miser.

(sig. Ss2)

18.　　In triuio mons est lapidum, supereminet illi
　　　Trunca Dei effigies, pectore facta tenus:
　　Mercurij est igitur tumulus, suspende uiator
　　　Serta Deo, rectum qui tibi monstrat iter.

> Omnes in triuio sumus, atque hoc tranute uitae
> Fallimur, ostendat ni Deus ipse uiam.
>
>   (1534, sig. F1)

[At the crossroads there is a mound of stones, and projecting above it the truncated image of the god as far down as the breast, Mercury; therefore this is the sepulchral mound, and the traveler hangs up a garland to the god who shows you the right way. We all are at crossroads, and we will be led astray in life's journey unless God himself shows the way.]

19. Alciati's 1549 *subscriptio* (sig. A5) in its entirety is

> La, doue molte vie diuersa strada
> Porgono a l'huom, sopra vn sassoso colle
> Posta è la Imagin di Mercurio. Bada
> Tu, ch'erri per terreno asciutto o molle;
> Ch'ei dimostra la dritta, onde si vada
> Per sicuro camin, ch'al giogo estolle.
> Tutti errano qua giu per questa valle
> Se la destra di Dio non mostra il calle.

20. Mercurij si quis subit antrum doctus amoenum:
 Quo cuiusque boni copia magna datur:
Pauperiem fugiens miseram, tristesque labores;
 Fert utraque manu commoda multa domum.
Musarum doctos qui versat saepe libellos:
 In quibus ars, virtus, ingeniumque latet:
Fit sapiens, doctus, dives, bonus, atque beatus:
 Fit clarus fama, dignus honore senex.
Mercurius tot opes donat venientibus ultro:
 Haud vacuum quenquam passus abire foras.
O miserum, quem non auctores cura legendi
 Afficit: & qui non haec bona sponte rapit.

[If anyone learned in the rites of Mercury approaches the
  pleasant cave
 where he is given great abundance of Mercury's gifts,
he escapes gloomy poverty and dismal work
 and carries home many good things in each hand.
Whoever often looks at the learned booklets of the Muses,
 art, virtue, and cleverness lie in these booklets,
he becomes wise, learned, wealthy, good, and blessed
 he becomes famous and, as an old man, worthy of honor.
Mercury gives so much wealth to those who come further,

and by no means does he go away empty-handed.
Oh poor man, who has no concern for the importance of
    making this choice,
Oh poor one, who doesn't immediately snatch up these gifts.]

CHAPTER THREE: ELIZABETHAN TEXTS TO 1595

1. Mercury as concord appears in the marginalium in Gabriel Harvey's annotated copy of Eliot (in the Huntington Library), Mercury's astrological symbol drawn next to the underscored phrase "en heureux paix" (sig. L1v). Harvey himself was something of a Mercurialist, of course.

2. Fraunce, *Yuychurch*, sig. K3v:

> Not long after this, *Phoebus* with *Mercury*; ioyned
> In faire-prowd *Chione: Chione* bare either a dearling:
> Th'one well knowne for a theefe, and th'other fit for a fiddle;

The first line and a half foreground the genital fraternization latent in this story of Ovid's, making it closer to the story of the engendering of Orion than it is in Ovid.

3. Although Daniel does not mention Mercury, Rosalind sees Io transformed, with Argus, engraved on a casket sent to her by Henry (ll. 400–493). James's second prefatory sonnet calls Mercury "Maias learned sonne" (sig. 2v). The octave of Sonnet 11 is a prayer to the learned god:

> And at your handis I earnestly do craue,
> O facound *Mercure*, with the *Muses* nyne,
> That for conducting guyde I may you haue,
> Aswell vnto my pen, as my Ingyne.
> Let Reders think, thy eloquence deuyne
> O *Mercure*, in my Poems doth appeare:
> And that *Parnassis* flowing fountaine fyne
> Into my works doth shyne lyke cristall cleare.
>
>   (sig. B4v)

4. Schrickx, *Contemporaries*, pp. 232–33, 236, discusses these passages from Nashe and Harvey as examples of "the 'hermetic' symbolism prevalent in the early nineties" (p. 236), in the light of which he argues that the motto ending *Love's Labour's* expresses "Shakespeare's disavowal of hermetic speculation," contrasting "the aspirations of a peculiarly esoteric type of learning with those of divinely inspired poetry" (pp. 237–38), overly simple conclusions that yet seem right in spirit.

5. Spenser is a Hermetic poet "in his partiality to mediated interpreta-

tions and recondite learning, in his preoccupation with the language of poetry and the poetry of etymology, and in his patronage of arts with an analogy to music" (Nohrnberg, *Analogy*, p. 730). Despite the keenness of Brooks-Davies's nose for Mercury, he has what seems a pair of perceptual blanks. He says nothing about the phonetic chime in the first syllables of Mercury and Merlin, and he ignores the false Florimell's constitution of snow, wax, "fine Mercury," and "perfect vermily" (*FQ* 3.8.6).

6. "La secreta intelligentia di questa favola, secondo alcuni, è, che nelle matrici delle donno sono sette le stanze che riogleno il seme dell'huomo: tre dalla parte destra, che producono i maschi, e tre dalla sinistra, che produnono le femine, & vna nel mezzo, laquale ricogliendo il seme, ha forza di procurre l'uno e l'altro sesso insieme, e per questa cagione, vogliono dire, che Hermaphrodito nascesse di Mercurio, hauendo Venere raccoloto il seme in quella stanza del mezzo: e pero sono chiamati & sono Hermaphradotiti tutti quelli che sono concetti nella medisima stanza" (Fraunce, *Yuychurch*, sig. N4).

7. For a succinct history of the use of mercury in the treatment of syphilis see Goldwater, *Mercury*, pp. 215–30. The first known printed work mentioning mercury as a specific for syphilis is Schelli[n]g, *Malas Morbum*, ca. 1490. Through the sixteenth century (and well after) it was the treatment of choice, administered in ointments, orally, and in the fumigating tubs. According to Goldwater (p. 226), "The use of mercury in the treatment of syphilis may have been the most colossal hoax ever perpetrated in the history of a profession which has never been free of hoaxes." Apropos of the nationality of the malady (which was of course also the Neapolitan bone ache), it may be worth mentioning three other links between Mercury and France. (1) While mythographers such as Cartari routinely mention the special esteem accorded Mercury in France, and also routinely describe Mercury as accompanied by a cock, the third side of the triangle is normally elided. Yet the association between the cock and France dates from the double signification of the Latin *gallus*, Gaulois, and cock. (2) The rebellion in Brittany of Philip Emanuel, Duc de Mercure, as well as the number of English soldiers killed fighting for the king, would have given the France-Mercury link an ominous resonance for the English in the early 1590s. (3) Caesar, *Gallico*, 54.5, recounts that the British abstained from eating the flesh of three animals they kept as pets: chickens, geese, and hares. Mercutio is associated with the first through Mercury, and he mentions the other two.

8. The fact that some part of *Dido* is Nashe's is not especially relevant here. To the small extent to which my argument here and below depends on linkage of Marlowe and the play's Mercury, joint authorship suffices.

9. For the significance of Marlowe's having written the play for the children, see especially Cope, "*Dido*," 1974. For the Mercury episode in *Hero*

and Leander, see especially Miller, "Epic," 1958, and Neuse, "Atheism," 1970. The five other references to Mercury or Hermes in Marlowe treat him for the most part conventionally, except for the most interesting reference, which is also the one Shakespeare is probably least likely to have seen by 1595. This is Lucan's mention of human sacrifice offered by the French to "fell Mercury" (l. 440) in Marlowe's translation (*Complete Works,* vol. 2) of *The First Book of Lucan* (see also l. 276 for the line's "interesting anomaly" in the 1600 quarto). See also below, chap. 5.

CHAPTER FOUR: ELOQUENCE AND LIMINALITY

1. While there is substantial consensus about a great deal in the field of pragmatics, there have also been enough disagreements for Altieri (*Act,* p. 69) to write in 1981, "This field is now in turmoil." Some of the turmoil is simply a function of the field's youth, size, and diversity. As the newly formed International Pragmatics Association announced: "Today, pragmatics is a large, loose, and disorganized collection of research efforts. . . . their contribution to our understanding of human verbal communication often does not reach its fullest potential as a result of the emerging theoretical, methodological, and terminological diversity" (*Journal of Pragmatics* 10 [1986]: 153). In addition, the form of Austin's *How to Do Things with Words* (1962), as we have it, has invited contradictory readings and attributions. It is a posthumous, sometimes fragmentary series of lecture notes, and it includes a sort of dialogic sequence of provision and revision. Hence for instance, Burton (*Discourse,* pp. 37ff.) is able to attribute to Austin the distinction between performatives and constatives without going on to explain that Austin introduces the distinction only to collapse it as untenable. See also Porter, "Pragmatics," 1986.

2. Speech act theorists for the most part use the word performative to mean "illocutionarily explicit speech act." But in the work of some pragmaticists, and still more in the work of some literary critics and theoreticians, performative simply means speech act. The confusion grows directly out of ambiguity resulting from Austin's dialogic exposition.

3. The first speech generally given to Benvolio may in fact be Mercutio's, as Capell suggested. The speech acts involved, the diction, and the scorn make it sound more like Mercutio (see Gibbons, 1.4.1n).

4. Rosaline will not be besieged by loving terms nor assailed by eyes, "Nor ope her lap to saint-seducing gold" (1.1.212). While not bawdy, the line is enough of a surprise for Gibbons (p. 93n) to comment at length, and not altogether persuasively, when he suggests that "we may suppose his [Romeo's] immaturity has allowed the conceit to get out of hand."

5. Goldman, *Shakespeare,* p. 37, contrasts "arias" given in company such

as the Queen Mab speech with the isolated ones of Romeo and Juliet. One of Queen Mab's accoutrements, incidentally—"Her chariot is an empty hazelnut" (l. 59)—carries a reference to the element mercury. "One of the most widespread uses of quicksilver has been to afford protection against the Evil Eye, 'spells' and related misfortunes. . . . A typical example . . . said to have been in practice since the middle ages, is to hollow out the kernel of a hazelnut and replace the contents with quicksilver. The amulet is to be hung around the neck, placed under the bedpillow or under the threshold of the door. . . . Hazelnuts . . . are frequently used as adjuvants to quicksilver" (Goldwater, *Mercury*, p. 26). Mercutio returns to the subject of hazelnuts when he tells Benvolio "Thou wilt quarrel with a man for cracking nuts, having no other reason but because thou hast hazel eyes" (3.1.18–20). Hazelnuts are mentioned only once elsewhere in Shakespeare, in conjunction with the only other appearance of the word "hazel" ("hazel-twig," *Shr.* 2.1.255).

6. By my count Mercutio has fifteen explicit references to speech acts apart from his three performatives. Five are his references to conjuring in 2.1. In addition he mentions asking (1.4.49, 2.1.98), prayer (1.4.87), swearing (1.4.87), challenging and answering (2.4.8, 10), jesting (2.4.63, 65, 78), and calling (3.1.58).

7. European hereditary surnames manifest a late medieval and Renaissance bourgeois familial impulse opposed to much of what Mercutio represents. The Normans brought the comparatively new practice to England, where the first hereditary English surnames are recorded in the Domesday Book (1086). While much has been written about the history of hereditary familial nomenclature, and about the histories of particular surnames, so far as I know the phenomenological or Foucauldian archaeology that would probe the evolution to any depth has yet to be done. "Arden," incidentally, is one of the earliest English hereditary surnames (Reaney, *Surnames*, p. 302).

8. "*One calls within: 'Juliet',*" 1.5.142 S.D.; "*Paris offers to go in and Capulet calls him again,*" 3.4.11 S.D. The second appears in Q1 but not in Q2–4, F. The word appears in only eight Shakespearean stage directions, twice in *Romeo* and once in six other plays. The word is frequent in the text of *Romeo*, and summoning with or without the word "call" happens a number of times without stage direction, as at 3.5.64–65.

9. The balcony scene answers the mock conjuration in ways beyond that already noted. The discussion of what to swear by (2.2.107–16) answers Mercutio's talk of conjuring by parts of Rosaline. And, as George Walton Williams has drawn to my attention, Mercutio's mocking "Cry but 'Ay me!'" (2.1.10) is answered by the first words Romeo hears Juliet speak from the balcony, "Ay me" (2.2.25). Nor are the echoes of Mercutio from 2.1 alone. Romeo's apostrophe (ll. 26–32) to Juliet as "a winged messenger of

heaven" (l. 28) not only invokes Mercury as angel but also in imagery and vocabulary strikingly echoes Mercutio's children of an idle brain speech discussed above.

10. How is it we know that Mercutio hasn't really misunderstood Benvolio? Perhaps because assuming he had would entail his seeming more lacking in common sense than we are willing to grant even though Benvolio seems willing to grant it. Mercutio's linkage with writing here and in the Capulet guest list, by the way, evinces a trace of Mercurian graphism. It may be objected that all four young men—the three friends and Tybalt—are linked to written messages on both occasions. However Mercutio alone here uses the word "write," doing so in a sentence without mention of any of the other three men, so that his linkage with writing is stronger than theirs. The situation brings him into the margins of the play's later fateful missives.

11. Gibbons (p. 105n) cites "To see him walk before a lady, and to bear her fan" (*LLL* 4.1.144) for the custom of carrying a fan. In some nineteenth-century productions, as in the silent-film version of 1908, the fan is made oversize for comic effect. Just possibly the fan Venus gives Mercury as a pledge in Peele, *The Araygnement of Paris* (1584), could have figured in Shakespeare's creation of the Nurse's fan. The Nurse and Mercutio are analogous in their bawdiness and fondness for oaths, their serving as advisers to the titular heroes, and even their names, "Angelica" standing to "Mercutio" as "angel" to "Mercury." The parallelism mustn't be pushed too far though. Where Mercutio achieves a kind of apotheosis in his death, the Nurse compromises herself pretty thoroughly in the last half of the play.

12. Line 36, Mercutio's last to Benvolio in the scene's first large movement, "By my heel, I care not," would bring the total of first-person pronouns there up to six if taken as part as that movement; I rather consider it transitional for, while it is addressed to Benvolio, it clearly manifests some of the hostile scorn Tybalt rouses in Mercutio. Line 54, "I will not budge for no man's pleasure, I," with its striking placement of the pronouns and late-as-possible caesura, exhibits some of the tragic and lonely egotism that reappears mutatis mutandis in Coriolanus's " . . . like an eagle in a dovecote, I / Fluttered your Volscians in Corioles. / Alone I did it" (*Cor.* 5.6.113–15).

13. A general dramaturgic theory of characters' limens or thresholds could be useful. It would need to take into account not only cases like Mercutio's, where reference to the character precedes his first entrance and follows his last exit, but also cases with no entrance or exit limen, where no reference precedes or follows the character's appearance onstage, and perhaps—though this raises problems—negative limens. The theory might take into account a given limen's comparative fullness (or emptiness) of

reference to the character. Mercutio's exit limen, for instance, especially in its beginning, seems comparatively full of reference to him. The theory could also be made to handle interliminal or subliminal spaces between a given character's onstage appearances.

14. "Brave" and "gallant," both favorite terms of approbation for Shakespeare, share a high degree of etymological obscurity. If the hypothesis that gallant is from an adaptation of an OHG word for wandering or going on pilgrimages (*OED*, s.v.) is correct, there is a suggestion (probably unavailable to Shakespeare) of Mercutio's becoming one of the *romei* himself here. "Gallant" is one of the notable links between Mercutio and Hotspur.

15. According to Meagher, "Economy," Lady Montague and the Nurse must both be absent in the final scene because their actors are present in other roles. Meagher bases his theory on the seemingly required doubling of roles imposed on Shakespeare by the size of his troupe, and on what he takes to be Shakespeare's exploitation of that limitation in his metatheatric use of the audience's presumed recognition of actors playing doubled roles. Because Lady Montague's absence "creates too obvious an asymmetry to be ignored," Shakespeare has Montague announce her death on the spot "rather lamely" (p. 12). But "one abrupt demise is enough; having eliminated Lady Montague explicitly, it would not be diplomatic for Shakespeare to try to get by with killing the Nurse through an analogous grief" (p. 12). Meagher holds that we in fact do miss the Nurse in the final scene. And see n. 16 below. In Q1, incidentally, Benvolio is mentioned in 5.3.

16. Meagher ("Economy," p. 13) has Mercutio doubled with Paris, but other arrangements are feasible. Mercutio's doubling with the Prince would "explain" the peculiar offstage death. Booth, *Tragedy*, pp. 142, 175n, does suggest that the roles of Mercutio and the Prince might have been doubled, or perhaps "tripled," since he asks us also to entertain the possibility that the same actor might have played Paris, an admitted improbability given the necessary legerdemain with Paris's body in 5.3 to permit the Prince's entrance in the same scene. While the proposed tripling would provide a pleasing reflection of the kinship of the three characters, Booth offers no more compelling reason for it. But Mercutio's exit to die offstage followed shortly by the Prince's entrance looks more like an accommodation to doubling than anything else in the play.

17. See Van Gennep, *Rites*, for the three stages of rites of passage (i.e., separation, margin or limen, and reaggregation) and Turner, "Betwixt" and *Ritual*, for an expansion of liminality to a border region incorporating some of Van Gennep's stage of separation, and for the liminal society: "The liminal group is a community or comity of comrades" ("Betwixt," p. 100). Bevington, *Action*, uses Turner notably.

CHAPTER FIVE: THE THIEF AND MARLOWE

1. See for instance Leech, "Venus," 1965, for the suggestion that Shakespeare read *Hero and Leander* in manuscript. Maclure (Marlowe, *Poems*) cites Leech, observes that Marlowe's "dwarfish beldam" resembles Shakespeare's Nurse, and cites comparison of *Romeo* 5.1.8, "And breath'd such life with kisses in my lips," with Marlowe's "He kist her, and breath'd life into her lips" (2.3n). The balcony scene, 2.2, itself perhaps visually alluding to Hero in her tower, contains additional textual echoes of *Hero*. Marlowe's

> And many poor excuses did she find
> To linger by the way, and once she stay'd,
> And would have turn'd again, but was afraid,
> In offering parley, to be counted light
>
> (2.6–9)

echoes in Juliet's "thou mayst think my haviour light" (l. 99) and "not impute this yelding to light love" (l. 105), as well as in her exits and re-entries. Marlowe's "Yet she this rashness suddenly repented" (2.33) echoes in the second line of Juliet's "I have no joy of this contract tonight: / It is too rash, too unadvis'd, too sudden" (ll. 117–18). Gibbons notes other echoes of *Hero* at 1.5.45 and 3.2.8–9, 12, 17. See also Walley, "Debt," 1942.

2. As Wilson, "Malone," p. 64, demonstrates, "the image of the crow decked out in the feathers of other birds was a stock jibe both of Greene and Nashe" and probably comes to them from Horace's third *Epistle*. As Chambers, *Stage*, 3:325 (cited by Wilson, p. 63), notes, Greene defended himself against a charge of literary dishonesty with an attack on the players. Greene was to be accused in print of literary theft in 1597 (see Bacon, Introduction to *Syrinx*, pp. lxxii–lxxiii).

3. For recent studies see especially Greene, *Light*, 1982. Though concerned primarily with Continental literature, it is proving influential in studies of the English Renaissance; see for instance Bellamy, "Broken Branch," 1986. Of course Bloom's work (*Anxiety*, 1973) on belatedness and influence antedates and influences these studies.

4. In Brooke, *Tragicall Historye*, 1562, class differences are taken for granted. The subject of class distinctions and Shakespeare has received considerable attention of late by scholars addressing the subject from widely varying perspectives. For a recent example see Leinwand, "killing," 1987.

5. Hartwig, *Analogical Scene*, pp. 67–112, discusses the Apothecary scene and those before and after, holding that "The Apothecary scene . . . acts out an emblem" (p. 103) of Melancholy.

6. One of the mentions of crows in 21 S.D. and 120 S.D. may be attributable to compositorial or other error in publication. See Gibbons.

7. White, *Plagiarism*, 1935, like a number of more recent commentators, chooses to read Greene's charge as one not of plagiarism but rather of uncompensated use of Greene's plays. The fact remains that Shakespeare in 1595 would have needed to take into account the public's perception of the charge, as exemplified by "R. B." writing in 1594 who (as White, p. 101, notes) takes Greene's attack as an unambiguous charge of plagiarism. Plagiarism, by the way, need not be restricted (as has generally been the case in the discussion of Greene's charge) to the theft of particular strings of words. As we know, devices, techniques, styles, and manners may be appropriated, as can, surely, the very authority of the author function. See also Bradbrook, "Beasts and Gods." Two important recent treatments of complexities of Renaissance literary proprietorship are Agnew, *Worlds*, 1986, and Evans, *Signifying*, 1986. Both naturally enough have occasion to write of Mercury.

8. Whether or not they beautify it, this discussion of the historical moment seems to have a particularly large number of stolen feathers, with Agnew, Benjamin, Evans, Foucault, Goldberg, and Orgel gratefully acknowledged locally, and with Barthes, Derrida, and others apparent passim, here gratefully acknowledged at a stroke.

9. "As Foucault says, the author is always a function of the text, and, classically, a name applied to a body of texts to signify their unity and propriety; at a certain point, when property defines the nature of the self, when copyright safeguards the text as the author's property, the author emerges as one whose existence is the transcendental guarantee for his texts" (Goldberg, *Voice*, p. 107). See Goldberg, pp. 107–8, 181n10, and passim for the Foucauldian (and Derridean and Barthesian) notion of the author function. As I mean the term, it encompasses Goldberg's reading of Foucault's pre-eighteenth-century author function, and also the notions of literary property rights apparent well before the eighteenth century.

10. The hint Shakespeare found in Brooke for Capulet's guest list is in the last line of

> No Lady fayre or fowle, was in Verona towne,
> No knight or gentleman of high or lowe renowne
> But Capilet himselfe hath byd unto his feast,
> Or by his name in paper sent, appointed as a geast.
>   (ll. 159–62)

In Shakespeare Tybalt's name is in the list but he, unlike Mercutio, has already appeared in person. For Rosaline and Valentine see above, "Introduction," and for Valentine see also Goldberg, *Voice*, pp. 68–81. For some of the richness of *mark*, see *OED*, s.v.; Derrida, "Writing," pp. 226–27; Goldberg, *Voice*, pp. 96–97, and passim. In addition to its meanings having to do with writing and reading, Mercutio's *mark* in its Germanic origins has the

Mercurial meaning still current in 1595 of border, boundary, or limen. Whereas, when the Chorus in l. 9 of the first "Prologue" speaks of the "death-mark'd love" of Romeo and Juliet the figure is reflexive inasmuch as the Chorus himself from his fatal extradramatic vantage has just informed us that "A pair of star-cross'd lovers take their life" (l. 6), the *mark* foreshadows Mercutio and the ways he marks the love with death including his own. Goldman, *Energies*, p. 38, writes that "significantly it is a list of names—all of which are read out—that is the villain."

11. Toward the end of the "battle of the Romeos" between Covent Garden and Drury Lane, on 11 October 1750 a writer in the *Daily Advertiser* (quoted in Pedicord & Bergmann, *Garrick*, 3:409) realized the metadramatic potential of Mercutio's malediction in

> Well—what tonight, says angry Ned,
>   As up from bed he rouses,
> Romeo again! and shakes his head,
>   Ah! Pox on both your houses!

12. In developing the present treatment of Shakespeare's Marlowe I have found especially valuable the annotated bibliography by Friedenreich, *Marlowe*, 1979, and studies by Bradbrook, Brooke, Brooks, Charney, Clemen, Cohen, Danson, Duane, Garber, Goldman, Greenblatt, Kernan, Levin, Longhurst, Parr, Ribner, Riggs, Shapiro, Waith, and F. P. Wilson, as well as discussions by some of these—Charney, Cohen, Danson, Garber, Goldman, and Shapiro—during the two-session seminar on "Marlowe and Shakespeare" chaired by Thomas Cartelli at the 1985 annual meeting of the Shakespeare Association of America. Commentators who have noted some of the Marlovianness in Mercutio include Klein, who maintains a bit simplistically that "Mercutio in all probability is Marlowe himself" ("Was Mercutio Marlowe?" p. 36), and Bradbrook, who suggests that "the tragic suddenness of his [Mercutio's] death may be taken to reflect Marlowe's own" ("Recollections," p. 202). *"A Poet & a filthy Play-maker": New Essays on Christopher Marlowe*, edited by Kenneth Friedenreich, Roma Gill, and Constance B. Kuriyama (New York: AMS, 1988), appeared after this book had gone to press.

13. In expanding the Apothecary incident from twenty-one lines in *Tragicall Historye* to forty-nine in *Romeo* (the two works being roughly the same length, 3020 lines in Brooke, *Romeo* 2964 lines), Shakespeare's most notable transmutation is of

> An Apothecary sate unbusied at his doore,
> Whom by his heavy countenaunce he gessed to be poore,
> And in his shop he saw his boxes were but fewe,
> And in his window (of his wares) there was so small a shew,

Wherfore our Romeus assuredly hath thought,
What by no friendship could be got, with money should be bought;
For nedy lacke is lyke the poore man to compell
To sell that which the cities lawe forbiddeth him to sell.

(ll. 2567–74)

Though beyond the scope of this study, all of what happens to these lines in *Romeo* 5.1 is of interest. Here, since it bears on the subject of the next chapter, we may simply note that Brooke's "frendship" (l. 2572) associated with Romeus migrates in Shakespeare to the Apothecary, and its absence becomes absolute.

14. Garber also speaks of "Hotspur—that most Marlovian (and Tamburlainian) of figures" in " 'Nothing Writ,' " 1984.

15. In addition to the generation traced here of Shakespeare's Mercutian Marlowe, Shakespeare uses Marlowe in many other ways. Riggs, *Histories*, p. 92, for instance, finds Richard III "in part the result of Shakespeare's continuing allusion to Marlowe," adding that "when Shakespeare alludes to Marlowe he usually does so for a specific reason, and not simply to fill out the page" (p. 96). Pistol in *2 Henry 4* 2.4.171–72 garbles his quotation of Tamburlaine from *Part 2*, 4.3.12, and is himself a kind of parody of the Marlovian hero. Nicholas Brooke, "Agent," p. 43, finds echoes of Tamburlaine in *Julius Caesar*, and Garber, "Vision," pp. 7–8, finds Tamburlainian echoes in the same play in *Antony*. See also Bradbrook, 1980, and, more recently, MacIntyre, 1986.

CHAPTER SIX: FRIENDSHIP AND LOVE

1. The treatment of love and friendship in this chapter is especially indebted to Foucault (*Use*), Mills, Rougemont, Sharp, and Whigam, and to recent psychoanalytic and feminist studies of Shakespeare including Adelman, Bamber, Dash, Kahn, and Novy.

2. Pequigney, *Love*, p. 231n26, stands out among Shakespeareans in his attention to Barnfield, whose defense—

Some there were, that did interpret *The affectionate Shepheard*, otherwise then (in truth) I meant, touching the subiect thereof, to wit, the loue of a Shepheard to a boy; a fault, the which I will not excuse, because I neuer made (*Cynthia*, sig. A3)

—is surely "curious and perfunctory."

3. See Smith, "Value," 1983, for a wide-ranging treatment of such canonization; and see Porter, "Marlowe," 1989, for an elaboration of the particu-

lar claim made here about Mercutio and the canonization of heterosexuality.

4. Since in Fiedler's view the primary force opposing marriage in Shakespeare is the father's love for the daughter, he slights fraternal bonding somewhat and speaks flippantly of Mercutio, who "manages to spare himself the pain of someone else's happy ending by dying before his beloved friend is quite Juliet's" (*Stranger*, p. 90). Additional feminist and psychoanalytic recognitions of the tension between friendship and love include Neely (*Nuptials*, p. 64) "Male resistance to marriage is more pervasive and persistent [than female resistance]," Novy (*Argument*, p. 63) on the "rivalry" between Antonio and Portia for Bassanio, and MacCary throughout *Friends*, 1985. All are more or less prescriptivist. Scarcely has MacCary (p. 3) seemed to take an admirably open-minded position, saying that Shakespeare "seems to say that every man's appetites and aversions are a law unto that man, i.e., that desire is a purely individual determination and that there can never be universal agreement on its objects" when he plunges (p. 5) into the standard heterosexual prescriptivist hierarchicalization of desire—"He [Shakespeare] carefully takes his young men through four stages of object-choice: first, they love themselves . . . then, . . . mirror images of themselves in twins or friends; after that, . . . those same images in transvestized young women; finally they learn to love young women. . . . [A lover's] identity must be a function of the objects he chooses—first parents, then friends, then lovers"—that continues through the study and, in particular, results in a peculiarly unpleasant approval of the marginalization of Antonio in *The Merchant of Venice*.

5. The elliptical quotation makes Gohlke say what she seems to mean to say. What she actually says is that *the feud* defines relations with women as controlling and violent. Her view of "relations among men as intensely competitive" is the standard psychological-feminist one that refuses to acknowledge friendship in the play. In her brief remarks about the play Gohlke does not mention Mercutio, but she finds that both Romeo and Juliet at moments express something of the intercourse-murder equation. Snow, in his Jungian-feminist "Language and Sexual Difference in *Romeo and Juliet*," p. 182, agrees with Kahn and others in (mistakenly, I maintain) transferring the play's opening equations whole-cloth to Mercutio, when he says that the Nurse's and Juliet's world of "vast interconnectedness" stands opposite to "the partially repressed realm of phallic violence that haunts the soldier's dream and Mercutio's reverie." But a kind of collapse of figuration happens if we turn all swords into Sampson's naked weapon. Any phallicism in the soldier's dream of cutting foreign throats seems more than partially repressed. In the speech's one explicit image of sexual intercourse the phallus is notably absent, or under erasure, as it is Queen Mab who presses maids when they lie on their backs.

6. "Not so fast," says the feminist concerned to put Mercutio in his place. "You're glossing over the aggressiveness of his 'hit the mark' at 2.2.33, and the reductiveness of that and of his 'a hole' at 2.4.93." As for "hit," while there may be some sexist aggressiveness in it, two further things should be said. First, a certain amount of aggressiveness, which is not necessarily sexist, is inherent in phallic sexuality. This truism needs saying here only because in feminist readings of *Romeo*, as of other texts, one senses in the margins of the discourse a myth of male heterosexuality that is nonphallic and nonintrusive. And second, in Mercutio's most elaborated talk of heterosexual intercourse, 2.1.24–29, while he talks bawdily of Romeo, Rosaline, and a male stranger, the only one he has taking action is Rosaline, who lays and conjures down the phallus of the stranger, who appears only in the phrase "Of some strange nature" identifying the phallus as not Romeo's, so that he becomes a mere site for a phallus that, rising in rather than into Rosaline's circle, seems so unintrusive as to be unrealistic. As for Romeo, he is not even present as a site for his phallus; he is the phallus in "I conjure only but to raise up him." As for Mercutio's "a hole," it, like the momentary reduction of Romeo to his phallus, certainly is a reductionist and therefore potentially sexist way to speak of the female party in the intercourse conjured up at 2.4.91–92. But reduction is arguably the lesser evil when the male party is "drivelling ... like a great natural that runs lolling up and down to hide his bauble." The speech, that is, seems far more antivenereal than sexist. Much the same seems generally true of Mercutio's rather parallel, though less energetic and picturesque, image of blind love's inability to hit the mark. In particular, given the *mark*-Mercutio correspondence at work in the play, the passage carries the subtextual message of Mercutio's invulnerability to love, and perhaps also it creates a fleeting suggestion of Mercutio's playing a "passive" role in homosexual intercourse.

7. Mercutio's "prick of noon" exhibits a Mercurial identification of phallus and graphic mark, since the dial's pricks are engraved marks.

8. Partride, s.v. "lay it," suggests an auditory allusion to the Latin *cunnus* and its English derivative (which he elsewhere rightly takes *OED* to task for excluding) in the "conjur'd" Mercutio gives to Rosaline at 2.1.26. The same allusion would presumably then also be present in Mercutio's "I conjure only but to raise up him [Romeo]" (l. 29), and here could have resonances with the postulated subliminal image of Mercutio containing Romeo's phallus. Partridge, of course, ignores the possible bawdiness of this "conjure," just as he provides an obfuscatory account of "raise up" (s.v.) in the line, because open recognition of the line's bawdiness could serve to compromise his claim that Shakespeare's bawdy is almost exclusively heterosexual. Pequigney recently, and generally rightly, takes Partridge and Colman to task for screening homosexual bawdy out of their accounts,

although (as mentioned) he has screened all sexuality out of the friendship between Mercutio and Romeo. Syntactically the line plays a trick with ambiguous modification. Officially Mercutio means "I conjure to raise up only but him" (i.e., Romeo and no one else). At the same time Mercutio's word order may suggest an unofficial subliminal meaning of "I only conjure but to raise up him"; that is, the only reason I'm talking (here and elsewhere) is to raise him up.

9. For the claim "That all they that love not Tobacco & Boies were fooles," attributed to Marlowe by Richard Baines in his list of charges against Marlowe sent to the queen three days after Marlowe's death, see Goldberg, "Sodomy." As Goldberg here points out, Bray (*Homosexuality*) lays bare some of the social mechanisms of Renaissance England in the context of which we can best understand the nature and force of Baines's charge.

10. Pequigney (p. 1) traces the ongoing attempt to protect Shakespeare and the *Sonnets* from "the embarrassment and scandal of homosexuality" from Benson's 1640 altered words and misleading titles through Auden's 1964 chiding of the homosexual reader determined to ally Shakespeare with "the Homintern" and the noncommitalism of Ingram and Redpath and of Booth, as well as in a smaller group of commentators who in the past twenty-five years have been willing to grant the persona of the *Sonnets* some erotic feelings for the young man. While Pequigney sometimes strains credibility, and has less than perfect command of the commentary—Giroux, *The Book Known as Q*, might have been included in the smaller group just mentioned—still he is often suggestive and sometimes persuasive in his all-out glosses of homosexual meaning in the *Sonnets*. See Sedgwick, *Between Men*, for a subtle and powerful treatment of relations among "homosocial" desire, gender, and power in the *Sonnets*.

11. "Prick love for pricking" suggests Romeo's penetration of love, perhaps preceded by love's of him. And then "you beat love down" strongly suggests masturbation, perhaps Romeo's of love. Conceivably there is another trace of sodomy in the last word of Mercutio's "Alas poor Romeo . . . the very pin of his heart cleft with the blind bow-boy's butt-shaft" (2.4.13–16). Partridge glosses "butt" in *Troilus* 5.1 as "buttocks."

12. "When the plays glance at sodomy it is with reticence and distaste. . . . Generally, . . . allusions to buggery are few in number and ambiguous in tenor . . . So far as one can judge . . . Shakespeare seems to have shared in the conventional disapproval of sodomy. . . . the subject was one that he seems to have preferred to avoid" (Colman, *Bawdy*, p. 7). I am in accord with all this. In his brief summary discussion of homosexuality and sodomy Colman (pp. 6–8) restates the conventional assurances about Elizabethan friendship, but admits here and in his chapter on the *Sonnets* the possibility of homosexual eroticism there. He finds Thersites's "preposter-

ous" (*Tro.* 5.1.22) the "one fully explicit reference" to sodomy. Part of the problem here is terminological; for Colman sodomy entails homosexuality, and when the act is heterosexual he calls it "anal intercourse," to which he also finds very few references in Shakespeare (p. 100).

13. The acceptance of "open-arse" in the Wilson and Duthie edition a mere year after Hosley (whose priority, along with that of Kökeritz, they acknowledge in their note on the line) suggests that they arrived at the emendation independently, and the wording of the last sentence of their note—about " 'or' as the seat of the [textual] corruption"—may acknowledge sodomy as the act Mercutio has in mind.

14. Colman (*Bawdy*) in his own way sacrifices Mercutio on the altar of young love—"Matters are so arranged that every time Mercutio tries to undercut Romeo's emotion, he fails" (p. 69)—but he is also sympathetic to Mercutio's "weird, fast-flowing current of indecent humour and extravagant fancy" (p. 70), and suggests that "*Romeo and Juliet* demands a good deal of critical reorientation if . . . Zeffirelli's . . . presentation of Mercutio is justified by the text" (p. 171). The remark seems prophetic of the present study, and might be generalized—the crux of course not being Zeffirelli (discussed below)—to the thesis that the play demands reorientation if *any* presentation of Mercutio is to be "justified by the text."

15. In the years intervening between 1595 and the present Marlowe elicits these and other kinds of mostly detrimental processing, including "explanation." Recent studies including those discussed in the preceding chapter undo some of that detrimental processing, and provide a climate in which we may find increasingly less tenable the line of claims running from Johnson's (Preface, p. 82) that Shakespeare "had no example of such fame as might force him upon imitation" to Bloom's that the anxiety of influence failed to touch Shakespeare.

CHAPTER SEVEN:
ADAPTATIONS, PROMPTBOOKS, PERFORMANCES

1. Of course the correlation between number of lines in a part and the amount of critical attention it receives is only rough and general across the canon, and there are many exceptional cases, some with a disproportionality greater than Mercutio's, as witness my namesake in *Macbeth*.

2. "Otway's play remains . . . the most absurdly incongruous of all the Restoration versions. . . . Of this . . . I am not aware that anything encouraging can be said. The execution of Otway's project is as grotesque as its conception" (Spencer, *Improved*, pp. 292, 296). Warner (*Otway*, p. 102) holds that "It is not difficult to understand why critics have given *Caius Marius* short shrift" but treats it far more sympathetically than do Odell

and Spencer. As Stephen Orgel reminds me, Spencer forgets Shakespeare's own "mixture of Roman and Renaissance" in *Cymbeline*.

3. For the play's mirroring of the current political scene, see Warner, *Otway*, pp. 32–36. Otway's sense of Roman politics depends not only on Plutarch but also on Shakespeare, particularly *Coriolanus*, for the portrayal of the plebeians, for instance, and also for the odd verbal echo, as when Lavinia speaks of being "Hooted by Slaves forth from thy gates, O *Rome*" (sig. F4; cf. *Cor.* 4.6.123–24).

4. Seeing Sulpitius described as both "the jolly tribune" (Odell, *Shakespeare*, 1:52) and "cynical and bloodthirsty" (Warner, *Otway*, p. 93) may lead one to suspect that at least one of the commentators has fallen victim to the trickster-god. Neither description seems quite on target, but in combination they suggest the survival and manifestation in Sulpitius of the laughing and potentially murderous god.

5. James "Nurse" Nokes had probably played the Nurse in D'Avenant's earlier revival of *Romeo*, and still earlier he had played a Nurse in *The Fatal Jealousie* (1672). For his "exuberant transvestitism" and alleged homosexuality, see Warner, *Otway*, p. 93. His textual feminization proceeds past his sobriquet to his title: while in the 1680 cast list the Nurse is played by "Mr. *Noakes*," the 1733 edition gives the role to "Mrs. Noakes."

6. Metellus speaks of "my daughters" because Otway has made Lavinia "My eldest born, her and the best of all / My fortune" (sig. B2v); Cibber in "our daughter" shifts the plural, restoring Juliet's uniqueness and including Lady Capulet in her parentage.

7. Cibber adopts Lavinia's soliloquy almost verbatim but balks at its conclusion

> Oh! I could . . .
> Tear up the Dead from their corrupted Graves,
> And dawb the face of Earth with her own Bowels
>   (sig. I4v)

which he replaces with lines from Lavinia's later speech to Marius Senior (sig. K1v).

8. Pedicord and Bergmann (Garrick, *Plays*) comment on relations among the Otway, Cibber, and Garrick adaptations, provide a scene-by-scene account of Garrick's divergences from Shakespeare, and assess the adaptation (3:406–13) with their text of the play accompanied by notes providing textual variants among the eighteenth-century printings of Garrick's two versions of his adaptation, 1748 and 1750 (the third, 1753, differs from the second only in the prefatory "Advertisement").

9. Compare Cibber,

> Help me into some House, *Benvolio*, or I shall faint; a Plague of both your Houses, they have made Worms-Meat of me: Curse your Houses. (sig. C8)

and Garrick,

> Help me into some house, *Benvolio*,
> Or I shall faint; a plague o' both your houses!
> They have made worms meat of me,
> I have it, and soundly too; plague take your houses;
> Your *Montagues* and *Capulets* together!
>
> (sig. B6)

(Here for Garrick I quote the 1750 edition directly for the close comparison.)

10. Discounting what are in effect duplications of others in the Folger collection (i.e., *Rom.* 10, *Rom.* Fo. 3, and *Rom.* Fo. 5), one arrives at a total of fifty promptbooks for *Romeo*, a number large enough to preclude the kind of error Shattuck warns about, error resulting from too small a sample. Shattuck describes 106 promptbooks, and lists 21 others, for a total of 125. Shattuck's total shrinks slightly if transcription and other duplication is discounted, and it grows slightly when the Folger books not listed by Shattuck (Folger *Rom.* 42, *Rom.* 43, *Rom.* 44) are added. The fifty promptbooks surveyed here, then, constitute a sizable proportion—something like 40 percent—of the entirety to 1961 that Shattuck surveys in 1965.

11. The Folger promptbooks without significant alteration of the role of Mercutio as printed are: *Rom.* 5, 6, 8, 11, 20, 23–26, 28, 30, 32, 34–36, 38, 40, 42; Bd.w. *Cymb.* 14; Fo. 1, 6, 7.

12. The 1763 edition of Garrick's adaptation, probably marked before ca. 1789; Shattuck [*Rom.* promptbook number] 3.

13. The Garrick adaptation published in New York by David Longworth, 1817. "Originally used by Brown at the National Theatre in Boston about 1838. Then used by Leman for nearly 50 years to play Mercutio and Friar Lawrence" (Shattuck, *Promptbooks*, p. 413); Shattuck 15. A fuller theater history of the role than that undertaken here would avail itself of the casting of Mercutio indicated in many of the promptbooks.

14. Text deriving from the 1904 production of E. H. Sothern and Julia Marlowe, the "Thorough promptbook record made by . . . the actor who played Balthazar, Capulet, Benvolio during several seasons beginning in January, 1906" (Shattuck, *Promptbooks*, p. 426); Shattuck 77, one of fourteen books Shattuck lists that derive from the Sothern-Marlowe production.

15. Based on the acting edition, London: Samuel French, n.d.; Shattuck 107.

16. 1877, based on the acting edition, London: Thomas Hailes Lacy, 1855; Shattuck 42.

17. 1847, based on the acting edition, London: T. Dolby, 1823; Shattuck 28.

18. 1876?, based on the Lacy edition; Shattuck 22.

19. *Rom.* 18: "Promptbook of a Shakespeare version used for many years" (Shattuck, p. 415), containing playbills for London and New York productions 1818–67; Shattuck 23. *Rom.* 17: 1887, based on the acting edition, New York: T. H. French, n.d.; Shattuck 17. *Rom.* Fo. 2: typescript deriving from the 1904 Sothern-Marlowe production; Shattuck 71.

20. *Rom.* 41: ca. 1900, based on New York: Samuel French, n.d. Promptbook of John Doud; ms. cast list with Doud as Mercutio; Shattuck 62. *Rom.* 19: 1845–77, based on the Garrick adaptation, London: John Cumberland, n.d.; Shattuck 22. *Rom.* 14: ca. 1860, based on New York: Wm. Taylor, n.d.; Shattuck 14. *Rom.* 37: n.d., based on New York: Samuel French, n.d.; Shattuck 107.

21. The Nurse calls her deceased husband a merry man at 1.3.40, but Romeo and Mercutio do not in the play use the phrase for Mercutio, nor does it seem especially accurate for him.

22. Based on the Garrick adaptation revised by J. P. Kemble, London. Printed for the Covent Garden Theatre, 1811, with additional markings indicating later use as a promptbook; not in Shattuck.

23. See n. 19 above.

24. See n. 20 above.

25. ca. 1852, based on New York: Wm. Taylor, n.d. Photocopy of Harvard Theatre Collection copy; Shattuck 31.

26. ca. 1904–6. Based on Israel Gollancz, ed. London: J. M. Dent, 1902. Spectator's copy deriving from the Sothern-Marlowe production; not in Shattuck.

27. The promptbooks affect Mercutio in other ways as well, of which there is room here for but a single example. Among various alterations of the conversation between Juliet and the Nurse about the guests departing from the ball (1.5.127–37), Folger Prompt *Rom.* 17 converts the Nurse's "Marry, that I think be young Petruchio" (l. 130) to "That, as I think is young Mercutio," thereby not only eliminating reference to the ghost Petruchio but also transferring his explicit youth to Mercutio.

28. See Stebbins, *Cushman*, pp. 58–64; Leach, *Star*, pp. 169–80.

29. Singer, 1826; Knight, 1838; Collier, 1842–44.

30. Kenneth Tynan interviewing Olivier in Burton, *Acting*, p. 17:

> *Which of those two parts did you prefer playing?*
> Oh, Romeo, Romeo.
> *That surprises me. I should have thought you were a natural Mercutio.*

Well, yes, perhaps that's why. But I saw myself as Romeo; I was
fighting a cause when I was playing Romeo.

I am grateful to Jill Levenson for the newspaper accounts of this and the
next two stage Mercutios discussed.

31. Brook cast Daphne Slater, eighteen, and Laurence Payne, twenty-
seven, as Juliet and Romeo. Jill Levenson has kindly reported to me that,
according to Brook's Temple edition promptbook, housed at the Shakespeare Centre in Stratford, he cut or transferred the following lines of Mercutio.

1.4. Mercutio speaks the second line as, "No, we shall in without apology." Line 13, "Nay, gentle Romeo" is given to Benvolio. Mercutio's lines
23–24, "And, to sink in it" are given to a masker. Most of lines 40–43,
"Tut, dun's the mouse . . . in our five wits" are cut.

2.1. Lines 12–14, "One nick-name" are cut, and at the end of the scene
"Mercutio laughs off, left."

2.4. Lines 19, "Oh, he's the courageous captain of compliments," and 72–
84, "Nay, if thy wits run the wild-goose chase . . . an ell broad," are cut.

32. "Scofield's Mercutio purred and roared; I remember him fighting,
flashing sword and an impossibly Douglas Fairbanks smile, tightened at the
corners with a touch of bitter mockery. The Queen Mab speech was a
scherzo. And here already was the typical Scofield delivery—the low mo-
notony, highlighted with almost unpredictable vocal flashes or irony. You
could hardly take your ears off him" (Clive Barnes, "The Faces of Scofield,"
Plays and Players [January 1963], p. 16; quoted in Levenson, *Performance*,
p. 70).

33. Jill Levenson, again, has kindly reported to me that, according to his
workbook at the Theatre Museum, Zeffirelli cut the following in his stage
version:

1.4. Lines 40–47 are cut.

2.1. Lines 34–36, "Now will he sit" are cut.

2.4. Lines 39–44, "Now is he for the numbers . . . to the purpose," and
63–84, "Now is he for the numbers . . . an ell broad," are cut.

3.1. Line 95, "Where is my Page? Go villain, fetch a surgeon," is cut.
According to Evans, *Romeo and Juliet*, p. 45n2, Zeffirelli considers Mercutio Shakespeare's self-portrait.

34. C. B. Young, "The Stage-History of *Romeo and Juliet*" (Wilson &
Duthie, *Romeo*, pp. xxxviii–lii), mentions the following additional players
of Mercutio: in London, Dyer (1750), Macklin (1750), Garrick (1761, after
he had ceased to play Romeo), Woodward (1748–76), Dodd (1765–76), Ellis-
ton (1807–22, after playing Romeo in earlier years), Charles Kemble (1829,
1836), Terriss (1882), Coghlan (1895), Beerbohm Tree (in his own production, 1913), Quartermaine (1919), Holloway (1926), and Milton (1928), and

at Stratford, Compton (1882), and Carrington (1919). See also Speaight, "Britain," pp. 187–88.

35. The same business with Mercutio's sword appears to happen in one of the other silent-film versions, directed by Barry O'Neill (?) in 1911, of which only the second half survives. Mercutio is not otherwise notable in the film. In the other silent, Italian version, directed by Geralmo Lo Savio in 1911–12, Mercutio has been almost entirely excised, appearing only with Romeo and Benvolio on their way to the ball.

36. The only important intervening film version is that directed by Renato Castellani in 1954. It was not generally well received or successful. Castellani's Mercutio, played without distinction by Aldo Zollo, is notable chiefly for the massive cuts, including the Queen Mab speech and the guying of the Nurse. See Jorgensen, *Film,* pp. 6–7. While I am excluding televised versions from this study (not to mention *Romeo and Juliet* ballets and other derived versions), a word may be in order here about the 1978 BBC production directed by Alvin Rakoff with Anthony Andrews as Mercutio. Even though its medium may have made it available to more viewers than the Zeffirelli film, it has proved nothing like so influential because of its general lack of distinction compared with some of the later BBC Shakespeares. Fenwick, "The Production" in the introduction to *The BBC TV Shakespeare: Romeo and Juliet,* bears possibly unintentional witness to the production's discounting of Mercutio; he writes of "the Romeo-Tybalt fight, where the play starts its slide into catastrophe" (p. 21).

37. Given the popularity of the film, and the amount of attention Evans gives it in his introduction to his edition in the New Cambridge Shakespeare, it is surprising that he implies that Stride and Dench, rather than Whiting and Hussey, played the leads (pp. 47–48).

38. The Apothecary scene itself is absent from the film, and that cut contributes much to the sense that Zeffirelli arrests Romeo's (and Juliet's) development far more than does Shakespeare.

39. Zeffirelli has Mercutio perform the obscene gesture under Benvolio's arm, a clear foreshadowing of the blow from Tybalt under Romeo's arm that mortally wounds Mercutio. And that foreshadowing manifests the phallus-sword equation made by Sampson and Gregory and realized visually by McEnery in the watering trough.

40. By cutting the lines following the soldier's dream Zeffirelli deprives Mercutio of touches of misogyny and uncanniness. Mercutio's death's-head petasos seems to have been planned carefully, inasmuch as at their first appearances Romeo, Benvolio, Tybalt, the Prince, Paris, the Nurse, Juliet, and Lady Capulet all have distinctive and characterizing headgear.

41. Arguably some sentimentalization also occurs in Zeffirelli's use of a subjective shot, at Mercutio's death, of Romeo's face blurring. If so, it seems at least a sentimentality more attuned than Barrymore's to Shake-

speare's Mercutio, and it also serves to link Mercutio cinematically with the Prince, to whom we attribute the next subjective shot, the view of the square with the dead Mercutio and Tybalt.

CHAPTER EIGHT: MERCUTIO'S SHAKESPEARE

1. There would be considerable agreement in the seventeenth, eighteenth, and nineteenth centuries as well, although numerous factors, notably including the establishment of the chronology of the canon, and Bradley's *Shakespearean Tragedy*, would tend to make twentieth-century agreement with Leech's general estimation more substantial. In the middle-to-late nineteenth century, when *Romeo and Juliet* seems to have had its best track record in the Shakespearean sweepstakes, it may have nosed past *Othello* and *King Lear*, but there was always *Hamlet*. The nineteenth-century ending of the play with Juliet's death, incidentally, could be seen as an attempt (which now looks abortive) to make the lovers' tale of woe more tragic by removing the "long-drawn-out ending" whose moralizing Leech, p. 73, finds antitragic.

2. "But we can guess that the speech prefigures the death [of Mercutio] and that Shakespeare knew . . . that its speaker was soon to die. That does not excuse the crassness of some recent directors who have made the actor of Mercutio's part show a trepidation of his own when, near the end of the speech, he refers to a soldier's dream: our anguish at his death is all the more poignant if he does not show fear or anticipation" (Leech, "Moral Tragedy," p. 74). As I read Zeffirelli's handling of the moment, however, Mercutio's trepidation is nothing like so self-centered as Leech suggests. Rather he seems to have a kind of passing premonition of all the woe to come.

3. Titularity and marginality converge similarly, and actually, in *The Merchant of Venice* with its other important resonances with *Romeo and Juliet*. Conceived as *The Tragedy of Mercutio*, Mercutio's play of course has a still longer drawn-out ending after the hero's death, an ending whose length is paralleled in Shakespeare only in *Julius Caesar*. While the length, in Leech's eyes, might be antitragic, the "ending" that follows Mercutio's death has an authentically tragic absence of rationalization and an equally authentic demonstration of deleterious effects of the hero's fall in his world.

4. The model of Victorian England could have affected Mercutio outside the empire as well as inside. A detailed comparison of what happens to him concurrently in the United States would be of interest.

5. Jehlen, "Archimedes," considers the importance for feminist criticism of this familiar difficulty faced by all movements born in reaction to a

prevailing injustice. "Denial always runs the risk of merely shaping itself in the negative image of what it rejects" (pp. 585–86). The current dichotomy in assessments of Mercutio derives not only from the nineteenth- and early-twentieth-century one apparent in the manifestations of Mercutio treated in chapter 7 but also from the dichotomy apparent in the criticism surveyed in McArthur, "Friend," p. 40: "If we . . . survey as a whole the field of criticism . . . we see that . . . the boundaries . . . are oriented about the Johnson-Dryden polarity of Shakespeare the immutable genius versus Shakespeare the clever but antiquated Elizabethan poet." With Johnson McArthur places Schlegel, Coleridge, Bernard Shaw, L. L. Schücking, E. K. Chambers, H. B. Charlton, and Dover Wilson; on Dryden's side stand Voltaire, Goethe, and Tieck. McArthur's own position is a sentimental recuperation of the "unity" of *Romeo* by demonstrating that "even the Queen Mab scene may be read as part of the whole" (p. 44; cf. Henley, "Mab").

6. These remarks about character and drama carry forward the inquiry begun in my *The Drama of Speech Acts*, pp. 162–66. Indeed the present study's general concern with the entity named Mercutio has many affinities with the earlier study's treatment of dramatic language as verbal action performed by actors such as Mercutio.

7. I have paid especially little attention to Paris. More than once, having given a colleague some account of the present study, I have then been asked, "But what will you do with Paris?" But the assumption that to do something with any character(s) in a play means that one must do something with all of them is a structuralist and modernist assumption that is unnecessary.

8. Considering these matters is a bit like "thinking the unthinkable" in some secluded room of the White House or the Pentagon. The occasional vague forecasts of Shakespeare's marginalization that I have encountered have for the most part been off-the-record, but it is easy to find their traces in print, as when Jehlen, "Archimedes," p. 579, claims that any feminism or protofeminism must automatically be devalued and discounted if it is discovered in Shakespeare since "from a feminist standpoint, he was a misogynist." Although the marginalization of Shakespeare does not seem to me particularly likely, it is certainly thinkable and there is precedent in the Western tradition, perhaps most notably in the effective marginalization of Virgil.

WORKS CITED

SHAKESPEARE
Romeo and Juliet

The BBC TV Shakespeare: Romeo and Juliet. New York: Mayflower, 1978.

Evans, G. Blakemore, ed. *Romeo and Juliet*. Cambridge: Cambridge University Press, 1984.

Gentleman, Francis, ed. *Romeo and Juliet*. London: John Bell, 1774.

Gibbons, Brian, ed. *Romeo and Juliet*. London: Methuen, 1980.

Hankins, John E., ed. *Romeo and Juliet*. Baltimore, Md.: Penguin, 1960. Reprinted in *William Shakespeare: The Complete Works*. See Harbage, ed., *Works*.

Hosley, Richard, ed. *The Tragedy of Romeo and Juliet*. New Haven: Yale University Press, 1954.

Spencer, T. J. B., ed. *Romeo and Juliet*. Harmondsworth, Middlesex: Penguin, 1967.

Turner, Robert K., Jr., and George Walton Williams, eds. *Romeo and Juliet*. Glenview, Ill.: Scott, Foresman, 1970.

Williams, George Walton, ed. *The Most Excellent and Lamentable Tragedy of Romeo and Juliet*. Durham, N.C.: Duke University Press, 1964.

Wilson, John Dover, and George Ian Duthie, eds. *Romeo and Juliet*. Cambridge: Cambridge University Press, 1955.

Other Works

Benson, John, ed. *Poems: Written by Wil. Shake-speare*. London, 1640.

Booth, Stephen, ed. *Shakespeare's Sonnets: With Analytical Commentary*. New Haven: Yale University Press, 1977.

Brooks, Harold F., ed. *A Midsummer Night's Dream*. London: Methuen, 1979.

Brown, John Russell, ed. *The Merchant of Venice*. 1955. Rev. ed. London: Methuen, 1961.

David, Richard, ed. *Love's Labour's Lost*. 1951. Rev. ed. London: Methuen, 1956.

Harbage, Alfred, ed. *William Shakespeare: The Complete Works*. 1969. Reprint. New York: Viking, 1977.

Honigmann, E. A. J., ed. *King John*. 1954. Reprint. London: Methuen, 1967.

Ingram, W. D., and Theodore Redpath, eds. *Shakespeare's Sonnets*. 1964. Reprint. New York: Barnes & Noble, 1968.

Jenkins, Harold, ed. *Hamlet*. London: Methuen, 1982.

Leech, Clifford, ed. *The Two Gentlemen of Verona*. London: Methuen, 1969.

Maxwell, J. C., ed. *Titus Andronicus*. 1953. Rev. ed. London: Methuen, 1968.

Pafford, J. H. P., ed. *The Winter's Tale*. London: Methuen, 1963.

Wilson, John Dover, ed. *Love's Labour's Lost*. 1923. Rev. ed. Cambridge: Cambridge University Press, 1962.

OTHER RENAISSANCE TEXTS

Adlington, William, trans. *The XI. Bookes of The Golden Asse Containing the Metamorphosie of Lucius Apuleius*. (London, 1566). Edited by Charles Whibley. 1893. Reprint. New York: AMS, 1967.

Alciati, Andrea. *Emblematum Libellus*. Paris, 1531, 1534.

———. *Diverse Imprese . . . .* Lyon, 1549.

Asclepius. In *Nova de Universis Philosophia* by Francesco Patrizi. Venice, 1593.

Bandello, Matteo. *Novelle*. 3 vols. Lucca, 1554.

Barnfield, Richard. *The Tears of an Affectionate Shepherd Sick of Love, or The Complaint of Daphnis for the Love of Ganymede*. London, 1594.

———. *Cynthia. With Certain Sonnets*. London, 1595.

Batman, Stephen. *The Golden Booke of the Leaden Goddes*. London, 1577.

Boccaccio, Giovanni. *De Genealogia Deorum*. Venice, 1472.

Bocchi, Achille. *Symbolicae Quaestiones*. Bologna, 1555, 1574.

Brooke, Arthur, trans. *The Tragicall Historye of Romeus and Juliet*. (London, 1562). In *Brooke's "Romeus and Juliet" Being the Original of Shakespeare's "Romeo and Juliet,"* edited by J. J. Munro. New York: Duffield, 1908.

Bullokar, William, trans. *Aesop's Fables*. London, 1585.

Cartari, Vincenzo. *Le Imagini de i Dei de gli Antichi*. Venice, 1556, 1571 (Reprint. New York: Garland, 1976), 1580, 1587; Lyon, 1581.

———. *Imagines Deorum*. Lyon, 1581.

———. *Les Images des Dieux des Anciens*. Lyon, 1581.

Casaubon, Meric. *A True and Faithful Relation of What Passed Between Dr. John Dee and Some Spirits*. London, 1659.

Caxton, William, trans. *Fables of Esope*. London [1484?, 1497?].

———, trans. *Eneydos*. (1490). Edited by W. T. Culley and F. J. Furnivall. London: Trübner, 1890.

Chapman, George, trans. *The Whole Works of Homer . . . his Iliads, and Odysses*. London [1616?].

———, trans. *The Georgics of Hesiod*. London, 1618.

———, trans. *The Crowne of all Homers Workes . . . His Hymns and Epigrams*. London [1642?].

Chettle, Henry. *Kind-Harts Dreame*. London, 1592.

Churchyard, Thomas. *A Discourse of the Queenes Maiesties Entertainment in Suffolk and Norffolk*. London, 1578.

Colonna, Francesco. *Poliphili Hypnerotomachia*. (Venice, 1499). Facsimile. London: Methuen, 1904.

———. *Poliphili Hypnerotomachia*. Translated by Jean Martin as *Discours du Songe de Poliphile*. Paris, 1546.

———. *Hypnerotomachia: The Strife of Loue in a Dreame*. London, 1592.

Comes, Natalis (Natale Conti). *Mythologiae*. Venice, 1551, 1567. Reprint. New York: Garland, 1976.

Daniel, Samuel. *The Complaint of Rosamond*. London, 1592.

Douglas, Gavin, trans. *The XII Bukes of Eneados*. London, 1553.

Du Choul, Guillaume. *Discours de la Religion des Anciens Romains Illustre*. Lyon, 1556.

Eliot, John. *Ortho-epia Gallica: Eliots Fruits for the French*. London: J. Wolfe, 1593.

Fraunce, Abraham. *The Third Part of the Countesse of Pembroke's Yuychurch*. London, 1592.

Gascoigne, George. *The Glass of Government*. London, 1575.

———. *A Briefe Rehearsall . . . of as Much as was Presented before Her Maiesti[e] at Kenelworth*. London, 1587.

Gerard, John. *Herball*. London, 1597.

Giovio, Paolo, and Gabriel Symeoni. *Sentiose Imprese*. Lyon, 1562.

Giraldi, Lilio Gregorio. *De Deis Gentium Varia . . . .* Basel, 1548.

Golding, Arthur, trans. *Ovid's Metamorphoses*. London, 1567.

Goldwel, Henry. *A Brief Declaratio[n] of the Shews . . . performed before the Queenes Maiestie . . .* London, 1581.

Greene, Robert. *A Briefe Apologie of the Sacred Science of Astronomie*. London, 1585.

———. *Planetomachia*. London, 1585.

———. *Perimedes the Blacke-Smith*. London, 1588.

———. *Groats-Worth of Wit*. London, 1592.

Hall, Arthur, trans. *Ten Books of Homer's Iliades*. London, 1581.

Harvey, Gabriel. *Pierces Supererogation*. London, 1593.

Henslowe, Philip. *Diary*. (1598). Edited by Walter W. Greg. 2 vols. London: A. H. Bullen, 1904–8.

James VI of Scotland. *The Essayes of a Prentise, in the Divine Art of Poesie*. Edinburgh, 1585.

Jonson, Ben. *Works*. Edited by C. H. Herford and Percy and Evelyn Simpson. 11 vols. Oxford: Clarendon, 1925–52.

Junius, Hadrianus. *Emblemata*. Antwerp, 1565.

La Perrierre, Guillaume de. *La Morosophie*. Lyon, 1553.

Linche, Richard, trans. *The Fountaine of Ancient Fiction*. London, 1599.

Lyly, John. *The Woman in the Moone*. London, 1597.

Marlowe, Christopher. *The Poems*. Edited by Millar Maclure. London: Methuen, 1968.

———. *The Complete Works of Christopher Marlowe*. 2 vols. Edited by Fredson Bowers. Cambridge: Cambridge University Press, 1973.

Middleton, W., trans. *Aesop: Fables in Englysshe*. London [1550?].

Nashe, Thomas. *A Pleasant Comedy, Called Summers Last Will and Testament*. London, 1600.

———. *The Works of Thomas Nashe*. 1904–5. Edited by Ronald B. McKerrow. 5 vols. Revised by F. P. Wilson. London: Blackwell, 1958.

———. "Preface to Greene's Menaphon." In Vol. 3 of *The Works of Thomas Nashe*. See Nashe, *Works*, 1958.

———. "Strange News." In Vol. 1 of *The Works of Thomas Nashe*. See Nashe, *Works*, 1958.

Nazari, Giovanni Battista. *Della Tramutatione Metallica Sogni Tre*. Brescia, 1572.

North, Thomas, trans. *The Lives of the Noble Grecians and Romanes by Plutarch*. (1579). Reprint. 8 vols. Oxford: Basil Blackwell, 1928.

Painter, William. *The Palace of Pleasure*. (London, 1566). Edited by Joseph Jacobs. London: David Nutt in the Strand, 1890.

Peele, George. *The Araygnement of Paris*. London, 1584.

Phaer, Thomas, trans. *The Nyne First Bookes of the Eneidos of Virgil*. London, 1558.

Porto, Luigi da. *Historia Novellamente Ritrovato di Due Nobili Amanti*. Venice, 1530.

Ralegh, Sir Walter. *History of the World*. London, 1614.

The Rare Triumphs of Love and Fortune. London, 1589.

Reusner, Nicolaus. *Emblemata*. Frankfurt, 1581.

Riche, Barnabe. *Dialogue, betwene Mercury and an English Souldier*. London, 1574.

Romei, Annibale. *I Discorsi*. (Venice, 1585). Translated by J. K[epers] as *Courtiers Academie*. London, 1598.

Salter, Thomas. *The Mirror of Modestie*. London, 1597.

Schelli[n]g, Konrad. *In Pustulas Malas Morbum quem Malum de Francia Vulgus Appelat.* Heidelberg: ca. 1490.

Sidney, Sir Philip. *The Countesse of Pembrokes Arcadia (The New Arcadia).* London, 1590. In *The Prose Works of Sir Philip Sidney.* 4 vols. Edited by Albert Feuillerat. 1912. Reprint. Cambridge: Cambridge University Press, 1963.

Spenser, Edmund. *The Faerie Queene.* Books 1–3. London, 1590; Books 1–6, 1596.

———. *Complaints.* London, 1591.

Stanyhurst, Richard, trans. *Richard Stanyhurst's Aeneis.* Leyden, 1582.

Stationers' Register: A Transcript of the Registers of the Company of Stationers of London; 1554–1640 A.D. Edited by Edward Arber. 5 vols. London: Privately printed [1875–77]. Birmingham, 1894.

Surrey, Henry Howard, Earl of, trans. *Certain Bokes of Virgiles Aenaeis.* (London, 1557). Edited by Florence H. Ridley. Berkeley: University of California Press, 1963.

Textor, Ravisius (Texier de Ravisi). *Officina Partim Historicis Partim Poeticis . . . .* Paris, 1520.

Tusser, Thomas. *Hundreth Good Points of Husbandrie.* London, 1557.

Valentine and Orson. (1503–4). Edited by Arthur Dickson. London: Oxford University Press, 1937.

Vallans, William. *A Tale of Two Swans.* London, 1590.

Whitney, Geoffrey. *A Choice of Emblemes.* London, 1586.

Wilson, Robert. *The Coblers Prophesie.* London, 1594.

CLASSICAL AND MEDIEVAL TEXTS

Apuleius. *The Metamorphoses or Golden Ass of Apuleius of Madaura.* Translated by H. E. Butler. 2 vols. Oxford: Clarendon, 1910.

———. *The Golden Ass.* Translated by W. Adlington. (1566). Revised by S. Gaselee. London: Heinemann, 1935.

Bennett, C. E., trans. *The Odes and Epodes.* See Horace, *Odes,* 1927.

Caesar, Caius Julius. *De Bello Gallico.* Translated by H. J. Edwards. London: Heinemann, 1917.

Chaucer, Geoffrey. *The Works of Geoffrey Chaucer.* Edited by F. N. Robinson. Boston: Houghton Mifflin, 1957.

Corpus Hermeticum. Edited by A. D. Nock, and translated by A. J. Festugière. 4 vols. Paris: Société d'édition "Les Belles lettres," 1945–54.

Fairclough, H. Rushton, trans. *Aeneid.* See Virgil, *Aeneid,* in *Eclogues, Georgics, Aeneid, Minor Poems,* 1934–35.

Henryson, Robert. *The Moral Fabillis of Esope . . . in . . . Scottis Meter.* Edinburgh, 1570.

_____. *The Testament of Cresseid.* (1593). In *Robert Henryson: Poems,* edited by Charles Elliott. Oxford: Clarendon, 1969.

Hesiod. *Works and Days.* In *Hesiod: The Homeric Hymns and Homerica,* translated by Hugh G. Evelyn White. 1914. Rev. ed. London: Heinemann, 1936.

Homer. *The Iliad.* Translated by A. T. Murray. London: Heinemann, 1930.

_____. *The Odyssey.* Translated by A. T. Murray. London: Heinemann, 1930.

Horace. *The Odes and Epodes.* Translated by C. E. Bennett. London: Heinemann, 1927.

_____. *Satires, Epistles, Ars Poetica.* Translated by H. Rushton Fairclough. London: Heinemann, 1929.

Hymn to Hermes. In *Hesiod: The Homeric Hymns and Homerica.* Translated by Hugh G. Evelyn-White. 1914. Rev. ed. London: Heinemann, 1936.

Martial. *Epigrams.* 2 vols. Translated by Walter C. A. Ker. London: Heinemann, 1943.

Martianus Capella. *The Marriage of Philology and Mercury.* Vol. 2 of *Martianus Capella and the Seven Liberal Arts.* See Stahl et al., *Martianus,* 1977.

Miller, Frank Justus, trans. *Metamorphoses.* See Ovid, *Metamorphoses.* 1921.

Ovid. *Metamorphoses.* Translated by Frank Justus Miller. London: Heinemann, 1921.

_____. *Ovid's Fasti.* Translated by James George Frazer. London: Heinemann, 1931.

Plautus. *Amphitruo.* In *Plautus.* 4 vols. Translated by Paul Nixon. London: Heinemann, 1916.

Virgil. *Aeneid.* In *Eclogues, Georgics, Aeneid, Minor Poems.* Translated by H. Rushton Fairclough. 2 vols. London: Heinemann, 1934–35.

OTHER WORKS

Adelman, Janet. "Male Bonding in Shakespeare's Comedies." In *Shakespeare's "Rough Magic": Renaissance Essays in Honor of C. L. Barber.* See Erickson & Kahn, *"Rough Magic,"* 1985.

Agnew, Jean-Christophe. *Worlds Apart: The Market and the Theater in Anglo-American Thought, 1550–1750.* Cambridge: Cambridge University Press, 1986.

Allen, Don Cameron. *Mysteriously Meant: The Rediscovery of Pagan Symbolism and Allegorical Interpretation in the Renaissance.* Baltimore: Johns Hopkins University Press, 1970.

Altieri, Charles. *Act and Quality: A Theory of Literary Meaning and Humanistic Understanding.* Amherst: University of Massachusetts Press, 1981.

Altman, Joel B. *The Tudor Play of Mind: Rhetorical Inquiry and the Development of Elizabethan Drama.* Berkeley: University of California Press, 1978.

Armstrong, Edward A. *Shakespeare's Imagination.* Lincoln: University of Nebraska Press, 1963.

Armstrong, Lilian. *Renaissance Miniature Painters & Classical Imagery: The Master of the Putti and His Venetian Workshop.* London: Harvey Miller, 1981.

Artaud, Antonin. *The Theatre and Its Double.* Translated by Caroline Richards. New York: Grove Press, 1958.

Attwater, Donald. *The Penguin Dictionary of Saints.* Baltimore: Penguin, 1965.

Austin, J. L. *How to Do Things with Words.* Edited by J. O. Urmson. Oxford: Clarendon, 1962.

Bach, Kent, and Robert M. Harnish. *Linguistic Communication and Speech Acts.* Cambridge: MIT Press, 1979.

Bacon, Wallace A. Introduction to *Syrinx* (1597), by William Warner. Edited by Wallace A. Bacon. Evanston: Northwestern University Press, 1950.

Bamber, Linda. *Comic Women, Tragic Men: A Study of Gender and Genre in Shakespeare.* Stanford: Stanford University Press, 1982.

Barnes, Clive. "The Faces of Scofield." *Plays and Players* 10 (January 1963): 15–17.

Bellamy, Elizabeth Jane. "The Broken Branch and the 'liuing Well': Spenser's Fradubio and Romance Error in *The Faerie Queene.*" *Renaissance Papers 1985* (1986): 1–12.

Benjamin, Walter. "The Work of Art in the Age of Mechanical Reproduction" (1936), translated by Harry Zohn. Reprinted in *Illuminations,* edited by Hannah Arendt, pp. 219–53. New York: Harcourt, Brace & World, 1955.

Berger, Thomas L., and William C. Bradford, Jr. *An Index of Characters in English Printed Drama to the Restoration.* Englewood, Colo.: Microcard, 1975.

Bevington, David. *Action Is Eloquence: Shakespeare's Language of Gesture.* Cambridge: Harvard University Press, 1984.

Biggins, Dennis. " 'Exit pursued by a Beare': A Problem in *The Winter's Tale.*" *Shakespeare Quarterly* 13 (1962): 3–13.

Bloom, Harold. *The Anxiety of Influence: A Theory of Poetry.* New York: Oxford University Press, 1973.

Booth, Stephen. *"King Lear," "Macbeth," Indefinition, and Tragedy*. New Haven: Yale University Press, 1983.

Bradbrook, Muriel C. "Beasts and Gods: Greene's *Groats-worth of Witte* and the Social Purpose of *Venus and Adonis*." *Shakespeare Survey* 15 (1962): 81–88.

———. "Shakespeare's Recollections of Marlowe." In *Shakespeare's Styles: Essays in Honour of Kenneth Muir*. Edited by Philip Edwards, Inga-Stina Ewbank, and G. K. Hunter, pp. 191–204. Cambridge: Cambridge University Press, 1980.

Bradley, A. C. *Shakespearean Tragedy*. 1904. Reprint. London: Macmillan, 1965.

Bray, Alan. *Homosexuality in Renaissance England*. London: Gay Men's Press, 1982.

Brooke, Nicholas. "Marlowe as Provocative Agent in Shakespeare's Early Plays." *Shakespeare Survey* 14 (1961): 34–44.

Brooks, Harold. "Marlowe and Early Shakespeare." In *Christopher Marlowe*, edited by Brian Robert Morris. London: Ernest Benn, 1968.

Brooks-Davies, Douglas. *The Mercurian Monarch: Magical Politics from Spenser to Pope*. Manchester: Manchester University Press, 1983.

Brown, John Russell. *Shakespeare's Plays in Performance*. 1966. Reprint. London: Penguin, 1969.

Brown, Norman O. *Hermes the Thief: The Evolution of a Myth*. Madison: University of Wisconsin Press, 1947.

Bullough, Geoffrey, ed. *The Narrative and Dramatic Sources of Shakespeare*. 8 vols. New York: Columbia University Press, 1957–75.

Burckhardt, Sigurd. *Shakespearean Meanings*. Princeton: Princeton University Press, 1968.

Burkert, Walter. *Greek Religion*. 1977. Translated by John Raffan. Cambridge: Harvard University Press, 1985.

Burton, Deirdre. *Dialogue and Discourse: A Sociolinguistic Approach to Modern Drama Dialogue and Naturally Occurring Conversation*. London: Routledge & Kegan Paul, 1980.

Burton, Hal, ed. *Great Acting*. New York: Hill and Wang, 1967.

Bush, Douglas. *Mythology and the Renaissance Tradition in English Poetry*. 1932. Rev. ed. New York: W. W. Norton, 1963.

Butler, H. E., trans. *The Metamorphoses or Golden Ass of Apuleius of Madaura*. See Apuleius, *Metamorphoses*, 1910.

Candee, Helen Churchill. *The Tapestry Book*. New York: Tudor, 1935.

Cercignani, Fausto. *Shakespeare's Works and Elizabethan Pronunciation*. Oxford: Oxford University Press, 1981.

Charney, Maurice. "Jessica's Turquoise Ring and Abigail's Poisoned Porridge: Shakespeare and Marlowe as Rivals and Imitators." *Renaissance Drama* n.s. 10 (1979): 33–44.

Cheney, Donald. "Tarquin, Juliet, and Other *Romei.*" *Spenser Studies* 3 (1982): 111–24.

Cibber, Theophilus. *Romeo and Juliet, A Tragedy, Revis'd, and Alter'd from Shakespear.* London, 1748.

Clemen, Wolfgang. "Shakespeare and Marlowe." In *Shakespeare 1971: Proceedings of the World Shakespeare Congress (Vancouver),* edited by Clifford Leech and J. M. R. Margeson. Toronto: University of Toronto Press, 1972.

Clements, Robert J. *Picta Poesis: Literary and Humanistic Theory in Renaissance Emblem Books.* Rome: Edizioni di Storia e Letteratura, 1960.

Cohen, Walter. "Marlowe and Shakespeare: Subversion and Containment." Paper presented at the annual meeting of the Shakespeare Association of America, Nashville, Tenn., March, 1985.

Colman, E. A. M. *The Dramatic Use of Bawdy in Shakespeare.* London: Longman, 1974.

Commager, Steele. *The Odes of Horace: A Critical Study.* New Haven: Yale University Press, 1962.

Cope, Jackson I. "Marlowe's *Dido* and the Titillating Children." *English Literary Renaissance* 4 (1974): 315–25.

Coudert, Allison. *Alchemy: The Philosopher's Stone.* Boulder, Colo.: Shambala, 1980.

Crosland, M. P. *Historical Studies in the Language of Chemistry.* Cambridge: Harvard University Press, 1962.

Culler, Jonathan. *Structuralist Poetics: Structuralism, Linguistics and the Study of Literature.* Ithaca, N.Y.: Cornell University Press, 1975.

Cumont, Franz. *Astrology and Religion among the Greeks and Romans.* New York: Putnam's, 1912.

Daly, Peter M. *Dichtung und Emblematik bei Catharina von Greiffenberg.* Bonn: Bouvier, 1976.

———. "A Note on Sonnet 116: A Case of Emblematic Association." *Shakespeare Quarterly* 28 (1977): 515–16.

———. *Literature in the Light of the Emblem: Structural Parallels between the Emblem and Literature in the Sixteenth and Seventeenth Centuries.* Toronto: University of Toronto Press, 1979.

Danson, Lawrence. "Christopher Marlowe: The Questioner." *English Literary Renaissance* 12 (1982): 3–29.

Dash, Irene G. *Wooing, Wedding, and Power: Women in Shakespeare's Plays.* New York: Columbia University Press, 1981.

David, Richard. *Shakespeare in the Theatre.* Cambridge: Cambridge University Press, 1978.

Davies, Stevie. *The Feminine Reclaimed: The Idea of Woman in Spenser, Shakespeare and Milton.* Lexington: University Press of Kentucky, 1986.

Dees, Jerome S. "Recent Studies in the English Emblem." *English Literary Renaissance* 16 (1986): 391–420.

Dent, R. W. *Shakespeare's Proverbial Language: An Index*. Berkeley: University of California Press, 1981.

Deonna, W. *Mercure et le Scorpion*. Brussels: Latomus, 1959.

Derrida, Jacques. "Freud and the Scene of Writing." 1967. In *Writing and Difference*, translated by Alan Bass. Chicago: University of Chicago Press, 1978.

Dickson, Arthur, ed. *Valentine and Orson*. (1503–4). London: Oxford University Press, 1937.

Dillon, Bert. *A Chaucer Dictionary: Proper Names and Allusions, Excluding Place Names*. Boston: G. K. Hall, 1974.

Dollimore, Jonathan. *Radical Tragedy: Religion, Ideology, and Power in the Drama of Shakespeare and His Contemporaries*. Chicago: University of Chicago Press, 1984.

Dollimore, Jonathan, and Alan Sinfield, eds. *Political Shakespeare*. Manchester: Manchester University Press, 1984.

Drakakis, John, ed. *Alternative Shakespeares*. London: Methuen, 1985.

Dryden, John. "Defence of the Epilogue; or, An Essay on the Dramatic Poetry of the Last Age." In vol. 1 of *Essays of John Dryden*, edited by W. P. Ker. Oxford: Oxford University Press, 1926.

Duane, Carol Leventen. "Marlowe's Mixed Messages: A Model for Shakespeare?" *Medieval and Renaissance Drama in England* 3 (1986): 51–67.

Dubrow, Heather. *Captive Victors: Shakespeare's Narrative Poems and Sonnets*. Ithaca, N.Y.: Cornell University Press, 1987.

Dusinberre, Juliet. *Shakespeare and the Nature of Women*. New York: Barnes & Noble, 1975.

Elam, Keir. *Shakespeare's Universe of Discourse: Language-games in the Comedies*. Cambridge: Cambridge University Press, 1984.

Eliot, T. S. "Philip Massinger." 1920. In *Selected Essays*. London: Faber & Faber, 1951.

Erickson, Peter, and Coppélia Kahn, eds. *Shakespeare's "Rough Magic": Renaissance Essays in Honor of C. L. Barber*. Newark: University of Delaware Press, 1985.

Evans, Malcolm. *Signifying Nothing: Truth's True Contents in Shakespeare's Text*. Athens: University of Georgia Press, 1986.

Fabiny, Tibor, ed. *Shakespeare and the Emblem: Studies in Renaissance Iconography and Iconology*. Szeged, Hungary: Dept. of English, Attila Jozsef University, 1984.

Fairchild, Arthur H. R. *Shakespeare and the Arts of Design*. University of Missouri Studies 12, no. 1. Columbia: University of Missouri Press, 1937.

Farmer, John Stephen, and W. E. Henley. *Slang and its Analogues, Past and Present.* 1903. Reprint. New York: Arno, 1970.

Ferguson, W. Craig. *Valentine Simmes.* Charlottesville: Bibliog. Soc. of the University of Virginia, 1968.

Festugière, André Jean. *La révélation d'Hermès Trismégeste.* 1944. Reprint. Paris: Gabalda, 1950.

Fiedler, Leslie A. *The Stranger in Shakespeare.* New York: Stein and Day, 1972.

Fineman, Joel. *Shakespeare's Perjured Eye: The Invention of Poetic Subjectivity in the Sonnets.* Berkeley: University of California Press, 1986.

Fish, Stanley E. "How to Do Things with Austin and Searle." *Modern Language Notes* 91 (1976): 983–1025.

Foucault, Michel. "What Is an Author?" 1969. In *Language, Counter-Memory, Practice: Selected Essays and Interviews by Michel Foucault,* edited and translated by Donald F. Bouchard and translated by Sherry Simon. Ithaca: Cornell University Press, 1977.

_____. *The Use of Pleasure.* Vol. 2 of *The History of Sexuality.* 1984. Translated by Robert Hurley. New York: Pantheon, 1985.

Freeman, Rosemary. *English Emblem Books.* London: Chatto & Windus, 1948.

Friedenreich, Kenneth. *Christopher Marlowe: An Annotated Bibliography of Criticism since 1950.* Metuchen, N.J.: Scarecrow, 1979.

Fripp, E. I. *Shakespeare Studies, Biographical and Literary.* London: Oxford University Press, 1930.

Frye, Roland Mushat. *The Renaissance Hamlet: Issues and Responses in 1600.* Princeton: Princeton University Press, 1984.

Garber, Marjorie. "Marlovian Vision / Shakespearean Revision." *Research Opportunities in Renaissance Drama* 22 (1979): 3–9.

_____. " 'Here's Nothing Writ': Scribe, Script, and Circumscription in Marlowe's Plays." *Theatre Journal* 36 (1984): 301–20.

Garrick, David. *The Plays of David Garrick.* Edited by Henry William Pedicord and Frederick Louis Bergmann. 7 vols. Carbondale: Southern Illinois University Press, 1980–82.

Gaselee, S., ed. *The Golden Ass.* See Apuleius, *Golden Ass,* 1935.

Gentleman, Francis. *The Dramatic Censor; or, Critical Companion.* London: John Bell, 1770.

Ghosh, Jyotish Chandra, and Elizabeth Gidlev Withycombe. *Annals of English Literature 1475–1925.* 1935. Revised by Robert William Chapman as *Annals of English Literature 1475–1950.* Oxford: Clarendon, 1961.

Gilbert, Allan H. "Falstaff's *Impresa.*" *Notes and Queries* 154 (1933): 389.

_____. "The Monarch's Crown of Thorns: The Wreath of Thorns in *Para-*

dise Regained." Journal of the Warburg and Courtauld Institutes 33 (1939–40): 156–60.

————. "The Embleme for December in *The Shepheardes Calender.*" *Modern Language Notes* 63 (1948): 181–82.

————. *The Symbolic Persons in the Masques of Ben Jonson.* Durham, N.C.: Duke University Press, 1948.

Giroux, Robert. *The Book Known as Q: A Consideration of Shakespeare's Sonnets.* New York: Atheneum, 1982.

Gohlke, Madelon. " 'I wooed thee with my sword': Shakespeare's Tragic Paradigms." In *The Woman's Part: Feminist Criticism of Shakespeare.* See Lenz et al., *Woman's Part*, 1980.

Goldberg, Jonathan. "Sodomy and Society: The Case of Christopher Marlowe." *Southwest Review* 69 (1984): 371–78.

————. *Voice Terminal Echo: Postmodernism and English Renaissance Texts.* New York: Methuen, 1986.

Goldman, Michael. *Shakespeare and the Energies of Drama.* Princeton: Princeton University Press, 1972.

————. *The Actor's Freedom: Toward a Theory of Drama.* New York: Viking, 1975.

————. "Marlowe and the Histrionics of Ravishment." In *Two Renaissance Mythmakers: Christopher Marlowe and Ben Jonson.* See Kernan, *Mythmakers*, 1977.

————. "Performer and Role in Marlowe and Shakespeare." Paper presented at the annual meeting of the Shakespeare Association of America, Nashville, Tenn., March, 1985.

Goldsworthy, William Lansdown. *Shake-speare's Heraldic Emblems: Their Origin and Meaning.* London: H. F. & G. Witherby, 1928.

Goldwater, Leonard J. *Mercury: A History of Quicksilver.* Baltimore: York, 1972.

Green, Henry. *Shakespeare and the Emblem Writers: An Exposition of Their Similarities of Thought and Expression.* London: Trübner, 1870.

Greenblatt, Stephen J. "The Improvisation of Power." Chap. 6 in *Renaissance Self-Fashioning: From More to Shakespeare.* Chicago: University of Chicago Press, 1980.

————. "Invisible Bullets: Renaissance Authority and Its Subversion." *Glyph* 8 (1981): 40–60.

Greene, Thomas. *The Light in Troy: Imitation and Discovery in Renaissance Poetry.* New Haven: Yale University Press, 1982.

Grice, H. P. "Logic and Conversation." In *Speech Acts*, edited by Peter Cole and Jerry L. Morgan. New York: Seminar, 1975.

Grimal, Pierre, ed. *Larousse World Mythology*, translated by Patricia Beardsworth. New York: Putnam's, 1965.

Haar, Dirk van der, ed. *Richard Stanyhurst's "Aeneis."* Amsterdam: H. J. Paris, 1933.

Hall, James. *A History of Ideas and Images in Italian Art.* New York: Harper & Row, 1983.

Halliday, F. E. *A Shakespeare Companion: 1564–1964.* Middlesex, England: Penguin, 1964.

Harbage, Alfred. *William Shakespeare: A Reader's Guide.* New York: Farrar, Straus, 1963.

_____. *Annals of English Drama 975–1700.* 1940. Revised by Samuel Schoenbaum. Philadelphia: University of Pennsylvania Press, 1964.

Hartt, Frederick. *Giulio Romano.* 2 vols. New Haven: Yale University Press, 1958.

Hartwig, Joan. *Shakespeare's Analogical Scene: Parody as Structural Syntax.* Lincoln: University of Nebraska Press, 1983.

Harvey, Paul. *The Oxford Companion to Classical Literature.* 1937. Reprint. London: Oxford University Press, 1940.

Hawkes, Terence. *That Shakespeherian Rag: Essays on a Critical Process.* London: Methuen, 1986.

Henderson, Archibald, Jr. "Family of Mercutio." Ph.D. dissertation, Columbia University, 1954.

Henkel, Arthur, and Albrecht Schöne. *Emblemata: Handbuch zur Sinnbildkunst des XVI and XVII Jahrhunderts.* Stuttgart: Metzler, 1967.

Henley, Elton F. "Relevance of Mercutio's Queen Mab Speech in 'Romeo and Juliet' I,iv,53–94." *University of South Florida Language Quarterly* 4 (1965): 29–32.

Holland, Norman N. "Mercutio, Mine Own Son the Dentist." In *Essays on Shakespeare,* edited by Gordon Ross Smith. University Park: Pennsylvania State University Press, 1965.

_____. "Shakespeare's Mercutio and Ours." *Michigan Quarterly Review* 5 (1966): 115–23.

Honigmann, E. A. J. *Shakespeare's Seven Tragedies: The Dramatist's Manipulation of Response.* London: Macmillan, 1976.

Hosley, Richard. "How Many Children Had Lady Capulet?" *Shakespeare Quarterly* 18 (1967): 3–6.

Hotson, J. Leslie. *The Death of Christopher Marlowe.* London: Nonesuch, 1925.

Hoyle, James. "Some Emblems in Shakespeare's Henry IV Plays." *English Literary History* 38 (1971): 512–27.

Hyde, Lewis. *The Gift: Imagination and the Erotic Life of Property.* New York: Random House, 1983.

_____. "Tricks of Creation." *Boston Review* 12, no. 1 (1987): 5–25.

International Pragmatics Association. "Announcements." *Journal of Pragmatics* 10 (1986): 153.

Jacobson, Howard. *Ovid's Heroides*. Princeton: Princeton University Press, 1974.

Jehlen, Myra. "Archimedes and the Paradox of Feminist Criticism." *Signs* 6 (1981): 575–601.

Johnson, Samuel, ed. Preface to *The Plays of William Shakespeare*. 1765. Reprinted in *Four Centuries of Shakespearian Criticism*, edited by Frank Kermode. New York: Avon, 1965.

Jones, Emrys. Review of *The Sources of Shakespeare's Plays* by Kenneth Muir. *Shakespeare Quarterly* 34 (1983): 359.

Jorgens, Jack J. *Shakespeare on Film*. Bloomington: Indiana University Press, 1977.

Jorgensen, Paul A. "Castellani's *Romeo and Juliet*: Intention and Response." *The Quarterly of Film, Radio, and Television (Film Quarterly)* 10 (1955–56): 1–10.

Kahn, Coppélia. "Coming of Age in Verona." In *The Woman's Part: Feminist Criticism of Shakespeare*. See Lenz et al., *Woman's Part*, 1980.

Kahn, Laurence. *Hermès passe: ou les ambiguïtés de la communication*. Paris: François Maspero, 1978.

Kaplan, Benjamin. *An Unhurried View of Copyright*. New York: Columbia University Press, 1967.

Kelly, Henry Ansgar. *Chaucer and the Cult of Saint Valentine*. Leiden: E. J. Brill, 1986.

Kernan, Alvin B., ed. *Two Renaissance Mythmakers: Christopher Marlowe and Ben Jonson*. Baltimore: Johns Hopkins University Press, 1977.

Klein, John W. "Was Mercutio Christopher Marlowe?" *Drama: The Quarterly Theatre Review* 60 (Spring, 1961): 36–39.

Knapp, Bettina L. *Theatre and Alchemy*. Detroit: Wayne State University Press, 1980.

Kökeritz, Helge. *Shakespeare's Pronunciation*. New Haven: Yale University Press, 1953.

———. *Shakespeare's Names: A Pronouncing Dictionary*. New Haven: Yale University Press, 1959.

Lathrop, Henry Burrowes. *Translations from the Classics into English from Caxton to Chapman, 1477–1620*. Madison: University of Wisconsin Press, 1933.

Leach, Joseph. *Bright Particular Star: The Life and Times of Charlotte Cushman*. New Haven: Yale University Press, 1970.

Leech, Clifford. "Venus and Her Nun: Portraits of Women in Love by Shakespeare and Marlowe." *Studies in English Literature* 5 (1965): 247–68.

———. "The Moral Tragedy of *Romeo and Juliet*." In *English Renaissance*

Drama: Essays In Honor of Madeleine Doran and Mark Eccles, edited by Standish Henning, Robert Kimbrough, and Richard Knowles. Carbondale: Southern Illinois University Press, 1976.

Leech, Geoffrey N. *Explorations in Semantics and Pragmatics.* Amsterdam: John Benjamins, 1980.

Leinwand, Theodore B. " 'I believe we must leave the killing out': Deference and Accommodation in *A Midsummer Night's Dream.*" *Renaissance Papers 1986* (1987): 11–30.

LeMoine, Fanny. *Martianus Capella: A Literary Re-evaluation.* Munich: Arbeo-Gesellschaft, 1972.

Lenz, Carolyn, Ruth Swift, Gayle Greene, and Carol Thomas Neely. *The Woman's Part: Feminist Criticism of Shakespeare.* Urbana: University of Illinois Press, 1980.

Levenson, Jill L. *Shakespeare in Performance: "Romeo and Juliet."* Manchester: Manchester University Press, 1987.

Lever, J. W. "Shakespeare's French Fruits." *Shakespeare Survey* 6 (1953): 79–90.

Levin, Harry. "Marlowe Today." *Tulane Drama Review* 8, no. 4 (1964): 22–31.

Levin, Richard. *New Readings vs. Old Plays: Recent Trends in the Reinterpretation of English Renaissance Drama.* Chicago: University of Chicago Press, 1979.

Lewis. C. S. *The Allegory of Love.* 1936. New York: Galaxy, 1958.

Longhurst, Derek. " 'Not for all time, but for an Age': An Approach to Shakespeare Studies." In *Re-reading English,* edited by Peter Widdowson. London: Methuen, 1982.

McArthur, Herbert. "Romeo's Loquacious Friend." *Shakespeare Quarterly* 10 (1959): 35–44.

McCall, John P. *Chaucer among the Gods: The Poetics of Classical Myth.* University Park: Pennsylvania State University Press, 1979.

MacCary, W. Thomas. *Friends and Lovers: The Phenomenology of Desire in Shakespearean Comedy.* New York: Columbia University Press, 1985.

MacIntyre, Jean. "*Doctor Faustus* and the later Shakespeare." *Cahiers élisabéthains* 29 (April 1986): 27–37.

Mauntz, Alfred Johannes Felix von. *Heraldik in Diensten der Shakespeare-forschung.* Berlin: Mayer & Müller, 1903.

Meagher, John C. "Economy and Recognition: Thirteen Shakespearean Puzzles." *Shakespeare Quarterly* 35 (1984): 7–21.

Miller, Paul W. "The Elizabethan Minor Epic." *Studies in Philology* 55 (1958): 31–38.

Mills, Laurens J. *One Soul in Bodies Twain: Friendship in Tudor Literature and Stuart Drama.* Bloomington, Ind.: Principia, 1937.

Mitchell, Charles. "Archaeology and Romance in Renaissance Italy." In *Italian Renaissance Studies*, edited by E. F. Jacob. London: Faber & Faber, 1960.

Muir, Kenneth. *The Sources of Shakespeare's Plays*. New Haven: Yale University Press, 1978.

Neely, Carol Thomas. *Broken Nuptials in Shakespeare's Plays*. New Haven: Yale University Press, 1985.

Neuse, Richard. "Atheism and Some Functions of Myth in Marlowe's *Hero and Leander*." *Modern Language Quarterly* 31 (1970): 424–39.

Newman, Paula, and George Walton Williams. "Paris: The Mirror of Romeo." *Renaissance Papers 1981* (1982): 13–19.

Nicholl, Charles. *The Chemical Theatre*. London: Routledge & Kegan Paul, 1980.

Nohrnberg, James. *The Analogy of "The Faerie Queene."* Princeton: Princeton University Press, 1976.

Novy, Marianne. *Love's Argument: Gender Relations in Shakespeare*. Chapel Hill: University of North Carolina Press, 1984.

Odell, George C. D. *Shakespeare from Betterton to Irving*. 1920. 2 vols. Reprint. New York: Dover, 1966.

Orgel, Stephen. "The Renaissance Artist as Plagiarist." *ELH* 48 (1981): 476–95.

Otway, Thomas. *The History and Fall of Caius Marius*. London, 1680. Reprint, 1733.

Parr, Johnstone. *Tamburlaine's Malady, and Other Essays on Astrology in Elizabethan Drama*. University: University of Alabama Press, 1953.

Partridge, Eric. *Shakespeare's Bawdy*. 1947. Reprint. New York: E. P. Dutton, 1955.

Peck, Harry Thurston, ed. *Harper's Dictionary of Classical Literature and Antiquities*. New York: Harper & Bros., 1897.

Pequigney, Joseph. *Such Is My Love: A Study of Shakespeare's Sonnets*. Chicago: University of Chicago Press, 1985.

Pharr, Clyde, trans. *The Theodosian Code and Novels*. Princeton: Princeton University Press, 1952.

Porter, Joseph A. *The Drama of Speech Acts: Shakespeare's Lancastrian Tetralogy*. Berkeley: University of California Press, 1979.

––––––. "Mercutio's Brother," *South Atlantic Review* 49, no. 4 (1984): 31–41.

––––––. "More Echoes of Eliot's *Ortho-epia Gallica*, in *King Lear* and *Henry V*." *Shakespeare Quarterly* 37 (1986): 486–88.

––––––. "Pragmatics for Criticism: Two Generations of Speech Act Theory." *Poetics* 15 (1986): 243–57.

––––––. "Marlowe, Shakespeare, and the Canonization of Heterosexuality." *South Atlantic Quarterly*, forthcoming, 1989.

Pratt, Mary Louise. *Toward a Speech Act Theory of Literary Discourse.* Bloomington: Indiana University Press, 1977.

Praz, Mario. *Studies in Seventeenth Century Imagery.* 2 vols. Studies of the Warburg Institute III. London: The Warburg Institute, 1939–47.

Pritchard, Alan. *Alchemy: A Bibliography of English-language Writings.* London: Routledge & Kegan Paul, 1980.

Purdon, Noel. *The Words of Mercury: Shakespeare and English Mythography of the Renaissance.* Salzburg: University of Salzburg, 1974.

Raingeard, Pierre. *Hermès psychagogue: Essai sur les origines du culte d'hermès.* Paris: Société d'édition "Les Belles lettres," 1935.

Reaney, P. H. *The Origin of English Surnames.* London: Routledge & Kegan Paul, 1967.

Reese, M. M. *Shakespeare: His World and His Work.* 1953. Rev. ed. New York: St. Martin's, 1980.

Ribner, Irving. "Marlowe and Shakespeare." *Shakespeare Quarterly* 15 (1964): 41–53.

Ridley, Florence H., ed. *The "Aeneid" of Henry Howard Earl of Surrey.* Berkeley: University of California Press, 1963.

Riggs, David. *Shakespeare's Heroical Histories: "Henry VI" and Its Literary Tradition.* Cambridge: Harvard University Press, 1971.

Root, Robert Kilburn. *Classical Mythology in Shakespeare.* 1903. Reprint. New York: Gordian, 1965.

Rougemont, Denis de. *Love in the Western World.* Translated by Montgomery Belgion. 1940. Rev. ed. New York: Fawcett, 1956.

Schoeck, R. J. *Intertextuality and Renaissance Texts.* Bamberg, W.Ger.: H. Kaiser Verlag, 1984.

Schoell, Frank Louis. *Etudes sur l'humanisme continental en Angleterre à la fin de la Renaissance: Bibliothèque de la Revue de littérature comparée.* Paris: Champion, 1926.

Schoenbaum, Samuel, ed. *Annals of English Drama 975–1700.* See Harbage, *Annals,* 1964.

Schrickx, W. *Shakespeare's Early Contemporaries: The Background of the Harvey-Nashe Polemic and "Love's Labour's Lost."* Antwerp: Nederlandische Boekhandel, 1956.

Scott, William O. "Another 'Heroical Devise' in *Pericles.*" *Shakespeare Quarterly* 20 (1969): 91–95.

Searle, John R. *Speech Acts: An Essay in the Philosophy of Language.* Cambridge: Cambridge University Press, 1969.

————. *Expression and Meaning: Studies in the Theory of Speech Acts.* Cambridge: Cambridge University Press, 1979.

Sedgwick, Eve Kosofsky. "Swan in Love: The Example of Shakespeare's Sonnets." Chap. 2 in *Between Men: English Literature and Male Homosocial Desire.* New York: Columbia University Press, 1985.

Sells, A. Lytton. *The Italian Influence in English Poetry: From Chaucer to Southwell*. Bloomington: Indiana University Press, 1955.

Seznec, Jean. *The Survival of the Pagan Gods: The Mythological Tradition and Its Place in Renaissance Humanism and Art*. 1940. Translated by Barbara F. Sessions. 1953. Reprint. Princeton: Princeton University Press, 1972.

Shapiro, James. "Revisiting *Tamburlaine: Henry V* as Shakespeare's Belated Armada Play." Paper presented at the annual meeting of the Shakespeare Association of America, Boston, Mass., April 1988.

Sharp, Ronald A. *Friendship and Literature: Spirit and Form*. Durham, N.C.: Duke University Press, 1986.

Shattuck, Charles Harlen. *The Shakespeare Promptbooks: A Descriptive Catalogue*. Urbana: University of Illinois Press, 1965.

Shirley, Frances A. *Swearing and Perjury in Shakespeare's Plays*. London: Allen & Unwin, 1979.

Smidt, Kristian. "Shakespeare's Absent Characters." *English Studies* 61 (1980): 397–407.

Smith, Barbara Herrnstein. "Contingencies of Value." *Critical Inquiry* 10 (1983): 1–35.

Smith, William, ed. *A Dictionary of Greek and Roman Biography and Mythology*. 3 vols. London: John Murray, 1869.

Snow, Edward. "Language and Sexual Difference in *Romeo and Juliet*." In *Shakespeare's "Rough Magic": Renaissance Essays in Honor of C. L. Barber*. See Erickson and Kahn, *"Rough Magic,"* 1985.

Snyder, Susan. "*Romeo and Juliet*: Comedy into Tragedy." *Essays in Criticism* 20 (1970): 391–402.

Speaight, Robert. "Shakespeare in Britain." *Shakespeare Quarterly* 28 (1977): 184–90.

Spencer, Hazelton. *Shakespeare Improved: The Restoration Versions in Quarto and on the Stage*. Cambridge: Harvard University Press, 1927.

Stahl, Harris, Richard Johnson, and E. L. Burge, eds. and trans. *Martianus Capella and the Seven Liberal Arts*. 2 vols. Vol. 1, *The Quadrivium of Martianus Capella: Latin Translations in the Mathematical Sciences, 50 B.C.-A.D. 1250*. Vol. 2, *The Marriage of Philology and Mercury*. New York: Columbia University Press, 1971–77.

Starnes, DeWitt T., and Ernest William Talbert. *Classical Myth and Legend in Renaissance Dictionaries: A Study of Renaissance Dictionaries in Their Relation to the Classical Learning of Contemporary English Writers*. Chapel Hill: University of North Carolina Press, 1955.

Steadman, John M. "Spenser's *Errour* and Renaissance Allegorical Tradition." *Neuphilologische Mitteilungen* 62 (1961): 22–38.

Stearns, Marshall W. "The Planet Portraits of Robert Henryson." *PMLA* 59 (1944): 911–27.

Stebbins, Emma, ed. *Charlotte Cushman: Her Letters and Memories of Her Life*. Boston: Houghton, Osgood, 1878.

Stone, Lawrence, *The Family, Sex and Marriage in England, 1500–1800*. New York: Harper & Row, 1977.

Sturrock, John. *Structuralism and Since: From Lévi-Strauss to Derrida*. Oxford: Oxford University Press, 1979.

Styan, J. L. *The Shakespeare Revolution: Criticism and Performance in the Twentieth Century*. Cambridge: Cambridge University Press, 1977.

Thomas, Sidney. "The Queen Mab Speech in *Romeo and Juliet*." *Shakespeare Survey* 25 (1972): 73–80.

Thomson, J. A. K. *Shakespeare and the Classics*. London: Allen & Unwin, 1952.

Thomson, Peter. "Shakespeare Straight and Crooked: A Review of the 1973 Season at Stratford." *Shakespeare Survey* 27 (1974): 143–54.

Tilley, M. P. *A Dictionary of Proverbs in England in the Sixteenth and Seventeenth Centuries*. Ann Arbor: University of Michigan Press, 1950.

Tobin, J. J. M. *Shakespeare's Favorite Novel: A Study of "The Golden Asse" as Prime Source*. Lanham, Md.: University Press of America, 1984.

Turner, Victor Witter. "Betwixt and Between: The Liminal Period in *Rites de Passage*." 1964. Chap. 4 in *The Forest of Symbols: Aspects of Ndembu Ritual*. Ithaca: Cornell University Press, 1967.

———. *The Ritual Process: Structure and Anti-Structure*. Chicago: Aldine, 1969.

Van Gennep, Arnold. *The Rites of Passage*. 1901. Translated by Monika B. Vizedom and Gabrielle L. Caffee. Chicago: University of Chicago Press, 1960.

Verschueren, Jef. *Pragmatics: An Annotated Bibliography*. Amsterdam: John Benjamins, 1978.

Waage, Frederick O. "Be Stone No More: Italian Cinquecento Art and Shakespeare's Last Plays." In *Shakespeare: Contemporary Critical Approaches*, edited by Harry R. Garvin. East Brunswick, N.J.: Associated University Presses, 1980.

Waddington, R. B. *The Mind's Empire: Myth and Form in George Chapman's Narrative Poems*. Baltimore: Johns Hopkins University Press, 1974.

Waele, F. J. M. de. *The Magic Staff or Rod in Graeco-Italian Antiquity*. Ghent: Drukkery Erasmus, 1927.

Waith, Eugene M. *The Herculean Hero in Marlowe, Chapman, Shakespeare and Dryden*. New York: Columbia University Press, 1962.

Walley, Harold R. "Shakespeare's Debt to Marlowe in *Romeo and Juliet*." *Philological Quarterly* 21 (1942): 257–67.

Warner, Kerstin P. *Thomas Otway*. Boston: Twayne, 1982.

Webster, Margaret. *Shakespeare Without Tears*. New York: McGraw-Hill, 1942.

Welch, Barbara L. *Ronsard's Mercury: The Arcane Muse*. New York: Peter Lang, 1986.

Whibley, Charles. Introduction to *The Golden Ass of Apuleius*. 1893. Reprint. New York: AMS, 1967.

Whigam, Frank. *Ambition and Privilege: The Social Tropes of Elizabethan Courtesy Theory*. Berkeley: University of California Press, 1984.

White, Harold Ogden. *Plagiarism and Imitation during the English Renaissance: A Study in Critical Distinctions*. Cambridge: Harvard University Press, 1935.

Wilson, F. P. *Marlowe and the Early Shakespeare*. Oxford: Clarendon, 1953.

Wilson, J. Dover. "Malone and the Upstart Crow." *Shakespeare Survey* 4 (1951): 56–68.

Wind, Edgar. *Pagan Mysteries in the Renaissance*. 1958. Revised 1967. Reprint. London: Faber & Faber, 1968.

Wood, Chauncey. *Chaucer and the Country of the Stars: Poetic Uses of Astrological Imagery*. Princeton: Princeton University Press, 1970.

Woodbridge, Linda. *Women and the English Renaissance: Literature and the Nature of Womankind, 1540 to 1620*. Urbana: University of Illinois Press, 1984.

Yates, Frances A. *A Study of "Love's Labour's Lost."* Cambridge: Cambridge University Press, 1936.

_____. *Giordano Bruno and the Hermetic Tradition*. London: Routledge & Kegan Paul, 1964.

_____. *Shakespeare's Last Plays: A New Approach*. London: Routledge & Kegan Paul, 1975.

Zimmerman, J. E. *Dictionary of Classical Mythology*. New York: Harper & Row, 1964.

uality; Houses; Limen, dramatic;
Phallicism (and phallocentrism);
Players, of Mercutio
Middleton, W., 212 (n. 5)
Miller, Frank Justus, 26, 30, 213
(n. 10)
Miller, Paul W., 226–27 (n. 9)
Mills, Laurens J., 146
Milton, John, 23
Minerva, 44, 64, 213 (n. 12), 223
(n. 17)
Misogyny, 121, 157–58, 170. See
also Mercury; misogyny of; Mer-
cutio: misogyny of
Mitchell, Charles, 218 (n. 1)
Montague (*Rom.*), 116, 137, 172,
181, 230 (n. 15)
Montemayor, Jorge de, 5
Muir, Kenneth, 142
Munday, Anthony, 208 (n. 10)
Munro, J. J., 207 (n. 2)
Mythographies, 48

Naming, act of, 107
Narrative, character in, 201
Nashe, Thomas, 25, 85, 86, 213
(n. 9), 225 (n. 4), 226 (n. 8), 231
(n. 2)
Nazari, Giovanni Battista, 39–40
Neely, Carol Thomas, 235 (n. 4)
Neoplatonism, 34
Neptune, 29, 84, 93
Neuse, Richard, 227 (n. 9)
Newman, Paula, 2
Nicholl, Charles, 217 (n. 24)
Niobe, 212 (n. 6)
Nohrnberg, James, 85, 87–88, 226
(n. 5)
Nokes, James "Nurse," 171, 239
(n. 5)
North, Thomas, 18
Novy, Marianne, 151, 234 (n. 1),
235 (n. 4)

Nurse (*Rom.*), 62, 64, 109, 110, 117,
125, 137, 142, 170–91 passim,
229 (n. 11), 230 (n. 15), 235 (n. 5),
239 (n. 5), 241 (nn. 21, 27), 243
(nn. 36, 40)

Odell, George C. D., 168, 184, 238–
39 (n. 2), 239 (n. 4)
Odysseus. See Ulysses
Olivier, Laurence, as Mercutio,
185–86, 241–42 (n. 30)
O'Neill, Barry, 243 (n. 35)
Orgel, Stephen, 131, 232 (n. 8), 239
(n. 2)
Orion, 29, 225 (n. 2)
Otway, Thomas, 168–72, 238–29
(nn. 1–6, 8), 239 (nn. 3, 6)
Ovid, 12, 15, 26–30, 81, 83, 89, 209
(n. 3), 213 (nn. 10, 12, 13), 223
(n. 17), 225 (n. 2)

Pafford, J. H. P., 45
Page (*Rom.*), 192
Painter, William, 4
Palestra. See Mercury: and gymnas-
tics
Pan, 30, 32, 213 (n. 11), 214 (n. 13),
215 (n. 17)
Paracelsus, 37
Paris (of Troy), 31, 44, 90
Paris (*Rom.*), 1, 101, 117, 120, 127,
137, 168, 179, 230 (n. 15), 245
(n. 7); presence at feast, 2; Trojan
overtones of name, 103
Parr, Johnstone, 216 (n. 22), 233
(n. 12)
Partridge, Eric, 161, 236 (n. 8), 237
(n. 11)
Pausanias, 51, 58, 62, 212 (n. 6)
Payne, Laurence, 242 (n. 31)
Peace (goddess), 49, 51, 64
Peck, Harry Thurston, 208 (n. 11)
Pedicord, Henry William, 174, 239

209 (n. 3); *King Lear*, 80, 141,
194, 217 (n. 24), 244 (n. 1); *Love's
Labour's Lost*, 13, 14, 117, 209
(n. 2), 210–11 (n. 4), 213 (n. 13),
225 (n. 4), 229 (n. 11); *Macbeth*,
194, 238 (n. 1); *Measure for Measure*, 167, 208 (n. 6); *The Merchant of Venice*, 35, 129, 143,
151, 213 (n. 13), 235 (n. 4), 244
(n. 3); *The Merry Wives of Windsor*, 15; *A Midsummer Night's
Dream*, 207 (n. 5); *Much Ado
About Nothing*, 208 (n. 12);
Othello, 194, 244 (n. 1); *The Rape
of Lucrece*, 45, 81, 110; *Richard
II*, 143, 208 (n. 12); *Richard III*,
13, 209 (n. 3), 234 (n. 15); *The
Sonnets*, 148, 149, 159–60, 237
(nn. 10, 12); *The Taming of the
Shrew*, 213 (n. 13), 228 (n. 5); *The
Tempest*, 81; *Timon of Athens*,
81; *Titus Andronicus*, 5, 12, 40,
81, 121, 209 (n. 2); *Troilus and
Cressida*, 14, 15, 81, 209 (n. 3),
210 (n. 3), 212 (n. 6), 213 (n. 13),
237 (n. 11); *Twelfth Night*, 39,
167; *Two Gentlemen of Verona*,
5, 7, 9, 138, 139, 207 (n. 4), 208
(n. 8); *The Two Noble Kinsmen*,
149; *The Winter's Tale*, 6, 15, 45,
63, 81, 115, 118, 129, 130, 149,
154, 210 (n. 3)
Shapiro, James, 233 (n. 12)
Sharp, Ronald A., 145–46, 234 (n. 1)
Shattuck, Charles Harlen, 177, 240
(nn. 10, 12–15), 241 (nn. 16–20,
22–27)
Shearer, Norma, 189
Shirley, Frances A., 110
Shylock, 204
Sidney, Sir Philip, 6, 118, 147
Sims [Simmes], Valentine, 208
(n. 11)

Sinfield, Alan, 204
Slater, Daphne, 242 (n. 31)
Smidt, Kristian, 1, 2
Smith, Barbara Herrnstein, 234
(n. 3)
Smith, William, 215–16 (n. 18)
Snow, Edward, 107, 145, 235 (n. 5)
Snyder, Susan, 14, 22, 99
Sodomy, 160–62, 189–90, 237–38
(n. 12). *See also* Mercutio: and
sodomy
Sothern, E. H., 240 (n. 14), 241
(n. 19)
Speaight, Robert, 243 (n. 34)
Speech acts, 227 (nn. 2, 3), 228
(n. 6). *See also* Mercutio: speech
acts of
Spencer, Hazleton, 168–69, 238–39
(n. 2)
Spencer, T. J. B., 161
Spenser, Edmund, 86, 87–89, 118,
122–23, 147, 225–26 (n. 5)
Stage, Mercutio on, 182–88
Stahl, Harris, 33–34, 216 (nn. 19,
20)
Stanyhurst, Richard, 23, 25, 106,
115, 212–13 (n. 8), 213 (n. 9)
Starnes, DeWitt T., 218 (n. 2)
Statue(s): of Hermione (*WT*), 15, 45,
48, 216 (n. 24); of Romeo and Juliet, 37, 139, 216 (n. 24); Egyptian, animated, 81
Steadman, John M., 221 (n. 13)
Stearns, Marshall W., 42
Stebbins, Emma, 241 (n. 29)
Steevens, George, 211 (n. 7)
Stone, Lawrence, 145
Stride, John, 187
Sturrock, John, 96
Styan, J. L., 147
Summoning, act of, 107, 114, 228
(n. 8)
Surnames, hereditary, 228 (n. 7)

Surrey, Henry Howard, Earl of, 23–24, 212–13 (n. 8)
Symeoni, Gabriel, 222 (n. 14)
Synod of gods, 66, 219 (n. 6)

Talbert, Ernest William, 218 (n. 2)
Textor, Ravisius, 48
Theft, 123, 125, 127–28, 129, 130–31, 165. *See also* Mercury: and theft
Thomas, Sidney, 132
Thomson, J. A. K., 14, 15, 214 (n. 13)
Thomson, Peter, 188
Thoth, 31, 208 (n. 1), 215 (n. 16)
Threshold. *See* Limen, dramatic
Tilley, M. P., 207 (n. 4)
Tobin, J. J. M., 214 (n. 14)
Tragedy, genre of, 194–95, 198, 244 (n. 3)
Travel, 117, 118, 127, 230 (n. 14)
Turner, Victor Witter, 118, 212 (n. 4), 230 (n. 17)
Tusser, Thomas, 19
Tybalt (*Rom.*), 1, 7, 8, 101, 108, 111, 112, 113, 114, 115, 116, 117, 125, 137, 138, 140, 141, 172, 179, 186, 189, 190, 191, 192, 193, 229 (n. 12), 232 (n. 10), 243 (nn. 36, 40), 244 (n. 41)
Tynan, Kenneth, 241 (n. 30)

Ulysses, 32, 102, 213 (n. 12), 223 (n. 17)
Underhill, Cave, 171

Valentine, Basil, 217 (n. 24)
Valentine (*Rom.*), 1–10, 114, 193, 208 (n. 8), 232 (n. 10)
Valentine (*TGV*), 138
Valentine and Orson (lost plays), 6, 208 (nn. 6, 10)

Valentine and Orson (prose romance), 5–6, 208 (n. 9)
Valentinianus and Valens, 6–7
Valgrisi, Vincenzo, 219 (n. 4)
Vallans, William, 85
Van Gennep, Arnold, 118, 230 (n. 17)
Venus, 31, 58, 84, 91–92, 213 (n. 13), 229 (n. 11)
Verschueren, Jef, 99
Victoria (queen of England), 196–97
Vining, Fanny, 184
Virgil, 14, 23–25, 102, 117, 211 (n. 6), 212–13 (n. 8), 245 (n. 8)

Waage, Frederick O., 218 (n. 2)
Waele, J. J. M. de, 211 (n. 7)
Waith, Eugene M., 233 (n. 12)
Walley, Harold R., 231 (n. 1)
Warburton, William, 175
Warner, Kerstin P., 169, 238 (n. 2), 239 (nn. 3–5)
Wars of the theaters, 131
Webster, Margaret, 182
Welch, Barbara L., 23, 211 (n. 2)
Whibley, Charles, 214 (n. 14)
Whigam, Frank, 131, 234 (n. 1)
White, Harold Ogden, 131, 232 (n. 7)
Whiting, Leonard, 190
Whitney, Geoffrey, 66, 75–76
Williams, George Walton, 2, 161, 228 (n. 9)
Wilson, F. P., 233 (n. 12)
Wilson, J. Dover, 161, 210–11 (n. 4), 231 (n. 2), 238 (n. 13), 242 (n. 34)
Wilson, Robert, 90, 209 (n. 2)
Wind, Edgar, 44–45, 223 (n. 17)
Withycombe, Elizabeth Gidley, 85
Wood, Chauncey, 38
Woodbridge, Linda, 146
Writing, and drama, 130–34, 201